Humor Us

HUMOR US

An Appeal for the Gospel of Relaxation

Donald Capps

CASCADE *Books* • Eugene, Oregon

HUMOR US
An Appeal for the Gospel of Relaxation

Copyright © 2016 Donald Capps. All rights reserved. Except for brief quotations in critical publications or reviews, no part of this book may be reproduced in any manner without prior written permission from the publisher. Write: Permissions, Wipf and Stock Publishers, 199 W. 8th Ave., Suite 3, Eugene, OR 97401.

Cascade Books
An Imprint of Wipf and Stock Publishers
199 W. 8th Ave., Suite 3
Eugene, OR 97401

www.wipfandstock.com

PAPERBACK ISBN 13: 978-1-4982-9037-1
HARDCOVER ISBN 13: 978-1-4982-9039-5
EBOOK ISBN 13: 978-1-4982-9038-8

Cataloging-in-Publication data:

Names: Capps, Donald.

Title: Humor us : an appeal for the gospel of relaxation / Donald Capps.

Description: Eugene, OR: Cascade Books. | Includes bibliographical references and index.

Identifiers: ISBN: 978-1-4982-9037-1 (paperback) | ISBN: 978-1-4982-9039-5 (hardcover) | ISBN: 978-1-4982-9038-8 (ebook).

Subjects: LCSH: Wit and humor—Religious aspects. | Wit and humor—Religious aspects—Christianity. | Wit and humor—Psychological aspects. | Psychology, Religious.

Classification: BR115 H84 C37 2016 (print) | BR115 H84 (ebook)

Manufactured in the USA

The author wishes to express his appreciation to Springer Publications for permission to use material from his articles published in *Pastoral Psychology*: "The Psychological Benefits of Humor" (2006), "Religion and Humor: Estranged Bedfellows" (2006), "The Placebo Effect and the Molecules of Hope" (2010), and "The Laborers in the Vineyard: Putting Humor to Work" (2012).

The author also wishes to express his appreciation to Springer Publications for permission to use material from his article published in *The Journal of Religion and Health*: "Gossip, Humor, and the Art of Becoming an Intimate of Jesus" (2012).

Scriptural quotations marked (NRSV) come from the New Revised Standard Version Bible, copyright 1989, Division of Christian Education of the National Council of the Churches of Christ in the United States of America. Used by permission. All rights reserved.

Scriptural quotations marked (RSV) come from the Revised Standard Version of the Bible, copyright 1952 [2nd edition, 1971] by the Division of Christian Education of the National Council of the Churches of Christ in the United States of America. Used by permission. All rights reserved.

Scriptural quotations marked (NIV) come from the Holy Bible, NEW INTERNATIONAL VERSION®, NIV® Copyright © 1973, 1978, 1984, 2011 by Biblica, Inc.® Used by permission. All rights reserved worldwide.]

Contents

Acknowledgments | vii

Introduction | ix

1. The Placebo Effect of Humor | 1

2. Humor as Moderator of Life Stress | 13

3. Religion and Humor: Estranged Bedfellows | 35

4. Did Jesus Have a Sense of Humor? | 67

5. Putting Humor to Work: The Laborers in the Vineyard | 87

6. Gossip, Humor, and the Joking Community | 117

7. Why the Long Face? | 148

Epilogue | 163

References | 167

Index of Names | 177

Acknowledgments

I want to express my appreciation to the editorial team at Cascade Books for their support, including K. C. Hanson, editor in chief; Jeremy Funk, copy editor; and Heather Carraher, typesetter. I also want to express my appreciation to James Stock, marketing director, and Mike Surber for the cover design.

I also want to express my appreciation to the Group for New Directions in Pastoral Theology for the inspiration it has provided over the years. I suggest in this book that Jesus and his disciples were a joking community and that this contributed in a positive way to the realization of their serious purposes and goals. The same suggestion applies to the Group for New Directions in Pastoral Theology. In fact, members have often alluded to the fact that the Group is composed of a similar number of participants, and this has naturally led to humorous suggestions that a participant has a certain likeness to one of the disciples. And, of course, there are suggestions that for purposes of organization and time management, someone needs to assume the role of Jesus. These suggestions invariably call to mind the following joke:

> A mother was preparing pancakes for her sons. The boys began to argue over who would get the first pancake. Their mother saw the opportunity for a moral lesson. "If Jesus were sitting here, He would say, 'Let my brother have the first pancake, I can wait.'" One of them turned to the other and said, "You be Jesus!"[1]

My Dad finished this book a few weeks before he died in August 2015. Helping prepare it for publication has been like looking over his shoulder, a welcome reminder of his sense of humor and his sometimes

1. Alexander et al., *Prairie Home Companion Pretty Good Joke Book* (5th ed.), 132.

maverick—and always deeply compassionate—approach to religion and pastoral care. Looking back it's obvious how he always thought of humor and religion as profoundly complementary: effective ways not just of coping with an uncertain world, but ways of achieving a flourishing human life.

My mother recently gave me copies of his high school writings. Some of these were earnest poems and short stories, often on religious themes. Others were parodies and satires poking fun at current events and American history. Reading these it became clear that working out the relationship between humor and religion was a life-long project for my father, one he pursued with both rigor and a light touch. This book is a good example of both, ranging from his discussions of Freud and recent psychological research, to his brilliant parody of Joyce Kilmer's "Trees."

In addition to everyone mentioned above—I really cannot adequately express my gratitude to the entire team at Cascade Books—I'd especially like to thank Evelyn Brister, Scot MacLean, and Regan Wylie for recent conversations and especially their good humor over the years.

—John Capps

Introduction

Stress: mental or emotional tension or strain characterized by feelings of anxiety, fear, threat, tension, pressure, etc.

Anxiety: a state of being uneasy, apprehensive, or worried about what may happen.

Humor: the quality that makes something seem funny, amusing, or ludicrous.[1]

William James, the psychologist and philosopher, presented an address to the 1896 graduating class of Boston Normal School of Gymnastics (a school for women intending to become teachers). The address was titled "The Gospel of Relaxation." It was published in *Scribner's Magazine* in 1899.[2] In the address he mentioned a comment that Dr. Thomas Smith Clouston, Scotland's "most eminent" asylum physician, made when he visited America many years earlier:

> "You Americans," he said, "wear too much expression on your faces. You are living like an army with all its reserves engaged in action. The duller countenances of the British population betoken a better scheme of life. They suggest stores of reserved nervous force to fall back upon, if any occasion should arise that

---

1. Adapted from Agnes, ed., *Webster's New World College Dictionary*, 1417, 64, and 696.
2. James, "Gospel of Relaxation." It was published in *Scribner's Magazine* in 1899, and the same year James included it in a collection of his lectures titled *Talks to Teachers on Psychology and to Students on Some of Life's Ideals*, 99–112. The following citations are from the book version.

requires it. This inexcitability, this presence at all times of power not used, I regard as the great safeguard of our British people. The other thing in you gives me a sense of insecurity, and you ought somehow to tone yourselves down. You really do carry too much expression, you take too intensely the trivial moments of life."³

Agreeing with Clouston, James said that "intensity, rapidity, vivacity of appearance" are "something of a nationally accepted ideal," and he mentioned a story he had read recently in a weekly newspaper in which the writer summarized the heroine's charms by pointing out that to everyone who observed her she gave the impression of "bottled lightning." James added that bottled lightning is "one of our American ideals."⁴ He devoted the rest of the address to the need for Americans to learn to relax. But he concluded the lecture with this cautionary note:

> Even now, I fear that some one of my fair hearers may be making an undying resolve to become strenuously relaxed, cost what it will, for the remainder of her life. It is needless to say that this is not the way to do it. The way to do it, paradoxical as it may seem, is genuinely not to care whether you are doing it or not. Then, possibly, by the grace of God, you may all at once find that you *are* doing it.⁵

I begin this book with this reference to James's "The Gospel of Relaxation" because I believe that in the intervening years we Americans have not changed. We are still living like an army with all its reserves in action, and if this means that we are at war, we are warring against ourselves. We are stressed out, anxious, tense, and unnerved.⁶ Knowing that this is nothing new, that we have been this way for a very long time, may help us to put it in perspective. But this knowledge does nothing to alleviate the problem. In fact, it can make us more resigned to the prospect of simply having to live with it. On the other hand, it can also inspire us to do something about it and, as James warns, the very ways we

---

3. Ibid., 103.
4. Ibid., 104.
5. Ibid., 112.
6. See Laird et al., eds., *Webster's New World Roget's A–Z Thesaurus*, 746. Two forms of stress are identified—pressure and mental tension—and after numerous synonyms for both forms of stress are given, these antonyms of stress are noted: *peace, calm, quiet.*

do this may simply cause us to become more stressed out, anxious, tense, and unnerved.

I suggest that this is where humor comes in. I want to make a case in this book for the role that humor may play in moderating stress and alleviating anxiety. Unlike many other ways recommended for moderating stress and alleviating anxiety, humor isn't likely to create its own stress and anxiety. On the other hand, most people are likely to think that humor is not an especially potent or effective means of moderating stress and alleviating anxiety. So, when I set out to write this book, I was fully aware that I had my work cut out for me. But I knew that in comparison to many of the topics that persons in my field write about, writing about humor is much less likely to create its own stress and anxieties. Also, the fact that I had already written a couple of books on humor offered grounds for thinking that this would be the case.[7]

Now, here a few words about the book itself: Chapter 1 rejects the idea that laughter is the best medicine, but it argues that humor can be an effective placebo as far as moderating stress and alleviating anxiety are concerned. To make this case, I discuss recent findings that placebos have real biochemical effects. In chapter 2 I discuss research studies on the psychological effects of humor, especially studies that show that humor moderates life stress and that it also alleviates anxieties. I also consider a study that shows that humor increases hope.

The fact that humor has these effects invites us to consider the relationship between humor and religion. Since we often turn to religion—in whatever form it is most meaningful to us—for help in alleviating our anxiety and stress, we might think that religion and humor would be allies in this regard. However, in chapter 3 I discuss the fact that the relationship between religion and humor has been a rather problematic one, and give particular attention to the empirical and theoretical studies by Vasilis Saroglou, a psychology professor at the Catholic University of Louvain in Belgium, in which he shows that religion and humor are negatively associated, largely because religion and humor draw upon conflicting personality characteristics and qualities. The chapter concludes with the proposal that although religion's mistrust of humor is to some extent warranted, there are grounds for viewing humor and religion as allies, especially in the face of life's ultimate incongruities.

---

7. Capps, *Time to Laugh*; Capps, *Laughter Ever After*.

In chapter 4 I focus on the question whether or not Jesus was a humorous person. Here I discuss an article by Henry F. Harris, published in 1908, in which he argues that Jesus was not humorous.[8] Then I discuss the view, especially as presented in Earl F. Palmer's *The Humor of Jesus* and Douglas Adams's *The Prostitute in the Family Tree*, that various parables and miracle stories in the Gospels reveal Jesus to have been a humorous person.[9]

To illustrate the fact that Jesus was a humorous person, I focus in chapter 5 on his parable of the Laborers in the Vineyard, a parable that centers on anxiety in the workplace. I note that Palmer and Adams see humor in the parable by focusing on the workers who worked only an hour, but then I draw on Richard Ford's interpretation of the parable and Sigmund Freud's views on humor to suggest that humorous possibilities also arise in the conversation between the landowner and the laborers who put in a full day's work.[10] In fact, if the disgruntled workers and the defensive landowner could have seen the humor in the situation, they could have reconciled their differences and given their "army" of nerves a rest. Thus, I suggest that the parable supports the view that Jesus was a humorous person who saw humor in the everyday experiences of life, and I also suggest that there is often more humor in his stories, whether overt or potential, than we tend to think there is. This, I believe, is due to the fact that we have been educated to think that the use of humor is incompatible with serious intentions.

Chapter 6 continues the emphasis in chapters 4 and 5 on humor in the life of Jesus by observing that gossip was the means by which word of his teachings and healings spread throughout the region, and that when gossip is infused with the spirit of humor it is much less likely to be smallminded and malicious and much more likely to be playful and gentle. I employ this association of gossip and humor to suggest that Jesus and his disciples were, in effect, a joking community, and that this was central to the intimacy they shared. Thus, whereas chapter 3 presents evidence that challenges the view that religion and humor are natural allies, chapters 4–6, by focusing on the person and ministry of Jesus, show that religion and humor are, in fact, allies and, moreover, that Jesus himself personifies their fundamental compatibility.

8. Harris, "Absence of Humor in Jesus."
9. Palmer, *Humor of Jesus*; Adams, *Prostitute in the Family Tree*.
10. Ford, *Parables of Jesus*; Freud, *Jokes and Their Relation to the Unconscious*; Freud, "Humor."

In chapter 7 I consider Jesus's reflections on worry (Matt 7:25–34) and suggest that they are fundamentally an expression of the gospel of relaxation. I also consider a poem by Rev. I. J. Bartlett titled "The Town of Don't-You-Worry," which leads to some reflections on Phillips Brooks's poem "O Little Town of Bethlehem," written when he was experiencing a downtime in his life. I conclude with his comments on preachers' inappropriate use of humor in their sermons and his countervailing view that humor, when appropriately introduced, may be "the bloom of the highest life" to which one's auditors aspire.[11] In the epilogue, I report on a dream of my own that displaced a long-standing anxiety by means of humor.

To conclude these introductory comments, I would like to note that my previous books on humor had the words *laugh* and *laughter* in their titles, and the word *humor* was relegated to their subtitles.[12] In this book *humor* is not only in the title, but the title itself—a play on words—is an attempt at humor. I indicate in chapter 1 that I have a specific reason for preferring the word *humor* over *laughter*, but here I note that humor is broader and more encompassing than laughter, and that there are situations that are humorous but when laughter is inappropriate. There are also humorous occasions that evoke a grin or chuckle but not outright laughter, and sometimes these occasions remain in our memory longer and have more lasting benefits than occasions that evoke a burst of voluntary or involuntary laughter.

This, then, is not a book about laughter. It is a book about humor and, more specifically, our need to be humored. No doubt I have become more conscious of this need in myself as I have become an older adult, and perhaps it is no accident that I have written this book just after writing a book in which I argued that older adulthood is a period of growth and development.[13] Surely some readers will view this book on humor as counterevidence of my argument in the preceding book, as being, instead, a sign that older adulthood is a period of regression and declining cognitive capacities. In response, I can only say that I can live with this view of what I have written here—and this being the case, perhaps I myself am no longer a stranger to the gospel of relaxation.

---

11. Brooks, *Lectures on Preaching*, 57.
12. Capps, *Time to Laugh*; Capps, *Laughter Ever After*.
13. Capps, *Still Growing*.

1

The Placebo Effect of Humor

"Laughter Is the Best Medicine" has been a long-standing feature of *Reader's Digest*. The book *Laughter: The Best Medicine*, published by the Reader's Digest Association in 1997, includes jokes and humorous anecdotes from fifty years of its publication.[1] However, the idea that laughter is the best medicine got a big shot in the arm, so to speak, when Norman Cousins, a journalist and editor, wrote about his affliction with Ankylosing spondylitis, a life-threatening degenerative disease involving the inflammation of the spine and large joints, resulting in stiffness and pain. Supported by his physician, he checked out of the hospital and into a hotel where he improvised a therapeutic regimen that included vitamin C, films by the Marx Brothers, and episodes of the television program *Candid Camera*. His book *The Anatomy of an Illness as Perceived by the Patient*, published in 1979, became a best seller.[2] He became a widely sought speaker on medical issues from the patient's perspective.

Later in life he moderated his laugh-your-way-to-better-health message, noting that humor should be viewed as a metaphor for the entire range of positive emotions. But the idea that laughter was the key factor in the remission of his disease is what everyone seemed to remember, and something about the scene of a sick man sitting in his hotel room watching videos, laughing his head off, and getting well has almost universal appeal. Moreover, there is scientific evidence that laughter has physical benefits. As Richard P. Olson notes in *Laughter in*

---

1. Reader's Digest Association, *Laughter: The Best Medicine*. See also Reader's Digest Association, *Laughter Really Is the Best Medicine*; and Reader's Digest Association, *Laughter Still Is the Best Medicine*.
2. Cousins, *Anatomy of an Illness as Perceived by the Patient*.

a Time of Turmoil, these physical benefits include lower blood pressure; release of brain chemicals (endorphins) that decrease pain; enhancement of the immune system; reduction of unhelpful hormones; and relaxation and improvement of muscle tone, of respiratory functioning, and of the cardiovascular system.[3] This is a very impressive list of physical benefits attributable to laughter.

On the other hand, Norman Cousins' later moderation of the laugh-your-way-to better-health message suggests that the idea that laughter is the *best* medicine is something of an exaggeration. In fact, the Bible is instructive at this point. Proverbs 17:22 says: "A cheerful heart is a good medicine; but a downcast spirit dries up the bones" (NRSV).[4] It does not say that laughter is the *best* medicine, only that a cheerful heart is a *good* medicine. In line with this more modest claim, I suggested in my previous book on humor, *Laughter Ever After*, that if *laughter* is probably not the best *medicine*, perhaps *humor* is the best *placebo*. In support of this claim, I noted that humor may not cure our bodily ills, but it can help us cope with them, and I cited the joke about the man who says to his doctor, "My back aches, I have chronic indigestion, my bowels are sluggish, and I don't feel so good myself." Humor won't remove the first three maladies, but it can do something for the fourth, and this can help him cope with the other three.[5] And this is where the placebo comes in. So in this chapter I want to expand on my earlier suggestion that humor may well be the best placebo.

Humor as Placebo

But what, exactly, is a placebo? The dictionary defines *placebo* as "a harmless, unmedicated preparation given as a medicine to a patient merely to humor him, or used as a control in testing the efficacy of another, medicated substance."[6] It is interesting that this definition includes the word

---

3. Olson, *Laughter in a Time of Turmoil*, 40–43.

4. Collicutt and Gray invoke this verse in "'A Merry Heart Doeth Good Like a Medicine': Humor, Religion, and Wellbeing." The quotation is from the King James Version.

5. Capps, *Laughter Ever After*, 101.

6. Agnes, *Webster's New World College Dictionary*, 1099. The dictionary also notes that "placebo" is "the first antiphon of the vespers for the dead, beginning with the word *placebo*," which is Latin for "shall please." This definition has relevance for the relationship of humor and death anxiety. I will comment on Thorson and Powell's "Relationships of Death Anxiety and Sense of Humor" in chapter 2.

"humor," and that it says that one of the placebo's purposes is to "humor" the person who is receiving it. This purpose has direct bearing on the title of this book: *Humor Us*.

But what does it mean to "humor" us? And why would a placebo be useful in this regard? To answer these questions I turned to the word *humor* in the dictionary. It has several meanings but the one that seemed the most relevant in this case is this: "To comply with the mood or whim of (another); indulge."[7] This definition seemed a bit patronizing as far as the prescribing of a placebo is concerned. So I consulted *The Merck Manual of Medical Information*, hoping that it would provide a better explanation of how a placebo may "humor" a person. This huge tome has a scant half-page on placebos.[8] It defines placebos as "substances that are made to resemble drugs but do not contain an active drug." It adds that a placebo "is made to look exactly like a real drug but is made of an inactive substance such as starch or sugar," and it notes that "placebos are usually used in research studies."[9] It explains their effects in this way:

> Placebos can result in or be coincidentally associated with many changes, both desirable and undesirable. This phenomenon, called the placebo effect, appears to have two components: anticipation of results, usually optimistic, from taking a drug (sometimes called suggestibility); and spontaneous change. Sometimes people improve spontaneously, without treatment. If spontaneous change—whether positive or negative—occurs after a placebo is taken, the placebo may incorrectly be credited with or blamed for the result.[10]

As for the first component (anticipation of results), the *Manual* notes that some people seem more susceptible to the placebo effect than others: "People who have a positive opinion of drugs, doctors, nurses, and hospitals are more likely to respond favorably to placebos than are people who have a negative opinion." Unfortunately, "some people who are particularly susceptible to placebos tend to become compulsive about using the drug; they tend to increase the dose, and they develop withdrawal symptoms when they are deprived of the placebo."[11]

---

7. Ibid., 696.
8. Beers et al., *Merck Manual of Medical Information*, 61.
9. Ibid.
10. Ibid.
11. Ibid.

When I read this statement about some people increasing the dose, I found it a bit puzzling: Does this mean that the placebo effect was no longer working at the original dosage? If so, why would this be? If the effect of the drug is due to the patient's suggestibility, why would a suggestible patient eventually need an increased dosage to experience the same effects? I was also a bit puzzled about the statement that if spontaneous change—whether positive or negative—occurs after the placebo is ingested, the placebo may incorrectly be credited with or blamed for the result. I wondered how anyone would know that the placebo *didn't* produce the positive spontaneous change, and I also wondered why anyone would blame the placebo for a negative spontaneous change. After all, the placebo, containing only an inactive ingredient, would seem to be harmless. (The dictionary definition actually states that it is harmless.) So the only blame that would seem to be reasonable would be the blame that the prescribing physician might be subject to for prescribing a placebo instead of a drug that had an active ingredient. But if the physician did not believe that the active ingredient would be health promoting, blaming the physician would seem inappropriate as well.

At the time, I simply wanted to make the case that humor may be an effective placebo, especially in reducing anxiety and stress, so I set these questions about the "real" placebos aside and did not pursue them any further. Instead, I focused on the *Manual*'s paragraphs on research studies, and especially its observation that when a new drug is being developed, "investigators conduct studies to compare the effect of the drug with that of a placebo because any drug can have a placebo effect, unrelated to its action," and therefore, "the true drug effect must be distinguished from a placebo effect."[12] Thus,

> Half the study's participants are given the drug and half are given an identical-looking placebo. Ideally, neither the participants nor the investigators know who received the drug and who received the placebo (this type of study is called a double-blind study). When the study is completed, all changes observed in participants taking the active drug are compared with those in participants taking the placebo. The drug must perform significantly better than the placebo to justify its use. In some studies, as many as 50% of the participants taking the placebo improve

12. Ibid.

(an example of the placebo effect), making it difficult to show the effectiveness of the drug being tested.[13]

To be honest, this conclusion was also a bit puzzling to me because it seems that the effectiveness of the drug being tested would be judged on the basis of whether those who took the drug experienced positive effects or not. On the other hand, I can see how the researchers might conclude that some of the participants who were given the drug were as suggestible as some of those who were given the placebo, so the placebo effect could not be ruled out in their case even though they had not received the placebo.

But this raises the question whether any studies have been conducted in which all the participants are given a placebo, but in which half are informed, and the other half are not informed, that it is a placebo. Does knowing that it is a placebo increase or decrease its "placebo effect"? This question had direct relevance to the claim that I am making here that humor may be the best placebo, especially with regard to the alleviation of anxiety and stress. If I "know" that humor is a placebo, do I receive greater—or lesser—benefits from humor than does a person who does not know that this is the case?

Another question relates to the danger of a person becoming compulsive about using a placebo and requiring steadily increasing doses and experiencing withdrawal symptoms when the placebo is unavailable: If the placebo is humor, does this mean that a person may need increasing doses of humor so that it will continue to have the same positive effect? And does it mean that a person may experience setbacks as far as the alleviation of anxiety and stress is concerned if humor is unavailable or, if available, is not being utilized? Conceivably, dealing with these two issues might require some careful self-monitoring because, to the best of my knowledge, there is no twelve-step program available for the placebo addict.

Finally, there is the question of relevance: Does humor have a better placebo effect when it addresses the unhealthy condition from which one is actually suffering? In the case that interests me here, are jokes that deal with anxiety and stress more effective than jokes on other topics and issues? Chapter 2 will present some evidence in support of this suggestion.

---

13. Ibid.

The Anomalies of the Placebo

As I noted, the placebo effect is generally attributed to the suggestibility of the recipient. After all, it consists of an inactive drug so it does not have the ingredients that have, or are expected to have, real physiological effects. Nor, for that matter, is it expected to have undesirable "side effects." But is it possible that a placebo may, in fact, have real biochemical effects? This issue is addressed in Michael Brooks' chapter on the placebo effect in *Thirteen Things That Don't Make Sense: The Most Baffling Scientific Mysteries of Our Time*.[14] Brooks is editor and consultant with the *New Scientist*.

He begins his chapter on the placebo effect with a quotation from Leo Sternbach, inventor of the antianxiety drug diazepam, marketed as Valium, the top-selling pharmaceutical in the United States from 1969 to 1982. Given our concern here with the effects of humor on anxiety and stress, it is significant that this drug combats anxiety. What Sternbach said was this: "It has brought me great comfort to know that I could, in some way, help people feel better."[15] This quotation is from the press release issued by Roche Pharmaceuticals when Sternbach died on September 30, 2005. Writing less than three years later, Brooks notes that what is only beginning to emerge is "just how much Leo Sternbach's drug depends on people helping themselves to feel better." He adds, "The strange thing is, it doesn't work unless you know you're taking it."[16]

Brooks goes on to cite an article published in the journal *Prevention and Treatment* the year that Sternbach died. The article reported on a study that demonstrated that diazepam had no effect on anxiety when it was administered without the patient's knowledge. The research was carried out in Turin, Italy, by Fabrizio Benedetti and his colleagues. Half of the trial subjects were informed by a doctor that it was a powerful antianxiety drug. The other half were hooked up to an automatic infusion machine and given the same dose of diazepam but with no other person in the room and no way of telling that they had received the drug. Two hours later, the subjects in the first group reported a significant reduction in their levels of anxiety. The second group reported no change. The

---

14. Brooks, *Thirteen Things That Don't Make Sense*, ch. 12.
15. Ibid., 164.
16. Ibid.

researchers suggested that "anxiety reduction after the open diazepam administration was a placebo effect."[17]

Noting that a sugar pill, a spoonful of sugar water, a saline drip, or a parade of doctors coming to your bedside to offer reassurances can trigger this effect, Brooks points out: "The power of placebo comes from the deceptive message that comes with it. You are told (or you sense) this procedure or ritual will have an effect on your body or state of mind, and if you genuinely believe it, taking the pill or the drink, or in some cases just seeing the doctor, will produce exactly that effect."[18] He adds that research has shown "that white coats and stethoscopes can produce surprisingly effective placebo effects—as can a good bedside manner. Doctors know that if patients feel they are getting suitable treatment, the treatment is enormously more effective."[19]

There is nothing really surprising about this research finding. But Brooks goes on to note that the same research team made another discovery. Whereas *The Merck Manual* attributes the placebo effect either to spontaneous change or to the suggestibility of the patient, Benedetti and his colleagues discovered that the chemistry of the drug "is being augmented by chemicals secreted in the brain—the effect of what Fabrizio Benedetti, the leader of the Turin group, calls 'the molecules of hope.'"[20] Brooks suggests that this new experimental evidence indicates that "where we once thought we had a handle on the placebo effect, it is now becoming clear that we don't."[21] In the past, "modern scientific medicine was constructed on the notion of the randomized double-blind, placebo-controlled trial, where drugs have to perform better than a dummy pill or inert saline injection.[22] As we have seen, *The Merck Manual* assumes the reliability of this model; it simply points to the dilemma that in some cases 50 percent or more of the persons who receive the placebo improve, thus complicating the task of showing the effectiveness of the drug being tested. But, as Brooks points out, matters are no longer quite so clear. The reason for this is that in some cases, the placebo effect is not due to

17. Ibid., 165.
18. Ibid.
19. Ibid.
20. Ibid.
21. Ibid.
22. Ibid., 165–66.

spontaneous change or to the patient's suggestibility but to the chemical effects of the placebo itself.[23]

The classic demonstration of this finding involves inducing pain in subjects, and, perhaps not surprisingly, the original test was carried out by dentists who extracted molars and administered a morphine drip to reduce the pain. Later, after the patients began to associate the morphine with pain relief, a saline solution was substituted for the morphine. The patients did not know that their "morphine" was nothing but salt water and, thanks to the placebo effect, they reported that their pain medication was still working fine. Then, however, when another drug, Naloxone, which blocks the action of morphine, was put into the drip, the Naloxone stopped the pain relief despite the fact that there was no morphine entering the patients' bodies. The patients, who had not been informed that the new drug had been put into the drip, next reported that they were in discomfort again.

How to explain the fact that a drug that blocks morphine stopped the pain relief that patients were actually receiving from the placebo? Brooks suggests: "The only possible explanation is that the drug that blocks morphine's pain-relieving power also blocks the saline's (placebo-based) pain-relieving power. Which means the saline was actually doing something—it wasn't all in the patient's imagination. *Or at least it means that imagination can have a physiological effect.*"[24] The dentists initially attributed the placebo effect to a stimulation of the body's endorphins—that is, to one of a group of natural opioids that use the same biochemical pathways that morphine (an opiate) does. They concluded that the expectation of pain relief was enough to trigger an endorphin release that did the job. Then, however, the Naloxone blocked the endorphins, and that is why the pain came back.

In fact, however, the explanation is more complicated than this. If ketorolac, a pain-killer that works via a completely different chemistry from that of morphine, is used in the conditioning, and is then replaced with saline, the addition of naloxone has no effect because the placebo pain relief is provided not by endorphins but by some other painkiller that the body produces. Or if patients are informed that they are getting morphine that is more diluted than usual when in fact they are receiving only saline, and then naloxone is introduced, the naloxone does

---

23. Ibid., 168.
24. Ibid., 169 (italics added).

not block the painkilling effect of the saline because the expectation of reduced pain relief has triggered some alternative mechanism. Brooks concludes: "The placebo effect pulls out all the stops; the expectation of pain relief can stimulate all kinds of natural pain-relieving chemicals."[25]

Brooks Decides to Find Out for Himself

At the time this new finding was being reported, Brooks was aware of important studies by two Danish researchers, Asbjorn Hrobjartsson and Peter Getzsche, who had performed meta-analyses of over one hundred clinical trials comparing placebo-treated patients with untreated patients. They concluded that there was "no evidence that placebo treatments had significant effects on health."[26] On the other hand, he also knew of an editorial by John Bailer of the University of Chicago, who contended that the conclusions of Hrobjartsson and Getzsche were too sweeping. To settle his mind on the issue, Brooks decided to visit the researchers in Turin and ask them to perform a placebo test on him.

Normally, Benedetti's team does not tell their trial volunteers what kind of experiment they are carrying out because such knowledge might skew the results. After all, they were studying the placebo effect. However, in this case, Brooks knew that they were testing the placebo effect because he had asked them to do so, and despite knowing this, the placebo effect was clearly evident. He describes in some detail the tests that were performed on him, noting that he knew there was some sort of deception involved in both, although he did not know its precise nature and was unable to figure out what it was. Nonetheless, in both cases he experienced the placebo effect, which took the form of significant pain reduction. The experimenter who conducted the first test acknowledged afterwards that she had not expected it to work on someone who actually knew what was going on.[27]

Note here that the experimenter had assumed the placebo would not work on someone who knows—or thinks he knows—that he is receiving a placebo. But this brings us back to our original question concerning the placebo effect of humor: Does the very "fact" that humor *is* a placebo increase or decrease its placebo effects? If I know that humor is a placebo,

25. Ibid.
26. Ibid., 171.
27. Ibid., 178.

do I receive greater or lesser benefits from humor than does a person who does not know this? I will return to this question in the conclusion to this chapter.

Brooks says that this visit to Turin "certainly cured me of any doubt about the reality of the placebo effect."[28] He adds that he was surprised that the experiments worked but that he really should not have been. After all, "the brain is an astonishing organ, a supremely complex collection of molecules that process signals—both chemical and electrical—to give us our sense of who we are and how we experience the world around us. With careful control of the signals going in, why shouldn't that sense be open to manipulation?"[29] Citing research on sufferers of Parkinson's disease, he concludes that "it's not just about positive thinking: it's about the chemical or electrical signals that positive thinking produces . . . Placebo, it seems, is all in the brain—and it is real."[30]

On the other hand, Brooks cautions against the belief that placebos can work wonders. He notes that placebos cannot, of course, cure cancer, slow the onset of Alzheimer's or Parkinson's disease, or make a malfunctioning kidney function again. He observes that patients are flocking to "complementary" therapists who unwittingly embrace placebos, and suggests that these same patients are probably unaware that their family doctor could quite intentionally embrace these same treatments, where appropriate. Therefore, the danger comes when the *complement* part of *complementary* disappears and patients visit practitioners who offer only "alternative" treatments: "If the patient's condition is simply not placebo responsive—even if many of the symptoms are—that could be life-threatening."[31] A better approach is to get the placebo out in the open and "find a way to make it an acceptable tool in the doctor's armory." Doing so could save lives "by keeping patients within the fold of efficacious, rational medicine" as long as we also acknowledge that, "for the moment at least, it's not quite as rational as we'd like."[32]

---

28. Ibid., 172.
29. Ibid., 173.
30. Ibid., 194.
31. Ibid., 181.

32. Ibid. Earlier, Brooks cited several studies that indicate that physicians do, in fact, prescribe placebos. The usual way in which they do this is not to prescribe sugar pills (as the patient would then be likely to know that a placebo was being prescribed) but to prescribe a medication that has something useful in it but whose licensed use is not to treat what is ailing the patient. He also cites an article in the *Journal of the*

Conclusion

In my earlier comments on humor as a placebo, I suggested that I *know* that humor has a placebo effect. In point of fact, I do not really *know* this. I simply *believe* it. But Brooks' discussion of the placebo effect in the case of medications serves as a useful analogy, and because it does, it also supports the idea that the placebo effects of humor are real. In chapter 2 I will cite studies that attest to the fact that humor may play a significant role in the reduction of anxiety and stress.

Also, I believe that the studies conducted by the Benedetti team in Turin provide a valuable explanation for why humor has this placebo effect. As I noted, Dr. Benedetti suggested that the chemicals secreted in the brain were the effect of "the molecules of hope," and Brooks indicates that the biochemical effects of the placebo point us to "the healing power of the imagination."[33] These observations invite the inference that humor is most effective as a placebo when it stimulates hope and the healing power of the imagination. This means that not all humor has a placebo effect. In fact, it could be argued that some humor actually undermines its placebo effect, and that this would be especially true of humor that either confirms the belief that things are hopeless or works against the healing power of the imagination. If this is so, there is a certain irony in the fact that the very claim that humor is a placebo appears, at first glance, to suggest that humor is not especially valuable—that it is, at best, a rather trivial affair. But Brooks' chapter on the placebo effect indicates that the placebo can play a very important role in the health of an individual, one that may even exceed the positive effects of "real" medications.

And this brings us back to the dictionary definition of *placebo*. As we saw earlier, the dictionary defines *placebo* as "a harmless, unmedicated preparation given as a medicine to a patient merely to humor him."[34] If the effect of humor, as a placebo, is to *humor* the person, I would suggest that this is no small achievement. In fact, one of the definitions of *humor*

American Pharmaceutical Association that offers advice to pharmacists who are aware that the prescription is a placebo. It suggests that the pharmacist say to the patient, "Generally, a larger dose is used for most patients, but your doctor believes that you'll benefit from this dose" (ibid., 168).

33. Ibid., 165, 179. In *Images of Hope*, William F. Lynch suggests that the imagination plays a critical role in the capacity to develop and maintain an attitude of hope; see Capps, "Imagining Hope"; see also Stotland, *Psychology of Hope*, who emphasizes the role that goals play in maintaining an attitude of hope.

34. Agnes, ed., *Webster's New World College Dictionary*, 1099.

is that it is "a person's disposition or temperament" or "state of mind."[35] It is also useful to consider that the word *humor* originally applied to the four fluids considered responsible for one's health and disposition.[36]

What Brooks' chapter invites us to consider is the fact that if humor *is* a placebo, its effects are not ephemeral or superficial. It is not a cure for everything that ails us. On the other hand, it is not inconsequential, and this being so, perhaps the real challenge that each of us faces is finding the right dose—not too much but not too little.

---

35. Ibid., 696.

36. Ibid. In their article "The Persistence of the Four Temperaments" Doody and Immerwahr note that "The theory of the four temperaments (sanguine, phlegmatic, choleric, and melancholic) has had a remarkable durability. From its development by Empedocles, Hippocrates, and Galen, the theory has survived virtually intact through every subsequent historical era in the West" (348).

2

Humor as Moderator of Life Stress

Now that we have established that a placebo may have real health-promoting effects, the next step is to determine whether this may also be true of humor and, if so, what these effects might be. As we have seen, Michael Brooks cautions against overestimating the beneficial effects of the placebo. It does not have curative powers. But it can reduce the symptoms of one's illness or disease, and it can help one cope more effectively with the illness. In this way it may contribute, indirectly, to the effectiveness of the drug that is normally prescribed for this particular illness or condition.

Similarly, humor is not a cure for anxiety and stress. But research studies have shown that it can, in fact, be helpful in alleviating anxiety and reducing stress. In this chapter, I will present their findings and offer some practical suggestions on how one might make use of humor's health-promoting properties in this regard.

As we consider these research studies, I feel I should forewarn readers that these studies are not particularly humorous or even amusing. In fact, I have spent hours familiarizing myself with these studies and have to confess that I rarely found myself laughing or even chuckling. While the subject of these studies is humor, the researchers who conducted the studies and wrote them up clearly mean business. They explain and defend their research methods, puzzle over results that they had not predicted or that even challenged their hypotheses, acknowledge the limitations of their research, and call for further research. All of this is standard fare, typical of psychological research reports, but it may strike readers—as it has me—that there is some incongruity here between topic and report, and maybe there is some humor in this very incongruity.[1]

---

1. In "A New Theory of Laughter," John Morreall identifies three philosophical

Nonetheless, these psychological studies of humor are worth reading. In some ways, they confirm what we believe or think we know about humor. In other ways, they teach us some things about humor that we either did not know or did not think to ask about humor.

Humor and Coping with Stressful Situations

The most extensively researched issue over the past several decades is the role of humor in moderating life stress. The originators of this line of research were Herbert M. Lefcourt, professor of psychology at the University of Waterloo, and Rod A. Martin, professor of psychology at the University of Western Ontario.

Their major monograph *Humor and Life Stress* is subtitled *Antidote to Adversity*.[2] In light of the view presented in chapter 1 that humor may be the best placebo, it is interesting that they, too, use a medical term—*antidote*—to characterize the effects of humor. The dictionary defines *antidote* as (1) "a remedy to counteract a poison," and (2) "anything that works against an evil or unwanted condition."[3] *The Merck Manual's* most

---

theories of humor: *superiority, incongruity,* and *relief.* The *superiority* theory goes back at least as far as Plato and Aristotle, and was given its classic formulation by Thomas Hobbes, who said that humor expresses "a sudden glory arising from some conception of some eminency in ourselves, by comparison with the infirmity of others, or with our own formerly" (Morreall, "A New Theory of Laughter," 129). The *incongruity* theory had its beginnings in some scattered comments in Aristotle, but did not come into its own until Kant and Schopenhauer: "The basic idea behind this theory is very simple. We live in an orderly world where we have come to expect certain patterns among things, properties, events, etc. When we experience something that doesn't fit these patterns, that violates our expectations, one reaction is to laugh. As Pascal said, 'Nothing produces laughter more than a surprising disproportion between that which one expects and that which one sees'" (ibid., 130). The *relief* theory goes back to Aristotle's comments on catharsis in comedy, but the idea that laughter is a release of nervous energy was not carefully worked out until the nineteenth century. Herbert Spencer observed that nervous energy tends to beget muscular action: in fear, we make movements of flight; in anger, we tend to make aggressive movements of fight. In contrast, laughter does not lead to practical action such as flight or attack. Instead, it is merely a release of nervous energy. It occurs when some emotion has built up but then is suddenly perceived to be inappropriate. If someone feels fearful because she thinks she hears an intruder in the house, then on discovering that it was only the cat, she might break out in laughter (Morreall, "A New Theory of Laughter," 131. See also Morreall, "Enjoying Incongruity"; and Marmysz, *Laughing at Nothing*).

2. Lefcourt and Martin, *Humor and Life Stress.*
3. Agnes, ed., *Webster's New World College Dictionary,* 61.

sustained discussion of antidotes is in its consideration of depression and, more specifically, the use of antidepressant drugs known as monoamine oxidase inhibitors (MAOIs). It notes:

> People taking MAOIs are usually instructed to carry an antidote, such as chlorpromazine or nifedipine, at all times. If a severe, throbbing headache occurs, they should take the antidote at once and go to the nearest emergency room. Because of the risk of stroke and difficult dietary restrictions and necessary precautions, MAOIs are rarely prescribed except for depressed people whose condition has not improved with other antidepressants.[4]

Clearly, the claim that humor is an antidote to adversity—which the dictionary defines as "a state of wretchedness or misfortune, poverty and trouble"[5]—is a much stronger claim than that humor is a valuable placebo. My own view is that a more modest claim for humor is preferable because this is less likely to set us up for disappointment. As we saw in the introduction, William James cautioned against a too strenuous commitment to the gospel of relaxation. The same caution applies to the gospel of humor.

Over the decade prior to the publication of *Humor and Life Stress* Herbert Lefcourt directed two doctoral dissertations on the subject of humor. But when the two students who wrote these dissertations graduated, humor research under his direction languished because he was more centrally engaged in research on the locus of control, a topic that has attracted great interest among empirically oriented psychologists of religion.[6]

However, an unexpected event prompted him to resume the humor studies. At his father's funeral, instead of the expected solemn occasion,

> the reuniting of disparate family members from far and wide proved to be an occasion for mirth and good will. This was not at all out of disrespect for the deceased, but was almost in his honor. He had always been one ready to make light of the grimmest circumstances, often with a joke or cliché that somehow

---

4. Beers et al., eds., *Merck Manual of Medical Information*, 618–19. The *Manual* also discusses the use of antidotes in cases of exposure to radioactive materials, 1660–61.

5. Agnes, ed., *Webster's New World College Dictionary*, 20.

6. This is largely because it has enabled them to study subjects' views on the influence of God in their lives. An example is Jackson and Coursey's "Relationship of God Control," which was published two years after the publication of Lefcourt and Martin's *Humor and Life Stress*.

would fit the occasion and would cause others to take the situation less seriously. The humor displayed at this funeral was very much in character with the way in which the deceased would have jested had he been there to take part.[7]

Humor and Life Stress begins with a discussion of theoretical approaches to the study of the sense of humor, and then it describes the authors' development of a sense-of-humor questionnaire titled "The Situational Humor Response Questionnaire" (SHRQ). The questionnaire is designed to measure respondents' propensity to smile and laugh in a variety of daily life situations. It is now widely used in humor research. It includes questions like, "If you arrived at a party and found that someone else was wearing a piece of clothing identical to yours" or "If you were eating in a restaurant with some friends and the waiter accidentally spilled a drink on you," followed by these choices:

a. I would not have found this particularly amusing.

b. I would have smiled occasionally.

c. I would have smiled a lot and laughed from time to time.

d. I would have found quite a lot to laugh about.

e. I would have laughed heartily much of the time.[8]

Lefcourt and Martin also developed a Coping Humor Scale that includes the following statements, to which respondents are asked to rate their agreement or disagreement:

a. I often lose my sense of humor when I'm having problems.

b. I have often found that my problems have been greatly reduced when I tried to find something funny in them.

---

7. Lefcourt and Martin, *Humor and Life Stress*, 1. See also Capps, "Nervous Laughter."

8. It is not surprising that the SHRQ does not include a funeral among the various situations that may evoke the propensity to smile and laugh, but if it had been distributed at his father's funeral, the responses would probably have been in the middle range of the choices offered, and the more extreme response—"I would have laughed heartily much of the time"—would have been viewed as inappropriate. This assumption suggests that considerations of social propriety play an important role in determining whether and to what extent a respondent has a propensity to smile or laugh in a given situation.

c. I usually look for something comical to say when I am in tense situations.

d. I must admit my life would probably be easier if I had more of a sense of humor.

e. I have often felt that if I am in a situation where I have to either cry or laugh, it is better to laugh.

f. I can usually find something to laugh or joke about even in trying situations.

g. It has been my experience that humor is often a very effective way of coping with problems.

These two instruments were then used to assess sense of humor as a moderator of life stress. The authors used a questionnaire designed for college students in order to establish a life stress score based on the number of stressful events the students had experienced during the preceding year and their assessment of the effect that each of these events had on their lives. Lefcourt and Martin also employed a questionnaire designed to assess the students' current mood levels. It considers negative moods of tension, depression, anger, fatigue, and confusion, and one positive mood of vigor.

The first study supported the hypothesis that humor reduces the impact of stress. Subjects with a high score on the SHRQ measure of sense of humor showed a weaker relationship between negative life events and depressed mood than did those with a lower sense of humor.[9] No gender differences were found in this initial study.

Because the initial study was based only on self-report measures of sense of humor, a second study involved an effort to obtain a more behavioral assessment of the subjects' actual ability to produce humor. They were seated at a table on which a dozen or so miscellaneous objects had been placed—a tennis shoe, a drinking glass, an aspirin bottle, and so forth—and were instructed to make up a three-minute comedy routine by describing the objects on the table as humorously as possible. They were rated according to the number of witty remarks they were able to produce and on their overall wittiness on a three-point scale. After analyzing the data, the authors concluded that the results provide further evidence for the stress-moderating role of humor: "Individuals who demonstrated an ability to produce humor 'on demand' in an impromptu

9. Lefcourt and Martin, *Humor and Life Stress*, 55.

comedy routine showed a lower relationship between life stresses and disturbed mood than did those who were less able to produce humor in this situation."[10]

The correlation between humor production and scenes in the situational humor response questionnaire (SHRQ) also indicated that "subjects who were able to produce a humorous monologue in the laboratory also tended to report that they exhibit mirth in a wide variety of life situations."[11] Lefcourt and Martin hypothesize that the subjects who had been rated as most funny in their monologues were those who had the most practice in creating humor in their everyday lives.

In a third study, the assumption that subjects with high scores on the humor measures would also make particular use of humor as a means of coping with the stressful experiences that they encounter in their everyday lives was directly tested by assessing their ability to produce humor when placed in a stressful situation. To create an experimental analogue of stress, the authors used the film *Subincision,* a movie that had been found to be mildly stressful and had been used by another researcher in his own work on stress.[12] The assumption was that the subjects who were best able to create a witty monologue while watching the film would be those who also tended to make use of humor in real-life stressful situations. This assumption was confirmed both by independent ratings of subjects' tape-recorded monologues and by their own responses to a questionnaire they were asked to fill out after watching the film. The questionnaire included the following statement and question: "You have just attempted to make up a humorous narrative while watching what is considered to be a rather stressful film. How likely would it be for you to normally use humor in this kind of situation?"[13]

Lefcourt and Martin conclude that these studies provide considerable support for the view that humor reduces the impact of stress. They acknowledge that this is only an initial attempt to investigate a hypothesis

---

10. Ibid., 59.

11. Ibid.

12. I have not been able to find out anything about the film, but I assume that it concerns a form of body modification in which the underside of the penis is incised and the urethra is slit open lengthwise. In many cultures, subincision is a ritual signifying that the individual has entered adulthood. Given that it is performed on males, I would assume that there were gender differences in terms of subjects' degrees of stress and their humorous responses.

13. Lefcourt and Martin, *Humor and Life Stress,* 60.

"that has long been maintained by a large number of humor theorists, psychotherapists, and laypersons alike, namely, that a sense of humor permits one to better cope with the aversive experiences of life."[14] They suggest, therefore, that further research is needed "to explore the specific processes involved in the stress-buffering effects of humor, the kinds of stresses with which humor is most effective and those with which it is less appropriate, the particular aspects or types of humor that are most effective in moderating stress, and the ways in which humor of this kind develops in individuals."[15] Answers to each of these questions would not only provide information specific to the stress-moderating role of humor, but would also "enlarge our general understanding of the ubiquitous but still largely unexplained human phenomenon called 'humor.'"[16]

Humor, Disability, and Self-Concept

In a subsequent study, Lefcourt and Martin took advantage of the fact that a young male student worked for a community-service organization that chauffeured physically disabled persons around their community.[17] Through his contacts and observations of his clients, Lefcourt and Martin were able to develop a study of the role played by a sense of humor in coping with physical disabilities. There were thirty disabled persons in the study, sixteen women and fourteen men, and they ranged in age from eighteen to seventy-eight. Fifteen were chronic cases whose disabilities were essentially lifelong, and fifteen were acute cases involving disabilities acquired in adolescence or adulthood a minimum of three years prior to the study. The level of disability was severe in all cases, with most subjects being paraplegic, quadriplegic, or, in the case of those with cerebral palsy, noticeably disabled. Potential subjects were asked about their willingness to participate in the study when they were being driven to their destination, and most expressed immediate interest in being involved. The interviews that formed the basis of the study took nearly two hours.

14. Ibid., 63.
15. Ibid.
16. Ibid.
17. In the following discussion of the study, I will not attempt to change the authors' references to the "handicapped," "crippled," and "disabled" to "physically challenged." I would simply remind readers that at the time their studies were carried out (the 1980s) the word "handicapped" was still in use but was being replaced by the word "disabled."

The first part of the interview involved scaling methods, and the second part consisted of open-ended questions. The scales were a locus-of-control scale and a disability self-concept scale. The first of these two scales included forced choice questions such as

a. Sometimes I impulsively do things which at other times I definitely would not let myself do.
b. I find that I can keep my impulses in control.
c. Self-regulation of one's behavior is always possible.
d. I frequently find that when certain things happen to me I cannot restrain my reaction.

A high score on this scale indicates a disbelief in one's ability to control one's own behavior.

The second scale included statements to which the respondent indicates agreement or disagreement on a five-point scale. Sample items are:

a. People look at me as if I were unusual.
b. People seem to feel sorry for me.
c. There is little future for a person who has been paralyzed.
d. It is unusual for a non-disabled person to be in love with a disabled person.

This scale essentially examined self-concept from two points of view: one's view of one's own personal worth and one's view of how one's personal worth is perceived by others. In terms of one's own self-perceptions, statements reflect personal self-confidence, the sense of personal adequacy, and beliefs about one's closeness to others. Concerning one's view of how one is perceived by others, the scale explores social acceptance, appearance to others, and relationships with others.

The second part of the interview involved a series of open-ended questions, and the responses were tape-recorded. In this segment of the interview, subjects were given the opportunity to discuss their feelings about their disabilities, how they deal with "normal" persons, their everyday activities, and how they are perceived by others. These questions were designed to reveal how subjects view themselves in comparison with nondisabled persons (the issue of equality), their possible feelings of bitterness about being disabled, their feelings of vulnerability about their disability and openness to discussing these feelings, their involvement in the community or in activities, their vigor and vitality, and their awareness and understanding of nondisabled persons' views concerning disabled persons. Their answers to these questions were rated by the interviewer and one of his coworkers in the community-service organization. The six factors (sense of equality, bitterness, openness, involvement, vigor, and awareness) were rated on scales of 1 to 10, and the total score was the sum of the five positive factors minus the one negative factor (bitterness).

Prior to setting up the tape recorder for each interview, the interviewer showed each subject two disability-related cartoons (for example, a gallows outfitted with a ramp for physically challenged persons) and asked them what they thought of them. Their responses to each cartoon were recorded and rated on a scale of 1–10, with 1 indicating a complete absence of humor and 10 indicating a hearty humorous response. Thus:

(1) No facial response, body rigid, verbal responses—if any—are negative

(2/3) Minimal smiling, no noticeable body response, no comments

(4/5) Soft chuckles, open smile, possible head shaking or verbal comments

(6/7) Soft laughter, chuckling, minimal body motions, verbal comments indicating approval

(8/9) Strong laughter and body motion, affirmative verbal comments

(10) Prolonged hearty laughter, marked body movement and strong verbal affirmative statements

The two cartoons made up the humor-eliciting aspect of the study.

On the assumption that there is a greater chance of coming to terms with disability over time, it was hypothesized that humor, as well as self-concept, vitality, and sense of control would be associated positively with the length of time that one had experienced the disability. Persons whose disabilities occurred more recently would be expected to exhibit more distress reflected in lower self-concept, sense of control, vitality, and humor.

The results were consistent with the earlier studies of humor and life stress. Humor was positively correlated with the disability self-concept scale and disability self-concept interview. Also, the relationship between humor and duration of disability was also positive. The one exception to these positive findings was the locus-of-control scale, as there were no relationships, positive or negative, between this scale and the other scales employed in the study. The research team had expected that this variable, the sense that one is able to self-regulate one's behavior and responses to situations, would be positively related to higher scores on the disability self-concept scale and self-concept interviews, and on the humor scores derived from the two cartoons. But they acknowledge that they were wrong in this regard, that it is more likely the case that disabled persons have to come to terms with the very fact that they are *unable* to exercise control over themselves and their lives. Thus, their higher self-concept and humor scores are a reflection of their having accepted this fact or truth about themselves.[18] In short, "humor was associated with greater vitality and positive self-concept, suggesting that there is greater acceptance and/or transcendence of their disabilities by those subjects who are able to express humor about the very state of being handicapped."[19]

Furthermore, the subjects who could laugh at cartoons that depicted their need for special facilities were clearly higher-functioning individuals. The very fact that these persons "have impressed others as being more vital and vigorous and that they respond to questions about their own circumstances in such a manner that they are viewed as being more confident, involved, and thriving indicates that there is something very meaningful about this display of humor in response to stimuli that are so relevant to their everyday difficulties."[20]

Lefcourt and Martin conclude this study with brief anecdotal comments on two of the subjects who received ratings of 10 on their humor responses to the two cartoons. One was a man who was born without arms and legs. The other was a man with a moderate case of cerebral

---

18. In terms of the three philosophical theories of humor noted in footnote 1, this finding would seem to support the *incongruity* theory of humor as opposed to the *superiority* and *relief* theories. The fact that one is disabled is likely to work against the *superiority* theory. As Thomas Hobbes said of humor, it is based on the sense of "a sudden glory arising from some conception of eminency in oneself, either by comparison with the infirmity of others or with one's own infirmity in the past" (Morreall, "A New Theory of Laughter," 129). After all, one is still disabled. It is also likely to work against the *relief* theory for the same reason. The *incongruity* theory is based on expectations of certain patterns among things, properties, and events, and the humor is in the fact that these expectations are violated. Physically challenged persons live with such violations every day of their lives, not only in relation to their disability but also in relation to how others perceive and behave toward them. The cartoon that depicts a gallows outfitted with a ramp plays on this sense of incongruity.

19. Lefcourt and Martin, *Humor and Life Stress*, 119.

20. Ibid.

palsy since childhood. The first had been reared in such a way that he seemed to accept dependency without bitterness or self-denigration in those situations where help from others was necessary and unavoidable: "As an adult, he retained a live-in nursing helper who carried him through all of those everyday routines that most of us regard as private, self-regulated, and automatic. This man, therefore, experienced what to a non-crippled person would seem to be a daily round of humiliations. To him, however, being aroused, bathed, toileted, fed, etc. had become automatic, semi-private events of little immediate significance."[21] What did matter to him "were his jobs, his avocations, and the fact that, in his words, 'there just aren't enough hours in a day.'"[22] In addition to being the executive director of a community-service organization, he regularly speaks on a local television program concerned with the ramifications of being physically disabled, and as an artist who uses his mouth to hold his brushes, he teaches art to nondisabled as well as disabled persons: "When this highly articulate, intelligent man looked at the cartoons related to physical handicaps, he laughed heartily and rejoined with his own jokes about handicaps."[23]

The other man, who could often be seen throughout his childhood riding a bicycle around the neighborhood, was difficult to understand and twisted in posture, the very epitome of someone affected by cerebral palsy. And yet, "as one came to know him, it was evident that he did not view himself as a pitiable victim . . . and that he had a highly developed sense of humor."[24] While laughing, he would often lose some control of his body, but what was most interesting "was his lack of self-consciousness or embarrassment about his features during a conversation, an indication perhaps of his positive self-concept. In the study this young man laughed heartily, scored highly on vitality and well-being (both self-concept measures), and admitted to externality with regard to self-control."[25] That is, he had come to terms with the fact that in various respects he was unable to exercise control over himself and his life.

How were these two men and others like them able to come to seem so confident and humorous in the face of such severe physical challenges?

21. Ibid., 120.
22. Ibid., 121.
23. Ibid.
24. Ibid.
25. Ibid.

Lefcourt and Martin speculate that a possible response to the hurts and humiliations they suffered as children would have been to become retiring and withdrawn, thus enabling them to "avoid the stares and not so subtle censure and revulsion seen in the faces of others."[26] But another response "was to accept the fact that in the eyes of others, they might be odd-looking; but in their own minds, they knew that they were the equals of others, even if they suffered limitations to their autonomy. Both men had become relatively well-educated, had hopes for their futures, and seemed buoyantly optimistic, reflecting their choice to be active in the pursuit of whatever opportunities that they felt were available to them."[27] To those who might see in these descriptions of the two men "clear evidence of denial, an assumedly unhealthy defense mechanism," Lefcourt and Martin counter that

> what we most readily perceive in these cases are examples of what Freud described as humor, the highest defense mechanism. By accepting limitations as a given and thereby regarding their life ambitions as being contingent upon others' help, and not solely in their own hands, it would be hard for these handicapped persons to become overly driven or too serious and proud. To be trapped in a non-functioning body should, on the other hand, provide one with a ready access to a "cosmic view" from which to look upon one's own struggles and problems.[28]

The authors are referring here to Freud's essay on humor in which he emphasized that, through humor, the ego demonstrates its refusal "to be hurt by the arrows of reality or to be compelled to suffer."[29] By repudiating the possibility of suffering, humor, according to Freud, "takes its place in the great series of methods devised by the mind" for "evading the compulsion to suffer," but unlike so many of these other methods (delusions, intoxication, and the like), humor achieves this evasion "without quitting the ground of mental sanity, as happens when other means to the same end are adopted."[30]

---

26. Ibid.
27. Ibid.
28. Ibid., 121–22.
29. Freud, "Humor," 265.
30. Ibid., 266.

For Lefcourt and Martin, how one finds humor in a predicament where the object of humor is oneself is itself a subject for further investigation. Meanwhile, they suspect that this humorous vantage point

> requires what Freud felt was the primary source of humor, the internalization of our parents' encouragement of our efforts as well as gentle tolerance of our failures. Freud judged this to be one of the wisest of legacies bestowable by parents upon their children . . . Likewise, handicapped individuals who aspire to lead something like a normal existence must be ready to forgive themselves for their failures to achieve many of their goals because their handicaps do in fact make accomplishments very difficult.[31]

Thus, persons who are not physically disabled and "who often forget that they are but mortal and heir to all the limitations associated with that condition, have much to learn about humor and grace from handicapped persons."[32] The authors posit, in other words, a positive relationship between a humorous sense of oneself and acceptance of the limitations that are inherent in the human condition itself. And in light of the close association of humor and grace, we learn what it means to be graceful from persons who are thought to be the very opposite of graceful in a physical sense.

Humor and Coping under Stress

Following Lefcourt and Martin's groundbreaking research, others have studied the relation between humor and coping with stress. An especially interesting study was carried out by Smadar Bizi, Giora Keinan, and Benjamin Beit-Hallahmi, professors of psychology at Tel Aviv University and the University of Haifa, in the late 1980s. They studied 159 Israeli soldiers, aged nineteen and twenty, who were taking part in a course for combat and defense forces.[33] In addition to a self-report questionnaire, there was a questionnaire in which crew members evaluated one another on two kinds of humor: *productive* humor (where one tells jokes and makes humorous comments and descriptions in a way that elicits

---

31. Lefcourt and Martin, *Humor and Life Stress*, 122. I will return to Freud's article on humor in chapter 5.

32. Ibid., 122.

33. Bizi et al., "Humor and Coping with Stress."

smiling or laughter in others) and *reactive* humor (where one mainly enjoys the jokes and humorous comments of others). There was also a companywide peer-rating questionnaire in which each respondent was asked to name ten soldiers in his company (numbering between forty-eight and fifty-two trainees), five whom they considered high in humor and five whom they considered low in humor. The coping-under-stress factor was also measured by means of peer-ratings and ratings by company commanders.

The self-rating questionnaire results did not support the prediction that persons who scored themselves higher in humor would also score higher in terms of coping under stress. The authors think this may have been due, in part, to the fact that there is "interpersonal variance in the degree of self-awareness which is a precondition for a valid self-report in general and concerning humor in particular."[34] Also, subjects might knowingly distort their own report for various reasons, such as the desire to present themselves in a positive light, which in this case would mean presenting oneself as more humorous than one actually is.[35]

On the other hand, the main positive finding of the study was that humor, as rated by peers, was positively related to performance under stress, and this was especially true for *productive* as opposed to *reactive* humor. Thus, the authors conclude that "there is a positive relationship between the degree of humor behavior, specifically active humor (production), and the quality of functioning under stress."[36] They suggest that further research is needed to establish the validity of theories that attempt to explain why humor may reduce stress, help personal relationships, facilitate the release of problematic feelings and thoughts, and serve as a cognitive active coping method. In other words, they have demonstrated that a positive relationship between humor and coping under stress exists, but why it exists is not self-evident.

---

34. Ibid., 955.

35. This raises an interesting question relating to the view, presented in ch. 1, that humor may be the best placebo. That is, might the very claim to have a more developed sense of humor than one actually possesses activate the placebo effect of humor? And, if so, might a person who seems rather humorless to others nonetheless experience the benefits of humor simply by claiming to have a sense of humor?

36. Bizi et al., "Humor and Coping with Stress," 956.

Humor and Worry: Partners in Coping

Another interesting study of humor as a means of moderating life stress was carried out by William E. Kelly, a member of the counseling department at the University of Nevada, Las Vegas. The results were published in 2002.[37] Kelly was especially interested in the relationship between humor and worry. He wanted to know if humor has a positive effect on worry—that is, whether humor causes a person to worry less. He used a worry questionnaire that assesses five worry areas: (1) relationships, (2) lack of confidence, (3) aimless future, (4) work concerns, and (5) financial concerns. He also used the sense-of-humor scale developed by James Thorson, a gerontologist at the University of Nebraska in Omaha, and F. C. Powell, for their own study of the relationship between sense of humor and death anxiety.[38]

Because this was an exploratory study and no previous studies had been undertaken on humor in relation to worry, Kelly made no predictions as to what he would find. But the use of these two instruments enabled him to try to identify any relationships that might exist between humor and worry.

The major finding of the study was a negative relationship between worry and sense of humor, leading to the conclusion that persons with a high sense of humor are less likely to worry. However, the primary reason that worry was negatively related to humor was the fact that worry had a strong negative effect on humor production. Because there was also a strong association between humor production and the lack-of-confidence domain of the worry scale, Kelly guesses that worries about self-confidence especially hinder persons from producing humor. In his view, this may be because "worriers would question their ability to produce humor in such a way that others would find favorable."[39] A similar explanation might be made for the negative relationship that was found between sense of humor and worries about personal relationships: "That

---

37. Kelly, "Investigation of Worry and Sense of Humor."
38. Thorson and Powell, "Relationships of Death Anxiety and Sense of Humor." Thorson and Powell also developed a multidimensional sense of humor scale that focuses on coping humor, humor generation or creativity, humor appreciation, and appreciation of humorous people. They found negative relationships, albeit rather slight ones, between death anxiety and all four dimensions of humor. As we might have expected in the case of death anxiety, the strongest of these negative relationships involved coping humor.
39. Kelly, "Investigation of Worry and Sense of Humor," 662.

is, individuals who worry about disrupting, or losing, relationships might be less inclined to use humor for fear that others will not approve of their humor."[40]

Although Kelly made no predictions as to what he would find, one finding of the study that one would not have predicted was that worry was *positively* related to one of the dimensions of humor, that of *coping* humor. That is, worry and coping humor were found to be compatible. It may seem surprising that worry and coping by means of humor would be positively related to each other, but Kelly cites another study demonstrating that worry is itself an active cognitive coping mechanism. Thus, "if worry and humor both serve as coping mechanisms, it is less surprising that worry and coping with humor are positively related."[41] This finding suggests that worriers are less likely to deal with stressful life experiences by thinking of something humorous to say, and more likely to employ humor as a way to mitigate the negative consequences or outcomes of these experiences. If situations that one cannot control are likely to produce anxiety and stress, worry and humor may both be ways to forestall or inhibit these reactions. The worrier does this by anticipating all the things that *could* go wrong, while the humorist does this by minimizing the importance or significance of what did *in fact* go wrong.

This conclusion is supported by Julie K. Norem's *The Positive Power of Negative Thinking*.[42] Norem contends that negative thinking—what is sometimes called "catastrophizing"[43]—is actually a positive coping mechanism for some individuals. Where others tend to minimize what might go wrong when they invite a group of friends over for dinner or organize a business conference, negative thinkers (what Kelly would call "worriers") think of all the things that might go awry and plan for these exigencies. If "non-worriers" suggest to worriers that their fears are groundless or that many of the things that they worry may happen are only remotely possible, the worrier may not disagree but still maintain that it is better to anticipate *all* the things that might go wrong than be taken by surprise.[44] Kelly's study suggests that worrying about these exigencies and remote

---

40. Ibid., 663.
41. Ibid.
42. Norem, *The Positive Power of Negative Thinking*.
43. See Beck and Emery, *Anxiety Disorders and Phobias*, 33.
44. The following joke is relevant in this regard: "The Jewish mother's telegram: 'Begin worrying. Details follow.'"

possibilities has the positive effect of reducing anxiety and moderating stress.

Thus, worry and anxiety are two very different psychological phenomena, and worry and humor may, in fact, be partners in coping with the stresses of life. And because personal relationships are among the potential contributors to stress, perhaps "humorists" and "worriers" need to develop greater tolerance and respect for one another. Also, since worry can escalate into anxiety, the worrier may find it useful to include a humor resolution with regard to the things that he or she worries about. This resolution, which would be based on the incongruity theory of humor, would involve planning in advance to consider amusing—rather than irritating, frustrating, depressing, and so forth—whatever happens that was *not* according to plan, that one's planning was, in fact, designed to keep from happening.

Translations of Jesus' admonition to his listeners not to be concerned about their life, what they will eat or drink, or what they will wear (Matthew 6:25–33) are interesting in this regard. The Revised Standard Version (RSV) uses the word "anxious" in this passage, and the New Revised Standard Version (NRSV) and New International Version (NIV) use the word "worry." The King James Version (KJV) avoids this problem by using the phrase "take no thought." These translation issues suggest that this passage may be a useful means to reflect on the anxiety/worry distinction and on Kelly's finding that worry may actually help in coping with anxiety. But humor is also important here, for humor can play an important role in keeping worry within the bounds of effective coping and not allowing it to develop into an anxiety that is debilitating and unproductive.

This does not, of course, mean that everything that might go wrong should simply be laughed off as inconsequential. The following joke from *Red Stangland's Norwegian Home Companion* is relevant in this regard:

> Ole and Lena had the Torkelsons over for lutefisk and lefse. Mr. Torkelson liked it with plenty of melted butter and pepper. Lena couldn't find the pepper, so she rummaged through the cupboard and found a container she thought was pepper. The next day Ole and Lena discovered it actually was gunpowder. So, Ole called Torkelson on the phone and told him the mistake. "Vell, I'm glad to find out what happened, becoss when ve got home

last night, I leaned over to tie my shoe and I accidently shot da cat."[45]

The very fact that this is a joke invites us to focus on the humorous side of the fact that things can go wrong at a dinner party no matter how careful one may be to anticipate such things in advance. On the other hand, we should not overlook the fact that the cat was the victim of Lena's mistaking gunpowder for pepper. But this simply underscores the point that was made in the previous chapter: that humor is a placebo, not a cure, and it cannot, in this case, restore life to the cat. On the other hand, we could probably forgive Ole for responding to Mr. Torkelson, "It's a good thing that you shot the cat and not the dog because, after all, cats have nine lives."

The Contagious Effect of Humor

Another interesting study of humor and its role in moderating stress is Marc Gelkopf, Shulamith Kretler and Micea Sigal's study of the potential therapeutic effects of humor on patients with schizophrenia.[46] The study involved thirty-four patients in two chronic schizophrenic wards in a mental hospital. Over a three-month period, the patients in Ward A were exposed to seventy humorous movies, while patients in Ward B were exposed to seventy movies of various kinds (action, romance, drama, and some comedies).

The main positive effect of exposure to a barrage of humorous movies was that patients in Ward A experienced a slight but statistically significant decrease in verbal hostility as perceived by members of the nursing staff. But there was also an unexpected result: that patients who "had been exposed to humor experienced a higher level of social support from the staff." The authors note that this "increased experienced support from the staff may have been initiated either by some humor-induced change in the patients or by some humor-induced change in the staff."[47] They add that in light of the fact that "the humorous films affected the staff to a larger extent than the patients," it might be advisable "to

---

45. Stangland, *Red Stangland's Norwegian Home Companion*, 291.
46. Gelkopf et al., "Laughter in a Psychiatric Ward."
47. Ibid., 288.

consider the possibility of affecting the patients by projecting humorous films with the staff as the target population."[48]

This finding suggests that humor may have indirect benefits and, if so, this very fact may have bearing on the other studies reported here. One would like to think that the researchers were themselves benefitted by their subjects' sense of humor. Lefcourt and Martin certainly imply that this was the case in their study of physically challenged persons. It is often said that humor is contagious, which is itself an interesting use of a medical term that usually has a negative connotation. However, this contagious effect may also mean that the effect of humor on the unknowing recipient—as demonstrated in the study by Gelkopf, Kreitler, and Sigal—may not be easy to detect or demonstrate empirically. But this, as we saw in chapter 1, is precisely what we would expect from a placebo.

Humor, Stress, and Hope

Finally, I would like to comment on a study by Alexander P. Vilaythong, Randolph C. Arnau, David H. Rosen, and Nathan Mascaro published in 2003 on humor and hope.[49] They were affiliated with Texas A&M University at the time the study was conducted. They begin their study by noting that "Negative life events, such as loss of employment, death of loved ones, or conflicts in the family, often lead to stress, which can then precipitate the onset of depression, anxiety, and many other psychological and physical ailments."[50] They cite Lefcourt and Martin's finding that "humor could alleviate stress by serving as a means of cognitively reframing situations, such as viewing a situation as more of a challenge rather than a threat."[51] They also note that humor has been shown to play an important role as a potential source of hope. They cite several studies showing that "as a coping mechanism, humor may competitively inhibit negative thoughts with positive ones, thereby fostering hope in individuals. Hence, humor and hope are potentially significant factors in one's overall sense of psychological and physical well-being."[52] On the other hand, they cite several studies that were unsuccessful in raising hopeful-

48. Ibid.
49. Vilaythong et al., "Humor and Hope." See also Capps, *Agents of Hope*.
50. Ibid., 79.
51. Ibid., 80.
52. Ibid.

ness through the use of humorous stimuli, and they suggest that a major factor in this regard is that the type of humor presented to subjects in the study can have a very strong influence on the outcome of the study.

The first objective of their study was to examine whether a humorous stimulus—a comedy video—can raise a person's level of hopefulness following a stress-inducing exercise of recalling stressful events in one's life. A second objective was to discern if any relationship exists between the number and degrees of stressors and one's overall sense of hopefulness. The measures used were the Multidimensional Sense of Humor Scale (MSHS), the College Chronic Life Stress Survey (CCLSS), the Snyder State Hope Scale (SSHS), the Self-Assessment Manikin (SAM), and a postvideo questionnaire.[53] One hundred eighty undergraduates (111 women and 69 men) who were enrolled in an introductory psychology course participated in the study.

The subjects completed the life-stress survey and then wrote about a stressful event or problem that occurred within the past month without describing its resolution. This enabled them to describe an event or problem that was not on the survey or to go into more detail about one that was on the survey. Then they filled out the hopeful-state survey. After this, they watched a video. Some watched a comedy while others watched a neutral video.[54] After watching the videos, the participants completed the hopeful-state survey again. The comedy video consisted of various segments of *Just Kidding*. These segments covered different aspects of humor, such as slapstick humor, but excluded sexual humor depicting nudity. The neutral control video was a clip from *Magic Eye*, without the music or sound.

The responses to the two videos were in the expected direction. The humorous video was rated as funnier, elicited more laughter, and was

---

53. For the Snyder State Hope Scale (SSHS) see Snyder et al., "Development and Validation of the State Hope Scale." See also Snyder, *Psychology of Hope*. For the Self-Assessment Manikin (SAM) see Bradley and Lang, "Measuring Emotion." The SAM consists of two sets of five cartoons depicting different levels of affective valence and arousal. The valence scores can range from 1 (most happy) to 9 (most unhappy), and the arousal scores can range from 1 (extremely excited) to 9 (very calm). Participants are instructed to place an X on or between the figures that best describes their emotional response to the video that they have been shown as part of the experiment.

54. It is perhaps worth noting that this method of having some students watch a humorous video and others watch a neutral video is similar to the studies we discussed in ch. 1 that employ a medication with an active ingredient and a placebo. We would expect that some of the same anomalies would occur in the video-watching study.

more relaxing than the neutral video. The fact that it was more relaxing has bearing on our discussion in chapter 1 of William James' article on "The Gospel of Relaxation," as it suggests that humor may contribute to a more relaxed state of mind. As for the hypothesis that humor would contribute to hopefulness, the results were somewhat mixed. The hypothesis that persons with a greater sense of humor, especially those with high ratings for using humor as a coping mechanism, would receive greater benefit from viewing the humorous video was not supported. However, there was a small but significant negative relationship between state-hope scores and the total severity of stressors experienced during the past month. In other words, those with higher stress scores were likely to have lower hope scores. Also, it was the felt severity of the stressors rather than the number of stressors that had this effect. Most important, viewing the fifteeen-minute comedy video resulted in a statistically significant increase in state-hope scores relative to the control group, who viewed the affectively neutral video. Thus, fifteen minutes of humor caused viewers to feel more hopeful, especially with regard to the stresses they were experiencing in their lives.

The authors note that future research is needed to determine whether the increase in hopefulness actually leads to a greater degree of successful positive resolution of stressful situations. This is a very important caveat, and one to which our discussion in chapter 1 of humor as a placebo is relevant. Skeptics—even realists—will say that it won't be long before the viewer's state of hopefulness returns to its previous level, and that there will not be any lasting effects of the watching of a fifteen-minute video. But do they know this for sure? Not really. And, this being so, can we not imagine that the viewers' hopefulness will survive the filling out of the researchers' questionnaires? If so, why not also imagine that it will play a role in the days and weeks to come?

Conclusion

I indicated earlier that readers who are hoping that the studies we would be reviewing in this chapter would be humorous or at least somewhat amusing are likely to be disappointed. I doubt that anyone who has read this chapter will disagree with me on this point. So I'm thinking that perhaps I owe it to these readers to end this chapter on a humorous note, but to do so in a way that actually supports the serious point that it makes—that humor can in fact help individuals moderate the stresses, tensions, and anxieties of life. Here are a couple of jokes about expectant fathers:

> A man speaks frantically into the phone, "My wife is pregnant and her contractions are only two minutes apart!" The doctor asks, "Is this her first child?" "Don't be silly!" the man shouts, "This is her husband!"[55]

> A young couple was nervously expecting their first child. As her contractions began in earnest, the wife calmly announced to her husband that it was time to get to the hospital. Noting that it was rush hour, he shouted as he ran out the door ahead of her, "Let's take both cars. That way, one of us is sure to make it in time!"[56]

Here's a joke about a man facing criminal charges:

> A man was arrested on a charge of horse theft and was indicted and brought to trial. When his day in court came, he was taken before the judge and the prosecuting attorney solemnly read the charge in the indictment to him. Then the attorney put the question: "Are you guilty or not guilty?" The man hesitated for a few moments before he answered, then said: "Well, isn't that the very thing we are about to try to find out?"[57]

All three men are in anxiety-producing situations, but the first two are frantic and the third is rather relaxed. Does this mean that expectant fatherhood is more anxiety-producing than being arrested for allegedly stealing a horse? Or is the difference due to temperament, especially as it manifests itself in situations in which others are in control? I tend to think that both explanations have merit. But I can't help thinking that the latter is more influential than the former—that the difference is due primarily to the fact that the alleged horse thief is able to live with ambiguity, and perhaps this is because he alone will be affected by whatever happens.

---

55. Becker et al., *Prairie Home Companion Pretty Good Joke Book* (3rd ed.), 178.
56. Capps, *Laughter Ever After*, x.
57. Lupton, ed., *Treasury of Modern Humor*, 439. I have slightly rewritten this joke.

3

Religion and Humor: Estranged Bedfellows

In chapter 2 we considered studies that show that humor moderates life stress and alleviates anxiety. As these benefits of humor are among the benefits that are often claimed for religion, it would seem that religion and humor would be considered allies. It is somewhat surprising, therefore, that the research literature on religion and humor does not support this assumption. Instead, it suggests that the relationship between religion and humor is ambiguous at best.

In the course of reading James Elkins' *On the Strange Place of Religion in Contemporary Art* I found a reference to a book on religion and art titled *Reluctant Partners*.[1] The phrase "reluctant partners" might also describe the relationship between religion and humor (with religion being the more reluctant partner), but I prefer the phrase "estranged bedfellows" (a play on the phrase "strange bedfellows") as this phrase seems a bit less pretentious, as befits the fact that one of the partners is humor. The following joke illustrates the situation:

> A guy goes into a bar and orders a triple Scotch whiskey. The bartender pours him the drink and says, "That's quite a heavy drink. What's wrong?" After downing his drink, the guy says, "I got home tonight and found my wife in bed with my best friend." "Wow," says the bartender, "No wonder you needed a stiff drink. The second triple is on the house." As the man downs his second triple Scotch the bartender asks him, "What did you do?" The guy says, "I walked over to my wife, looked her straight in the eye, and told her we were through and to get the hell out."

---

1. Elkins, *On the Strange Place of Religion in Contemporary Art*, 117; Heller, *Reluctant Partners*.

The bartender says, "That makes sense, but what about your best friend?" "Oh, I walked over to him, looked him straight in the eye, and said, 'Bad dog!'"[2]

We could, of course, simply declare that this is a "bad joke" and let it go at that. But perhaps it is worth noting that it not only plays on the "a dog is a man's best friend" cliché but also parodies the recommended method for housebreaking a dog, thus placing the discovery of one's dog in bed with one's wife on the same moral scale as discovering that the dog has soiled the carpet.

But there is a deeper issue here as well: If boys and their dogs have a habit of sleeping together as loving and loyal bedfellows, this joke suggests that as both have aged, something has come between them. The dog remains the man's best friend, but an element of mistrust has entered into their relationship. This, I suggest, is what the research literature on religion and humor documents. According to it, they are not enemies or adversaries. They are "estranged bedfellows."

The purpose of this chapter is to identify the reasons for this estrangement and thereby find ways to overcome it. Also, as this research literature will show, the mistrust between them may go both ways, but religion's mistrust of humor seems to be more deeply felt. This, of course, is to be expected, for we tend to think that religion itself is more deeply felt than humor. Perhaps, though, this is where humor can offer assistance to religion, for as we saw in chapter 1, we Americans have a tendency to overtax ourselves and to experience difficulty relaxing. Perhaps this is also true of religion, and if so, it needs to relax and not take itself quite so seriously.

Making the Case for Humor

It is important to note that this mistrust of religion toward humor is not, by any means, universal. In fact, many theologians and religion scholars have made a case for humor. They include Conrad Hyers, who has written two books on humor and edited a third on the relation between religion and the comedic sense of life; Ignacio L. Götz, author of a book on faith and humor; and Robert C. Roberts, who has written significant articles on the sense of humor as a virtue.[3] Also, the fact that *Salvation by*

---

2. Tapper and Press, *Guy Goes into a Bar . . .* , 132.
3. See Hyers, *And God Created Laughter*; Hyers, *Holy Laughter*; and Hyers,

Laughter by Dudley Zuver was published in 1933 attests to the fact that this is not a new issue for theologians and religion scholars.[4]

However, in these and other books and articles by theologians and religion scholars, a sense emerges that they are engaged in a valiant effort to make a case for humor, that they know that they are fighting an uphill battle. For example, in his article titled "Toward a Theology of Humor," Wilbur H. Mullen devotes much space to explaining why the works of many theologians "are so lacking in comic sense."[5] Similarly, in her article on religion and humor Doris Donnelly notes that "something has gone wrong with our perception of the alliance between being religious and having a sense of humor."[6] She suggests that because "Jesus, for one, was witty, unpredictable, fully alive, and a person who delighted in, celebrated with, and was open to surprise," it is "safe to say that divorcing humor from religion is potentially destructive of true religion."[7] On the other hand, her article illustrates the affinities of humor and hope (as noted in chapter 2), for she characterizes the situation we now confront as one in which the "divine quality of humor is peeking its fragile head through centuries of humorless Christianity," and she concludes her essay with nine recommendations for strengthening and revitalizing our sense of humor, the final and most important one being to look for humor in the Scriptures.

Also instructive is Reinhold Niebuhr's essay on humor and faith.[8] For him, humor has a place in religion, but it is rather circumscribed and marginal. He notes that the "intimate relation between humor and faith is derived from the fact that both deal with the incongruities of our

---

Spirituality of Comedy; see also Götz, *Faith, Humor, and Paradox*; and Roberts, "Humor and the Virtues"; and Roberts, "Sense of Humor as a Christian Virtue."

4. Zuver, *Salvation by Laughter*.

5. Mullen, "Toward a Theology of Humor," 9.

6. Donnelly, "Divine Folly," 386.

7. Ibid., 388. As I noted in the introduction, chapter 4 will be devoted to Jesus as an ally of humor.

8. Niebuhr, "Humor and Faith." Niebuhr refers to this and the other essays in *Discerning the Signs of the Times* as "sermonic essays" (ix). They are based on sermons actually preached in American colleges and universities, but they were not written until after they were delivered. In the process of putting them in written form, Niebuhr made them somewhat more theological, and theoretical points were elaborated in some cases beyond the limits usually deemed advisable in the traditional sermon (ix). I will simply refer to "Humor and Faith" as an essay.

existence."⁹ But he then goes on to make a distinction between the immediate incongruities with which humor is concerned and the ultimate incongruities of life, with which faith is concerned. Thus, "laughter is our reaction to immediate incongruities and those which do not affect us essentially," and "faith is the only possible response to the ultimate incongruities of existence, which threaten the very meaning of our life."¹⁰ With this distinction between that which does not affect us essentially and that which does, Niebuhr effectively downplays, even, perhaps, downgrades humor while elevating faith to a position of highest importance and significance. He concludes his essay with a rather qualified endorsement of humor:

> Insofar as the sense of humor is a recognition of incongruity, it is more profound than any philosophy which seeks to devour incongruity in reason. But the sense of humor remains healthy only when it deals with immediate issues and faces the obvious and surface irrationalities. It must move toward faith or sink into despair when the ultimate issues are raised. That is why there is laughter in the vestibule of the temple, the echo of laughter in the temple itself, but only faith and prayer, and no laughter, in the holy of holies.¹¹

I will return to Niebuhr's essay at the end of this chapter.

Peter L. Berger presents a similar view in *A Rumor of Angels*.¹² In his chapter on theological possibilities he makes a distinction between *deductive faith*, which begins with ideas that precede experience, and *inductive faith* that begins with the facts of human experience. In other words, "inductive faith moves from human experience to statements about God, deductive faith from statements about God to interpretations of human experience."¹³ He suggests that there are "signals of transcendence within the empirically given human situation," and identifies several of these signals: One is the "created *order* of society" that, "corresponds, in one way or another, to an underlying order of the universe, a divine order that supports and justifies all human attempts at ordering."¹⁴ A second is the experience of *play*, whose "intrinsic intention points beyond itself and

---

9. Ibid., 112.
10. Ibid.
11. Ibid., 130–31.
12. Berger, *Rumor of Angels*, 49–75. See also Berger, *Redeeming Laughter*.
13. Berger, *Rumor of Angels*, 57.
14. Ibid., 53.

beyond man's 'nature' to a 'super-natural' justification."[15] A third is the experience of *hope,* which "has always asserted itself most intensely in the face of experiences that seemed to spell utter defeat, most intensely of all in the face of the final defeat of death."[16] A fourth is the experience of *outrage* (which Berger calls "the argument from damnation"), which refers to experiences "in which our sense of what is humanly permissible is so fundamentally outraged that the only adequate response to the offense as well as to the offender seems to be a curse of supernatural dimensions."[17]

Finally, there is the experience of *humor,* which "not only recognizes the comic discrepancy in the human condition" but "also relativizes it, and thereby suggests that the tragic perspective on the discrepancies of the human condition can also be relativized."[18] In other words, "at least for the duration of the comic perception, the tragedy of man is bracketed. By laughing at the imprisonment of the human spirit, humor implies that this imprisonment is not final but will be overcome, and by this implication provides yet another signal of transcendence—in this instance in the form of an intimation of redemption."[19]

Like Niebuhr, Berger affirms the relevance of humor to religion, and, in a certain sense, he makes a stronger case than Niebuhr does for humor because he identifies it as a "signal of transcendence." On the other hand, he presents a much stronger case for *hope* as it relates to human tragedy than he does for *humor.* This is basically because he views them both as responses to human tragedy, and suggests that whereas hope asserts itself most intensely in the face of tragedy, humor "brackets" the tragedy altogether. To be sure, humor "implies" that the "imprisonment of the human spirit is not final but will be overcome," but it lacks the intensity and conviction exhibited in hope. As Berger says of hope, "in a world where man is surrounded by death on all sides, he continues to be a being who says 'no' to death—and through this 'no' is brought to faith in another world, the reality of which would validate hope as something other than illusion."[20]

15. Ibid., 60.
16. Ibid., 61.
17. Ibid., 65.
18. Ibid., 70.
19. Ibid.
20. Ibid., 64.

Berger does not say that humor *is* an illusion—which, for him, is clearly negative—but neither does he suggest that humor's "bracketing" of the tragedy of man brings us to faith in another world, the world in which human tragedy is overcome. As a "signal" of transcendence, humor, in comparison to hope, is quite weak and ineffectual. He does not consider the possibility that humor may, in fact, make a significant contribution to one's spirit of hopefulness. Also, although he suggests that humor, like play, "can be seen as an ultimately religious vindication of joy,"[21] faith, in his view, is generally accorded much greater importance than joy in religion.

I am not suggesting that Berger overestimates the power of hope. Rather, my point is that even when a positive case for humor in relation to religion is being made, authors tend to make this case in a qualified way. For Niebuhr, humor is consigned to the vestibule, and for Berger, humor enables us to "bracket" human tragedy, "at least for the duration of the comic perception."[22]

Religion and Humor Creation

Having cited several examples of the qualified way in which theologians and religion scholars tend to speak in behalf of humor, I would now like to turn to empirical studies on the relation of religion and humor. I will especially focus on studies carried out by Vassilis Saroglou, a professor in the department of psychology at Catholic University of Louvain, in the late 1990s and early 2000s. I will discuss several of his empirical studies, then focus on an article of his that takes a more theoretical approach to religion's historical mistrust of humor.[23] I will conclude with a brief consideration of the legitimate and illegitimate grounds for religion's mistrust of humor.

In his first empirical study, which he coauthored with Jean-Marie Jaspard, Saroglou hypothesized that humor would be negatively affected by religion. The rationale for this prediction was that despite "the presence of humor in religion, mistrust exists in many religions toward laughter and humor. One may suspect that, from a psychological perspective, this

---

21. Ibid., 70.
22. Ibid.
23. Saroglou, "Religion and Sense of Humor."

attitude is not an historical accident, but reflects a deeper reality."[24] This deeper reality is the fact that "many components substantial to humor as well as many personality traits related to humor are, respectively, prohibited by, and related in an opposite direction to, religion."[25]

For example, humor is defined by or linked to the perception and enjoyment of incongruity, a playful and gratuitous attitude, the tolerance of ambiguity, low conservatism, and low dogmatism. Also, aggression and sexuality are inherent, at least to some extent, in humorous phenomena. In contrast, religion expresses the need for the reduction of uncertainty and is associated with a risk-avoidance attitude, orderliness, the need for control, conservatism, and dogmatism. Aggression and sexuality are not encouraged. Thus, "although contemporary Christian religion does not present an explicit anti-humor discourse, one may hypothesize that the number of traits mentioned above [with citations] is so important that religion may be negatively correlated with spontaneous humor creation as a response to hypothetical daily associations."[26]

What Saroglou and Jaspard wanted to know was, "Does this association reflect a causal relation between religion and humor? In other words, and because it is hard to consider that humor abilities have an impact on religion, it seems appropriate to test empirically the alternative, more intuitive hypothesis, that religion affects the tendency to create humor."[27] Thus, the authors hypothesized "that religious stimulation might have an 'inhibiting' effect on participants' spontaneous humor production in response to daily hassles," and that, in contrast, "a humorous stimulation may have an opposite, promoting effect on humor creation."[28] In light of the fact that the studies reported in chapter 2 centered on the role of humor in moderating life stress, it is noteworthy that this study focused on the creation of humor in response to hypothetical daily hassles, the everyday situations that cause stress and anxiety.

The subjects of the study were fifty-six students (thirty-two women, twenty-four men) at the Catholic University of Louvain. It was advertised as a "study in coping and the ways in which individuals cope with

---

24. Saroglou and Jaspard, "Does Religion Affect Humor Construction?," 33.
25. Ibid.
26. Ibid., 34.
27. Ibid.
28. Ibid.

stressful situations."[29] Two experimental groups were formed. The first group watched a religious video while the second group watched a humorous one. A third, control group performed the same tasks as the other groups but without any specific stimulation.

Both videos were fifteen minutes long. The religious video contained segments of a documentary film on pilgrims to Lourdes, scenes from the life of Jesus in the film *Jesus of Montreal,* and a discussion between a journalist and a monk about religious and spiritual issues. It was "representative of positive common religiosity and thus respectful of religion," yet presented in such a way that the sensitivities of nonreligious persons would not be offended.[30] The humorous video consisted of scenes from a famous French comedy, sketches by a famous French comedian, including an ironic sketch of Belgians (the nationality of the subjects of the study) as the target, and extracts from the comedy routines of a very well-known group of French comedians. It included convivial humor, comedy, irony, and satire, and no obscene or sick humor. The control group was not given a "neutral" video, such as a documentary film, because it could unintentionally have characteristics inherent to a humorous or religious stimulus. The authors cite an earlier study in which "persons high on reported humor seemed to have found the documentary almost as amusing as the film that was intended to be funny."[31]

After the video exposure, the two experimental groups were presented the twenty-four pictures in Rosenzweig's Picture-Frustration Test depicting frustrations in daily life situations.[32] They were instructed to imagine how they would react in the situations depicted. Responses were evaluated by raters as humorous or nonhumorous and were assumed to indicate the degree to which the person would be prompted to use humor spontaneously as a reaction to situations involving daily hassles. For example, one of the pictures presents a woman returning to a shop for the third time to complain that the clock she bought there a week earlier would stop just as soon as she carried it into her home. The subject's task is to supply the shopkeeper's response. If the subject has him say, "That's

29. Ibid., 36.

30. Ibid., 36–37.

31. Ibid., 37. See Nevo and Nevo, "What Do You Do When You Are Asked to Answer Humorously?"

32. Rosenzweig's article, "The Treatment of Humorous Responses in the Rosenzweig Picture-Frustration Study," explains how the investigator is to treat humorous responses to these pictures.

certainly not normal. I'll examine it," the response is rated as nonhumorous. But if the subject has him say, "You're lucky; time stands still in your home"; or, "This was the only way I could devise to make you come back"; or, "Seems the clock has been here so long it has developed separation anxiety," the response would be rated as humorous.

Next, subjects were ushered into another room ostensibly to contribute to a different research study, and were administered a religious fundamentalism scale, a postcritical-belief questionnaire, and a religiosity index investigating the importance of God to the individual, religion's place in the subject's daily life, and the frequency of the individual's prayer. Finally, subjects were tested on a scale based on the five-factor model of personality developed by H. J. Eysenck.[33]

The main finding was that persons who were exposed to the humorous video produced more humor in comparison with those who watched the religious video or no video at all. This result was not statistically significant, but the authors had hypothesized that the effects of the video presentations would diminish over time, so when they compared the subjects' scores on the first of the twenty-four pictures, they found that humor creation was considerably stronger among subjects who watched the humorous video, and that humor creation was considerably weaker among those who watched the religious video.

Thus, the main hypothesis of the study—that religious stimulation inhibits humor creation—was confirmed. Also, humorous stimulation promoted more spontaneous use of humor in comparison with the religiously conditioned and control groups. Gender differences were also found. The mean score for men on humor creation after exposure to the humorous video was especially high. Conversely, the men who did not receive humorous stimulation but instead received religious stimulation or no stimulation at all did not differ from the women in their respective groups in terms of humor production. This suggests that men are more suggestible than women where humor is concerned. But this, of course, could be due, at least in part, to the likelihood that the comedians in the video were male, or to the type of humor employed, or both. It would not be appropriate to draw any conclusions concerning men and women's basic sense of humor from the greater suggestibility of men in this particular study.

---

33. See Eysenck, "Appreciation of Humor"; see also Saroglou, "Religion and the Five Factors of Personality."

As for the impact of personality on humor creation, the authors found that persons who score high on *conscientiousness* are unlikely to create humor spontaneously when faced with hypothetical daily hassles. As *conscientiousness* was the only personality trait that was related (in this case, negatively) to humor creation, the fact that religiosity has been shown in earlier studies to be associated positively with *conscientiousness* (and also *orderliness*) suggests that the religiosity of individuals may have an indirect effect on humor creation via the personality trait of *conscientiousness*. On the other hand, the main negative influence on humor creation was the religious video that subjects watched prior to being presented with the daily hassles test. This suggests that the situational context and not the person's inherent religiosity— or nonreligiosity—exerts the greatest influence on humorous responses to the frustrations of daily life.

Since the presentation of the religious video was an artificial stimulation, one that is unlikely to occur with any degree of consistency in ordinary life, we *might* be tempted to argue that the negative effect of religion on humor is negligible. But it seems more useful to view the results of this study from the opposite perspective and to note that neither the religious condition (video) nor the inherent religiousness of the subjects contributed in a positive way to the creation of humor. If humor, as shown by the studies presented in chapter 2, can have a positive effect on coping with negative life experiences, then the *failure* of religion to promote humor production on a test that concerns the daily frustrations of life is really the issue. This is particularly noteworthy when we consider that the studies reported in chapter 2 suggest that there is a positive relationship between humor creation and humor as a coping mechanism.

But this also raises a question that the Saroglou and Jaspard study does not address. This is the question whether the humorous comments and remarks of the participants were helpful as far as coping with the situation is concerned. For example, if I were the person who brought the clock back for a third time, I would probably view myself, not the shopkeeper, as the one who was experiencing greatest frustration. This being the case, would I prefer that the shopkeeper would make a joke ("Time seems to stand still in your home") or that he would respond, "That's not normal. I'll examine it," or even better, "Then we need to replace it at no cost to you"? I would undoubtedly prefer the *nonhumorous* response—as it proposes a way of solving the problem, although if the shopkeeper's joke was designed to set my mind at ease before proposing a solution, I would then, no doubt, welcome the *humorous* response.

In any event, the fact that participants in the experimental group who watched the religious video were less disposed than participants who watched the humorous video to offer a humorous response *could,* at least in certain situations, be a point in favor of religion. Also, the fact that the personality trait of conscientiousness was the only trait that had any bearing on the results may indicate the judgment of many of the subjects that a humorous response is unlikely to be a conscientious response. It may, for example, appear to be an attempt to trivialize the frustration which, in this instance, the woman who bought the clock was experiencing. While humor production may well have its own intrinsic rewards, the assumption underlying the psychological studies reviewed in chapter 2 is that humor has some tangible benefits. If the shopkeeper's tone of voice while making the humorous comment was one of empathy and understanding, we can well imagine that it contributed to a good feeling between the woman and the shopkeeper. But if it was spoken wittily or casually, the woman may well have taken offense.

It may also be noted that the influence of the humorous video on subjects' responses to the picture-frustration test was greatest at the outset and then began to diminish as the test continued. One could argue that this means that the very benefits of humor are relatively short-lived. In effect, this takes us back to our earlier observation that Peter Berger seems to present humor, at least in comparison with hope, as a relatively weak response to human tragedy. To be sure, the picture-frustration test deals with situations that could hardly be viewed as tragic, but perhaps the same implicit assessment of humor is applicable here as well. On the other hand, the study showed that the impact of the religious video on subjects' responses to the picture-frustration test also diminished as the test continued, and this does not speak especially well for religion, for we might have expected that, given its serious intent, the effects of the religious video would have been longer-lasting than those of the humorous video.

Religion, Coping Styles, and Sick Humor

A second study by Saroglou, coauthored by Lydwine Anciaux, focuses on sick humor.[34] Sick humor was defined as humor that makes fun of death, disease, deformity, and the disabled. This definition enabled them to distinguish sick humor from other closely related humor styles such as aggressive and provocative humor. They note that aggressive humor may focus on another person's character and behavior and may have nothing to do with death, disease, deformity, and disabilities, and this may also be true of provocative humor, such as humor against established authorities.

The authors suggest that one way of attempting to understand appreciation for sick humor is to ask what functions this kind of humor serves. It is usually assumed that sick humor allows individuals to distance themselves emotionally from uncontrollable, unpredictable, and harmful objects, events, and situations, but similar proposals have been made about humor in general, so we learn nothing about sick humor specifically when we simply assume that sick humor helps individuals to cope with stressful situations. We need, therefore, to examine more specifically what may be the particular coping styles that seem to be associated with sick humor. Thus, the first aim of the study was to investigate the specific coping styles employed by persons who like sick jokes in their everyday lives.

Its second aim was to investigate whether religion is negatively associated with appreciation for sick humor. The authors note that in recent years a great deal of theoretical and empirical evidence has pointed to the role of religion in coping with death, suffering, failure, frustrations, and meaninglessness. Also, religion, especially religion that promotes a coping style involving collaboration with God, has the intention of assisting individuals in taking responsibility, reacting actively when faced with stress, and attempting to take control over the situation. However, it is unclear whether humor also leads to active coping. There is mixed evidence in this regard. Humor tends to relate negatively to avoidance of stressful situations, but it relates positively to disengagement. In addition, even if sick humor implies, at least to a certain extent, the positive reframing of a harmful situation, this reframing does not ordinarily use the mechanism of "glorification" of the situation (i.e., finding what is positive when confronted with a disaster, looking for challenges in the face of harmful events) as does religion when it promotes positive reframing and

---

34. Saroglou and Anciaux, "Liking Sick Humor."

active coping. Moreover, even if sick humor implies to a certain extent the positive reframing of a harmful situation, we may assume that this reframing does not promote an active and willing acceptance of the situation's challenges. Rather, the key mechanism of sick humor is diminishment: that is, it makes fun of death, disease, deformity, and disability by making them appear even worse, for "sick humor implies the use of negative hyperbole."[35]

Another reason for predicting that religion will be negatively associated with appreciation for sick humor is that religiousness is positively associated with values emphasizing conservation of the social order: "We can thus expect religious people not to be prone to appreciate sick humor, which usually constitutes a transgression of social norms."[36] Also, low appreciation of sick jokes on religious grounds can be hypothesized on the basis of sensitivity to disgust in general. Rituals of purification in many religious traditions suggest a high concern in religion with cleanliness and purity, and many studies confirm that the religious personality is marked by traits of orderliness and cleanliness. Thus, on the basis of evidence indicating that religion promotes a high sensitivity to disgust, we may expect that "the religious ideal of universal harmony is broken by the disorder, deformity, and chaos introduced by disgusting things, including disgusting jokes."[37] In addition, religion, especially Christian religion and theology, tends to emphasize human beings' distinctiveness from animals and thus the need to maintain a distance from everything that reminds them of animal life, such as eating, excrement, reproduction, injury, decay, and death itself. This distancing is likely to contribute to a resistance to disgusting things, including disgusting jokes.

The study involved 256 adults ranging from seventeen to eighty-eight years of age, and included 131 men and 124 women (and one unidentified respondent). The humor-appreciation measure employed in the study was a selection of jokes found on the web that represented sick humor involving the following specific thematic categories: death-related jokes, jokes where the target is a disabled person, and disgusting jokes. Some neutral nonsick jokes were also included. In all, there were twenty-four jokes, eighteen of which were sick.[38] To address the first hypothesis

35. Ibid. 261.
36. Ibid.
37. Ibid., 261–62.
38. A few examples of sick jokes are provided. In a death-related joke a lawyer asks a coroner whether he took the man's pulse and checked to see if his heart was

relating to coping, a 28-item coping measure was employed. The religion measures included a two-item index of religiosity (importance of God and importance of religion in one's life) and a one-item index of spirituality (importance of spirituality in one's life), which was included in order to explore whether respondents viewed religion and spirituality differently.

The major finding was that both religiosity and spirituality were negatively correlated with sick humor and were unrelated to neutral humor. Also, use of religion as a coping mechanism was negatively related to appreciation of sick humor. In addition, religion was positively associated with several coping styles (including acceptance, positive reframing, active coping, and planning) and negatively associated with substance use. It was also found that men tend to like sick humor more than women do. With regard to the coping styles of persons who like sick jokes, those styles positively associated with appreciation for sick humor were venting, seeking social support for emotional and instrumental reasons, and self-distraction. Active coping, positive reframing, and acceptance were correlated with neutral humor but not with sick humor. Also, persons who liked sick humor tended to appreciate humor in general and to report high use of humor in coping.

The authors conclude that individuals who appreciate sick jokes seem not to use highly adaptive coping strategies (i.e., active coping and positive reframing), but neither do they use highly negative coping strategies (such as denial). Also, the authors suggest that the strong correlation between appreciation for sick humor and the use of emotional supports for coping may be understood in at least two ways. One way is that people who enjoy sick jokes may allow themselves to express publicly what others repress or express less easily, and this may include ease in playing with disgust, an emotion that usually elicits avoidant behavior. Another way to understand the correlation between sick-humor appreciation and emotional support for coping is that telling sick jokes in spite of the discomfort this causes others may be understood as a way of trying to get attention and communicate with others. Thus, enjoyment of sick jokes may be a sign of some aspects of emotional instability or difficulty

---

still beating, and whether he was still breathing before signing the death certificate. When the coroner replied that he had done none of these things, the lawyer said, "So you signed this death certificate without performing any of the recommended tests for establishing whether a person is really and truly dead." The coroner replies, "Well, yes. But why are you asking? Did you find his head?"

with emotional regulation. On the other hand, a moderate appreciation of sick humor may correspond to moderate social expression of emotions and thus have an adaptive coping value.

What seems especially clear is that persons who appreciate sick humor tend to be more emotional as far as coping with stressful situations is concerned. Thus, the coping styles used by persons who seem to enjoy sick humor may help us to understand the role of religiousness in sick-humor appreciation. If religion tends to involve a positive problem-focused approach to stressful situations in terms of active coping, planning, positive reframing, and acceptance, sick humor tends to diminish rather than idealize these approaches to stressful situations. It focuses on the stressful situation itself and suggests that attempts to overcome the situation are likely to end in frustration and failure. Thus, sick humor seems to suggest that perhaps the best that one can do is bring attention to the situation, even if one makes others uncomfortable in doing so, and makes oneself liable to the charge that one lacks sensitivity to the suffering of others.

This study focuses on a form of humor that is especially problematic as far as religion is concerned. Yet, the study reveals that sick humor addresses emotional needs that religion is also concerned to address. While we may take the view that persons who identify with religion should have nothing to do with sick humor because it transgresses values that emphasize conservation of the social order, is disgusting, and emphasizes our animal nature, it could also be argued that persons who identify with religion should take a more sympathetic view toward sick humor—or, at least, toward those who enjoy it—as it can play a useful role in helping persons who are incapable of using the more mature forms of coping that religion supports to deal with the anxieties and stresses of life. However, this tentative conclusion invites us to consider another article of Saroglou's, one that addresses the issue of religion and humor from a more theoretical point of view.[39]

---

39. As we move to this more theoretical article, it should be noted that Saroglou has conducted other empirical studies of the relation of religion and humor. Especially noteworthy are "Humor Appreciation as a Function of Religious Dimensions"; "Being Religious Implies Being Different in Humor"; and "Religiousness, Religious Fundamentalism and Quest as Predictors of Humor Creation."

Are Religion and Sense of Humor Inherently Incompatible?

The article, titled "Religion and Sense of Humor: An a Priori Incompatibility? Theoretical Considerations from a Psychological Perspective," is basically concerned with the influence of religion on individuals' sense of humor.[40] The abstract notes that the article is concerned with religion's mistrust of humor and that the approach taken to explore this mistrust is a psychological one:

> Although humor is not absent from religion, one may wonder whether religion's historical mistrust of the comic is not accidental, but reflects a deeper reality. Based on theory and research on both psychology of humor and psychology of religion, as well as on the psychological anthropology of early Christianity, the present paper inspects the ways in which religion is related to personality traits, cognitive structures and social consequences associated with sense of humor.[41]

Saroglou begins with the observation that humor is present in religion, noting that scholars from different fields have explored humor in biblical texts, in the lives of holy figures such as Christ and the saints, and in religions other than Christianity.[42] Thus, it is not the case that humor and religion are absolutely opposed or antithetical to one another. On the other hand, relationships between humor and religion have not been studied, either theoretically or empirically, from a psychological perspective, and the issue he wants to address is not the presence and function of humor in a religious context but rather the question whether "it can be argued that religion may *influence* the sense of humor, and this in a negative, intuitive, direction, or at least whether religiousness may be associated with low propensity for humor."[43] Attempts have been made "to valorize positive links between the comic and religion from a theological, religious, or spiritual point of view,"[44] but "an empirical science such as

---

40. Saroglou, "Religion and Sense of Humor."
41. Ibid., 191.
42. Ibid. He cites Morreall's "Comic and Tragic Religions"; Apte's *Humor and Laughter*; and Davies' "Protestant Ethic and the Comic Spirit of Capitalism." They represent the fields of philosophy, anthropology, and sociology respectively.
43. Ibid., 192.
44. Ibid. He cites Berger's *Redeeming Laughter*; Hyers' *Spirituality of Comedy*; and Kuschel's *Laughter*.

psychology should be prudent as to whether the reality of everyday life fits these theoretical, theological, and ideological assertions."[45] In this regard, "a deeper historical examination of the relationship between religion and the comic seems to justify the intuitive hypothesis of religion's suspicion of laughter and humor."[46]

His introductory comments conclude with the suggestion that "a promising way to investigate the possible incompatibility between humor and religion seems to be to inspect how religion is associated with personality traits, cognitive structures and social attitudes which are theoretically considered to be characteristic of, or empirically found to be associated with, humor."[47] In his view, this comparison is legitimate because both humor and religiousness may be viewed as characteristics of personality.[48] In the discussion that follows these introductory comments Saroglou considers five characteristics of humor and then discusses how each is viewed by religion or a religious perspective. They include (1) incongruity, ambiguity, and nonsense; (2) playfulness; (3) novelty, sensation seeking and risk; (4) emotional aspects and self-control; and (5) tendentious aspects.[49]

Concerning *incongruity, ambiguity, and nonsense*, Saroglou notes that humor involves the perception and enjoyment of incongruity, tolerance of ambiguity, and entertaining the possibility that life is ultimately nonsensical. As he points out, "humor is marked by the ambiguity and limits of meaning."[50] In contrast, religion is especially concerned with the search for meaning and for evidence of order and purpose, and it looks for answers where, objectively speaking, there is no information (i.e., as to the origin and the end of the human being and of the world itself). This

---

45. Ibid.

46. Ibid. He cites several authors in support of this suspicion, including Eco's *The Name of the Rose*; Hausherr's *Penthos*; Le Goff's "Laughter in the Middle Ages"; and Ménager's *La Renaissance et la Rire*.

47. Ibid.

48. Ibid. He cites in this connection Ruch, ed., *Sense of Humor*; and Beit-Hallahmi and Argyle, *Psychology of Religious Behavior*.

49. The dictionary defines *tendentious* as "characterized by a deliberate tendency or aim, especially advancing a definite point of view," Agnes, ed., *Webster's New World College Dictionary*, 1474. This is a rather neutral definition. However, in the case of humor, the word *tendentious* may have a more negative connotation, as the "aim" may be to ridicule, cause discomfort, or cause offense. Lampoons and satires are considered examples of tendentious humor. Sick humor would also be considered tendentious.

50. Saroglou, "Religion and Sense of Humor," 193.

need for meaning is fundamental to religious persons, and religion itself is characterized by a need for the reduction of uncertainty, especially in matters of ultimate importance. Thus, "it seems reasonable to suspect that religion may not be attracted to a celebration of incongruity, ambiguity, and, most importantly, possibility of nonsense."[51] Or, to put it in more strictly cognitive terms, "one may hypothesize that the perception, or at least enjoyment, of incongruity is not encouraged by religion."[52]

Concerning *playfulness*, Saroglou suggests that in order to be perceived as humorous, "incongruity needs to be perceived in a secure, playful framework."[53] He notes that D. E. Berlyne has applied to humor the criteria developed by Jean Piaget to distinguish play from nonplayful activities, and that these criteria include the fact that play is an end in itself, is spontaneous, is an activity for pleasure, has a relative lack of organization, is free from conflicts, and is overmotivated.[54] Saroglou emphasizes the fact that humor, like play, is an activity for pleasure and is an end in itself,[55] and he observes that these characteristics of playfulness are counterindicative to religion and religiousness. This observation, he suggests, is supported by the psychological understanding of the religious personality as well as the psychological anthropology of early Christianity and its suspicion of laughter. He points out that "the lack of finality and usefulness inherent to humor seems incompatible with the religious faith," for "religiousness is structured by a need for integration with, and subordination of everything to, the faith." Thus, "it is not surprising that Gregory of Nyssa (4th century) considers laughter an enemy of man, because laughter is neither a word nor action ordered towards any possible

---

51. Ibid., 195.

52. Ibid.

53. Ibid. He cites in this connection Suls, "Cognitive Processes in Humor Appreciation."

54. Saroglou, "Religion and Sense of Humor," 195. See Berlyne, "Laughter, Humor, and Play." The claim that play is free from conflicts is one that child psychoanalyst Erik Erikson would question. See my chapter, "The Power of Play," in Capps, *Resourceful Self*, 96–124. This is also true of some expressions of humor. However, this fact does not invalidate the more general observation that humor is a form of play.

55. For example, Morreall points out that unlike animals for whom "incongruity provoked by negative emotions and puzzlement implies motivation for change in order to survive," human beings "are capable of enjoying incongruity, an enjoyment which is defined by a lack of motivation for change" (Morreall, "Enjoying Incongruity," 196).

goal."[56] Also, "the importance of being engaged, and of acting on that engagement, is especially present in a religious context."[57] Unlike humor, religion is purposeful, and this sense of purpose is typically informed by moral or spiritual judgment. Religion is also sensitive to an engagement with truth, an engagement that humor characteristically lacks or makes light of.

Concerning *novelty, sensation seeking, and risk,* Saroglou notes that a sense of humor implies openness to novelty. Also, research evidence suggests that "sensation seeking"—the need for varied, novel, and complex sensations and experiences, and the willingness to take physical and social risks for the sake of such experiences—predicts a high sense of humor, a high appreciation of nonsense humor, and a low appreciation for incongruity-resolution humor.[58] Furthermore, risk is inherent to play,[59] and one can therefore assume that humor, given its affinities with play, will also be linked to a preference for risk. Thus, we may anticipate that this characteristic of humor will not play a significant role among most religious persons, who tend to be conservative and to attach great importance to values of tradition, security, and conformity, and low importance to the value of stimulation (excitement, novelty, and challenge).[60]

Concerning *emotional aspects and self-control,* Saroglou refers to an article by Howard Leventhal and Martin A. Safer that makes a plea for greater integration of emotional aspects in humor theories.[61] On the other hand, he cites John Morreall's contention that humor is not an expression of emotion, for humor does not have a practical orientation and is not followed by action. In Morreall's view, emotions typically give rise to actions.[62] However, in Saroglou's view, Morreall's insistence on the motivation to action and change as a criterion in defining emotion is problematic. Saroglou notes, for example, that emotions also seem to

---

56. Saroglou, "Religion and Sense of Humor," 195.

57. Ibid., 197.

58. Ibid. 198. See Zuckerman, *Sensation Seeking*; and Deckers and Ruch, "Sensation Seeking and the Situational Humor Response Questionnaire (SHRQ)."

59. Saroglou, "Religion and Sense of Humor," 198. Dufflo makes this point in *Jouer et Philosopher.*

60. Ibid. See Miller and Hoffmann, "Risk and Religion."

61. Saroglou, "Religion and Sense of Humor," 199. See Leventhal and Safer, "Individual Differences, Personality, and Humor Appreciation."

62. Saroglou, "Religion and Sense of Humor," 199. See Morreall, "Humor and Emotion."

be characterized by a need for mental rumination, which can be seen as contrary to action, especially when action is defined by Morreall as "doing something other."[63] Also, recent work on the psychology of emotions has shown that people need to relive emotional experiences, both positive and negative, by sharing them with others.[64] Saroglou suggests that humor and laughter resemble emotions in this respect, for people often "report to their friends the humorous and amusing things that have happened to them, and jokes and witticisms they have either recounted or heard."[65]

Saroglou also notes that surprise "is a typical element of emotion in general: subjects perceive a discrepancy between expectations and events-stimuli, and afterwards evaluate whether the stimulation is agreeable or not."[66] Even joy may be considered a surprise in the sense that expectations are surpassed or unexpected stimuli turn out to conform to one's goals. Also, the emotional aspect of surprise implies a momentary loss of control, and this is also true of humor. Laughter, after all, is typically an involuntary reaction. He cites Berger's observation that the comic, although it can be deliberately constructed, "very often simply happens or befalls the individual,"[67] and Freud's observation that "we speak, it is true, of 'making' a joke; but we are aware that when we do so our behavior is different from what it is when we make a judgment or make an objection. A joke has quite outstandingly the characteristic of being a notion that occurred to us 'involuntarily.'"[68] In contrast, religion is associated with a need for control:

> In early Christian ascetic literature and, more generally, the entire patristic thought of early Christianity, the ideals of self-mastery and vigilance are extremely important. For example, suspicion of dreams is explained by the fact that dreaming was considered an experience beyond the control of the dreamer because the intellect was not awake and therefore incapable of controlling the soul's wanderings.[69]

63. Saroglou, "Religion and Sense of Humor," 199.
64. Ibid. For example, Rime et al., "Social Sharing of Emotion."
65. Saroglou, "Religion and Sense of Humor," 199.
66. Ibid., 200. Saroglou cites in this regard Scherer, "Les Émotions."
67. Ibid. See Berger, *Redeeming Laughter*, 14.
68. Saroglou, "Religion and Sense of Humor," 200. See Freud, *Jokes and Their Relation to the Unconscious*, 167.
69. Ibid., 201. Saroglou cites here his own unpublished master's thesis titled "Rêve

Also, since religiousness has been shown in empirical studies to be associated with orderliness, conscientiousness, and low impulsivity, "one may hypothesize that such an experience where laughter erupts, almost without 'premeditation', may appear suspect to religion."[70] Not surprisingly, therefore, the mistrust of the comic found in early Christianity appears to be based on the need for self-control. Not only negative emotions (e.g., fear, sadness, and anger) but also positive emotions (e.g., joy) are viewed with suspicion because of their unpredictable character. Also, laughter and humor are seen as a failure of self-mastery. Thus, Basil the Great, writing in the fourth century, noted that "raucous laughter and uncontrollable shaking of the body are not indicative of a well-regulated soul, or of personal dignity, or self-mastery."[71]

Taken together, the emotional aspects of humor—the absence of a motivation to achieve change, the tendency to relate one's humorous experiences to others, the fact that humor has an element of surprise, and the related fact that humor tends to conflict with self-mastery—cause humor either to conflict with religion or to invite religion's mistrust of it. What especially stands out here is the conflict between surprise and self-mastery and the role that this conflict plays in the emotional incompatibility between humor and religion.

Concerning the *tendentious aspects* of humor, Saroglou notes that significant amounts of humor have aggressive and sexual components. Beginning with its aggressive component, he cites a study that indicates that humor works against the *inhibition* of aggression.[72] Since aggressive humor is very common, Saroglou suggests that the critical question is whether aggression is typical of only some or of all types of humor, and he cites theoretical and empirical evidence suggesting that all types of humor have a propensity for aggression. For example, Freud distinguished between innocent and tendentious (i.e. hostile and/or sexual) humor, but wondered if perhaps all humor, no matter how innocent it may appear to

---

et Spiritualité chez Jean Climaque." His doctoral thesis, also on the subject of humor, is titled "Humor, Religion, and Personality."

70. Ibid.

71. Saroglou, "Religion and Sense of Humor," 201. See Basil, "Long Rules," 271.

72. Ibid., 202. See Nevo and Nevo, "What Do You Do When You Are Asked to Answer Humorously?" Saroglou also cites two studies that suggest that humor may actually reduce an aggressive mood: Dworkin and Efran, "Angered"; and Ziv, "Effect of Humor." However, he notes that this is a different issue and does not directly challenge the findings reported in the Nevo and Nevo study.

be, is actually tendentious.[73] Similarly, George Christie argues that both humor and irony have an aggressive element.[74] Saroglou adds that we may even wonder whether what is usually called "philosophical irony" constitutes "a kind of ritualized, sublime expression of aggression or rebellion towards the incongruity of the world and human existence."[75] Furthermore, humor may be viewed as a means to get out of a closed and structured system, and this "exit," if not a demonstration of overt aggression, is at least an expression of power and dominance, for the person who introduces humor in an interpersonal context demonstrates that he knows that exiting from the defined framework is possible, that he is at this moment the first and perhaps the only one who is able to exit, and that he is in a position to decide the moment and the norms that are to be transgressed in order to achieve it. Thus, it is not surprising that the personality trait of dominance is associated with a sense of humor.[76]

Turning to sexuality as a prominent component of humor, Saroglou notes that when factor analyses of humorous materials are conducted, sexual humor constitutes a specific type of humor. However, he suggests that sexuality or pleasure involving a sexual connotation may characterize more than one type of humor. For example, Freud analyzed the forepleasure that characterizes humor in general, a characteristic of humor that may explain the role of humor in sexual seduction.[77] Also, a study by Willibald Ruch and Franz-Josef Hehl found that people high on sexual satisfaction and permissiveness were also high in humor appreciation.[78]

Saroglou concludes that aggression/dominance and sexuality not only constitute specific and important humor types "but also seem to constitute an important element of humor in general."[79] Given this con-

---

73. Saroglou, "Religion and Sense of Humor," 202. See Freud, *Jokes and Their Relation to the Unconscious*, 106–39. Freud introduces the distinction between tendentious and innocent jokes in chapter 3—"The Purposes of Jokes"—and identifies four classes of tendentious jokes: exposure or obscene; aggressive or hostile; cynical, critical, or blasphemous; and skeptical.

74. Saroglou, "Religion and Sense of Humor," 202. See Christie, "Some Psychoanalytic Aspects of Humor."

75. Ibid.

76. Ibid. See Thorson and Powell, "Sense of Humor and Dimensions of Personality."

77. Saroglou, "Religion and Sense of Humor," 203. See Freud, *Jokes and Their Relation to the Unconscious*.

78. Ibid. See Ruch and Hehl, "Attitudes to Sex, Sexual Behavior, and Enjoyment of Humor."

79. Ibid.

clusion, and the fact that aggression and sexuality are usually considered to be the two universal themes of social prohibition, "one has to seriously consider that the enjoyment of humor may essentially be an enjoyment of the transgression of moral rules."[80] And this is where religion comes in.

Saraglou begins his discussion of religion's view of aggression and dominance by noting that although the relationship between religion and violence is complex, there is no doubt that in its explicit discourse, religion prohibits aggression. In fact, "religious ideals of tolerance, forgiveness, and universal charity may be supposed to have a prohibiting effect on aggression and eventually on dominance, as well as a promoting effect on altruism."[81] In fact, the tendency of the religious personality to high altruism and low interest in dominance and power may help to explain why early Christianity condemned ironic and hostile humor. Also, "the biblical distinction between permitted laughter, reflecting joy and well-being, and laughter which is hostile and denigrating, and therefore prohibited, gave way to a generalized suspicion towards laughter in the first medieval period."[82] However, this is not only the case in ancient Christianity, for "when we look at contemporary works of Christian spirituality, the distinction between good, morally appreciated humor, and bad, hostile humor, disrespectful to other people, is made very clear."[83]

With regard to religion and sexuality, Saroglou notes that religion's suspicion towards sexuality seems obvious, but for those in doubt, "it is interesting to note that, while the contemporary discourse of various religious denominations tends to valorize the body and its sexuality, empirical research indicates that religiousness still affects and prohibits to some

---

80. Ibid. Saroglou notes that the transgression of the subjective moral order is an important condition in Thomas C. Veatch's humor theory. See Veatch, "Theory of Humor."

81. In a footnote Saroglou observes that religion may also encourage aggression (especially out-group aggression), but he points out that religion is considered a social mechanism that promotes universal brotherhood and fraternity and, in this way, it widens the limits of natural kinship.

82. Saroglou, "Religion and Sense of Humor," 204. He cites in this connection Le Goff, "La Rire dans les Règles Monastiques du Haut Moyen Age."

83. Ibid. Derville's "Humor" is a case in point. It is perhaps worth noting that Saroglou's earlier suggestion that humor may be inherently aggressive (or at least dominance-oriented) may pose problems, at least theoretically, for these contemporary efforts to distinguish good, morally appreciated humor and bad, hostile humor. In fact, one could argue that bad, hostile humor is at least open about the real intentions and motivations of humor.

extent sexuality, even among young people."[84] For example, religiousness predicts low permissiveness of premarital sex, a preference for nonrevealing clothing, and low attraction to absolute sexual freedom in young persons of many European countries.[85] He also cites several examples of early patristic writers' association of laughter and voluptuous pleasure, shameless gazing and immoderate laughing, and concludes: "If humor may be considered as a transgression of rules and especially of the two universal 'taboos' concerning sexuality and aggression, religion on the contrary is supposed to express these prohibitions and both theoretical and empirical evidence suggests that it succeeds in doing so."[86]

Saroglou concludes his study of the incompatibility of religion and sense of humor with the observation that when religion is viewed from a psychological, and especially a personality-psychology, perspective, it has a negative association with personality traits, cognitive structures, and social consequences typical of humor, including incongruity, ambiguity, and nonsense; low dogmatism and low authoritarianism; playfulness, spontaneity, and attraction to novelty and risk; lack of truthfulness and finality; affective and moral disengagement; loss of control and order as implied by emotionality; and transgression, especially of prohibitions related to aggression, dominance, and sexuality. Of course, there may be other traits associated with humor that have positive affinities with religiousness. In fact, although this was not the purpose of the article, he notes that the one personality trait that emerged in the course of his investigations is that religion and sense of humor share an optimistic view of life. However, this quality has only recently been strongly associated with religion; previously, it was only associated with sense of humor.[87] And, in any event, the evidence he has presented indicates that, overall, religiousness is negatively associated with sense of humor.

Saroglou acknowledges that one could object that most of the arguments he has presented are based on empirical research and religious ideas found in Christianity. However, he believes that the hypothesis of a negative association between religion and sense of humor is likely to be

84. Saroglou, "Religion and Sense of Humor," 204.

85. Ibid. See Haerich, "Premarital Sexual Permissiveness and Religious Orientation"; Edmonds and Cahoon, "Effects of Religious Orientation and Clothing Revealingness on Women's Choice of Clothing"; and Campiche, *Cultures Jeunes et Religions en Europe*.

86. Saroglou, "Religion and Sense of Humor," 205.

87. Ibid. See Diener et al., "Subjective Well-Being."

true of other religions, for most if not all of the personality correlates of religiousness presented in this article are also present in other religions. He also anticipates the objection that in fact some religious people have a good sense of humor. He does not disagree. But he suggests the possibility that religious persons may have a good sense of humor *despite* and not *because* they are religious.

Legitimate and Illegitimate Grounds for Religion's Mistrust of Humor

As we have seen, the abstract of Saraglou's article "Religion and Sense of Humor" refers to religion's "historic mistrust of the comic." He does not discuss whether or in what sense this mistrust is legitimate. Quite likely, he believes that this is not a psychologist's prerogative, that it is a task of theologians and ethicists. But this is a question well worth pursuing, and in the remaining pages of this chapter I will suggest that there are both legitimate and illegitimate grounds for religion's mistrust of humor. I will use the five characteristics of humor that he identifies to guide this exploration.

I will begin with the *tendentiousness* of humor, as this seems to be the characteristic of humor that most merits religion's mistrust. While it may be the case that all humor has an aggressive element, some humor is hostile and degrading toward others, and it is altogether appropriate that religion would disapprove of it. The same point may be made with regard to sexual humor. Much sexual humor is rather innocent, but the fact that the humor sections of local bookstores contain anthologies of "dirty jokes" as well as anthologies of "good clean jokes" suggest that distinctions can be made on moral grounds between types and expressions of sexual humor.

Contemporary theologians and ethicists have not had much to say about this issue, so we lack contemporary guidelines for deciding what counts as innocent sexual humor and what is morally objectionable. Even so, I believe that most of us would contend that religion's strongest case against humor, and thus its best rationale for mistrusting humor, relates to tendentious humor. And, as Saroglou points out, there is both theoretical and empirical evidence suggesting that religion does in fact have an inhibiting effect on humor that involves themes of aggression and sexuality. The question is whether this inhibiting effect is sufficiently discriminating. Does it inhibit only morally objectionable forms of tendentious humor, or does it also inhibit innocent expressions as well? If by censuring tendentious sexual humor, religion tends to inhibit innocent sexual humor as well, then religion may negatively affect the educational value of humor.

The *novelty, sensation seeking, and risk* characteristic of humor may also provide warrant for religion's mistrust of humor. If sensation seeking, including the willingness to take physical and social risks, is a predictor of high reported sense of humor, this may be reason for religion to raise questions about humor or, at least, the forms of humor that have the greatest appeal to those for whom sensation seeking also has appeal. While it may not be the case that sensation seeking is inherently problematic, religion has a natural and legitimate aversion to the tempting of fate, and therefore promotes an attitude toward life that is prudent and thoughtful. As Saroglou suggests, this may be a reflection of the fact that religious people tend to be conservative, but it may also be a reflection of religion's commitment to the conservation of life itself.

On the other hand, religion's very opposition to novelty, sensation seeking, and risk is reflected in its preference for types and expressions of humor that involve negligible social risk. The humor presented in church newsletters and denominational magazines consists, to a large extent, of humor resulting from typographical errors in church bulletins, or of the unintentional humor of children (such as a child's innocent answer to a question posed by the minister or a church school teacher about God, Jesus, or the Bible). Thus, persons of high reported sense of humor may find that religion is too conservative precisely in regard to the kinds of humor it promotes and, by implication, discourages. As a result, such a person may deem religious people to be relatively dull and uninspiring, citing in support official church publications' preference for humor that is quite innocuous.

Concerning the other characteristics of humor, the mistrust of religion toward humor becomes, in my view, less defensible. With regard to *emotional aspects and self-control,* Saroglou emphasizes the element of surprise in his consideration of the emotional aspects of humor, and notes that humor tends to evoke an involuntary reaction. This, he observes, tends to cut across the grain of religion's association with the need for control. But Lefcourt and Martin's study of persons who are physically challenged (which we discussed in chapter 2) is especially instructive in this regard, for the subjects in this study did not use humor to gain greater control over events but instead used it to express a certain equanimity and acceptance of their very *lack* of control.[88]

Here, then, the motivations for having recourse to humor are markedly different from, perhaps antithetical to, motivations for being religious. But this very difference between humor and religion is not grounds for religion's mistrust of humor. Rather, it is grounds for humor's mistrust of religion. This is not because surprises are inherently good or valuable (few of us like surprise parties given in our behalf), but because our lives are replete with surprises, some of which are positively valued, and others of which are inconvenient, painful, or even tragic. Humor is therefore reflective of this important fact about human life, and of the fact that we are often thrown by these surprises, for even positive surprises can be disorienting.

I think here of the male student who was thrown for a loop when his girlfriend, in a role reversal, proposed marriage to him.

"What did you do?" I asked.

"Well, I told her that I needed to sit down on the sofa and collect my thoughts. I just wasn't prepared for this."

Or, consider in this regard the story that Jesus tells about a treasure hidden in a field, which a man found and covered up; then in his joy went and sold all he had and bought the field (Matthew 13:44). This was truly a surprising discovery, which produced a joyful emotion. Of course, there was also a moral issue involved with regard to his failure to reveal his discovery to the owner of the field. But this is not the point of the story as Jesus tells it. To the extent, then, that religion manifests and even encourages the need for control, both with regard to self and to life's exigencies, humor provides a valuable countermeasure, and religion is therefore impoverished to the extent that it takes a negative or mistrustful view of humor's witness to the surprising events and unpredictable experiences of life.

Much the same point may be made about the *playfulness* of humor. Religious mistrust of humor is based, in part, on its own view that life, after all, is serious business, and that our behavior has important consequences, for good or ill. In contrast, humor shares with play the fact that, in the larger scheme of things, it is inconsequential and gratuitous. Telling a good joke is not in the same league, ethically and morally, as speaking out against an injustice. Also, as Saroglou points out, humor is

---

88. Lefcourt and Martin, *Humor and Life Stress*.

characterized by its nonengagement in action, and thus its tendency to fail to motivate persons to initiate or enact needed change. Furthermore, humor, as playful, is more aligned with fiction than with truth. Jokes and cartoons are funny because they imagine events that have never happened, or as happening in ways other than how they actually happen.

Because religion is aligned with truth and with real consequences, it is natural that it should mistrust humor. Yet, religion also has a vital interest in what *might* have been or what *could* be so, and religious visions of a better or brighter future in this world are the work of the same mental process—the imagination—that humor employs. Thus, there is reason for religion to take a more trustful view of humor in its affinity with play, and there is also reason for humor to mistrust those expressions and forms of religion that are prejudiced against the play of the imagination.[89] As Saroglou points out, "religion is particularly sensitive to engagement with truth and moreover, *literal* truth."[90] The importance of truth to religion is not to be minimized or treated casually. After all, Jesus himself declared that he is "the way, *the truth,* and the life" (John 14:6; italics added). But truth is not merely what is or what happens to be the case at any given moment. Truth is created out of the possibilities that we are able to imagine, and this is why a commitment to the "literal truth" can be so disabling, discouraging, and disempowering. In suggesting that it *could* have happened *this* way, improbable as this may be, humor challenges the tyranny of "literal truth"—mere factuality—over the play of the imagination, the envisioning of different outcomes from those with which we are already familiar.[91] As we saw in chapter 2, humor may

89. See Pruyser, *Play of the Imagination.*

90. Saroglou, "Religion and Sense of Humor," 197 (italics added). He adds that Christ's command to let what you say be simply "yes" or "no" for anything more than this comes from evil (Matt 5:37) seems to hold true, for religiosity and religious orthodoxy are associated with honesty and unwillingness to cheat on one's taxes, 197–98.

91. In his chapter on illusion processing in religion in *The Play of the Imagination* Paul W. Pruyser relates that when he was a young boy and it was his turn to say the Lord's Prayer at the family dinner table, he would sometimes utter the phrase "Our Father, Who art in heaven" with a giggle while "casting a sideways glance at my natural [deceased] father's photograph—it dominated the dining room table—supported by the stifled laughter of my siblings, checked instantly by my mother's glances of dismay" (160). He notes that this "kind of act was neither religious, nor plain talk about the family tree, but belonged to the sphere of joking—all the more risqué on account of the sacred power of these two venerable figures" (ibid.). In any event, the reader of this story cannot help feeling that Pruyser is imagining, through humor, that his father is present at the dinner table and is thus expressing feelings of loss that he is unable to

contribute to one's ability to imagine a more hopeful future than would otherwise have been the case. Also, given its own interest in matters that are beyond rational thought and human comprehension, religion has an ally in humor, whether in the form of illogical jokes or the behavior of a clown who is variously entranced, awestruck, and fearful as he watches his circus colleagues engaged in a dangerous high-wire act some fifty feet above him.

It may also be noted that even as there are forms and expressions of play that do not manifest the characteristics that Saroglou mentions, so there are forms and expressions of humor that actually counter these play characteristics. If humor is mistrusted by religion because it manifests the playful qualities that Saroglou identifies, then it would seem that religion would have some obligation to view more positively the forms and expressions of humor that have the opposite qualities or features. In fact, this is the assumption behind Saroglou's own research in which subjects' attitudes toward incongruity-resolution and nonsense are compared. In the context of play, such attitudes may take the form of a preference for games in which skill predominates versus games in which luck is the predominant factor. Jokes about a dog that plays poker or chess (with the inevitable punch line, "Oh, he's not so smart; I beat him three out of five games.") assume the priority of skill over luck. The punch line is supposed to end the discussion. One *could*, however respond, "Which only proves that humans are luckier than dogs," thus invoking the priority of luck over skill, and suggesting that the original assumption—that the dog is smarter than his owner—is true after all.[92]

Finally, there is the characteristic of humor—*incongruity, ambiguity, and nonsense*—that is widely regarded in theories of humor as its central quality, namely, the perception and enjoyment of incongruity. The theological literature on humor tends to focus on the role of incongruity in humor, and this is the primary basis for its ambivalent attitude toward humor—its receptiveness, on the one hand, and its mistrust, on the other.

Reinhold Niebuhr's essay on "Humor and Faith," mentioned at the beginning of this chapter, is a representative example of this ambivalence. In the first paragraph of the essay, Niebuhr agrees with critics who "regard Scripture as deficient in the sense of humor," and who "point to the

---

express in any other way.

92. See Rescher, *Luck*.

fact that there is little laughter in the Bible."[93] But he disagrees with these critics' view that this constitutes a weakness of the Bible. On the contrary, this "supposed defect will appear less remarkable if the relation of humor to faith is understood." He explains that "humor is, in fact, a prelude to faith; and laughter is the beginning of prayer," and, therefore, "laughter must be heard in the outer courts of religion; and the echoes of it should resound in the sanctuary," but "there is no laughter in the holy of holies" for in the holy of holies "laughter is swallowed up in prayer and humor is fulfilled by faith."[94]

As I noted earlier, Niebuhr goes on to say that the "intimate relation between humor and faith is derived from the fact that both deal with the incongruities of our existence," but "humor is concerned with the immediate incongruities of life and faith with the ultimate ones."[95] Thus, toward the end of the essay, he contends that the "Christian faith declares that the ultimate order and meaning of life lies in the power and wisdom of God who is both Lord of the whole world of creation and the Father of human spirits," and "it believes that the incongruities of human existence are finally overcome by the power and the love of God and that the love which Christ revealed is finally sufficient to overcome the contradiction of death."[96]

> Faith is therefore the final triumph over incongruity, the final assertion of the meaningfulness of existence. There is no other triumph and will be none, no matter how much human knowledge is enlarged. Faith is the final assertion of the freedom of the human spirit, but also the final acceptance of the weakness of man and the final solution for the problem of life through the disavowal of any final solutions in the power of man.[97]

While Niebuhr makes a compelling case for the power of faith to triumph over incongruity, I believe that his argument that faith is concerned with the ultimate incongruities of life while humor is concerned with the immediate incongruities of life fails to take account of the fact that humor does, in fact, concern itself with the ultimate incongruities as well. Think, for example, of jokes that focus on the themes of suffering

---

93. Niebuhr, "Humor and Faith," 111.
94. Ibid., 111–12.
95. Ibid., 112.
96. Ibid., 129.
97. Ibid., 130.

and death, such as jokes about terminal illnesses and funerals, and humorous epitaphs.[98] Or consider humor concerned with the afterlife, such as jokes that focus on petitioners for admission to heaven who must first pass through the pearly gates and therefore satisfy Saint Peter's admission policies. Since theses jokes have their "immediate" counterparts in immigrants' and travelers' encounters with immigration authorities and border guards, the firm distinction that Niebuhr draws between the immediate and the ultimate tends to collapse.

But, more important, humor addresses the same uncertainties about *ultimate* matters with which faith is also concerned, and, like faith, it refuses to resolve them. To be sure, humor and faith represent two different ways of recognizing that such uncertainties can never be resolved this side of death itself, but they share in common their very acceptance of this fact. Both recognize this to be a matter that is beyond our control. Humor, then, *mistrusts* the very religious claims that faith also mistrusts, namely, those that assert that our existential questions about pain, suffering, and death are illegitimate, that no mysteries remain. Niebuhr says that the Christian faith "*believes* that the incongruities of human existence are finally overcome by the power and the love of God and that the love which Christ revealed is finally sufficient to overcome the contradiction of death."[99] However, to say that it *believes* is different from saying that there is an absolute certainty, or that there are no grounds for doubt or uncertainty that this may not, in fact, be the case.

Thus, I see no reason why faith would allow laughter in the vestibule of the temple but refuse it entry in the holy of holies. Both humor and faith are born of human anxiety concerning the ultimate incongruities of human existence and their more immediate manifestations throughout the journey of life.[100] I would think that faith would not want to be without its sidekick—humor—especially when it enters the holy of holies and stands, as it were, shaking in its boots.

---

98. See my chapter titled "Aging, Illness, and Death: 'A Time to Weep / A Time to Laugh,'" in Capps, *Laughter Ever After*, 88–110.

99. Niebuhr, "Humor and Faith," 129 (italics added).

100. For a similar argument see Collicutt and Gray, "'Merry Heart Doeth Good Like a Medicine: Humor, Religion, and Wellbeing.'"

Conclusion

The foregoing discussion of the mistrust of religion toward humor could be expanded and carried on at much greater length. However, I hope that it at least makes a plausible case against any blanket mistrust of humor on religion's part, and a case for religion taking expressions of humor on a case-by-case basis. In my view, the major loser in the estrangement of religion and humor is religion itself, as religion is impoverished to the extent that it holds humor at arm's length, failing to recognize that the two have often shared the same bed together. No doubt, they have always made *strange* bedfellows, but perhaps this very fact redounds to their credit. One could, in fact, cite in this regard the many jokes that play on the idea that the two individuals who have somehow come to occupy the same bed together make a rather incongruous or implausible couple. However, this fact is not treated in these jokes as cause for alarm or censure, but as affording opportunities heretofore unimagined. At the very least, the bedfellows make the best of the situation in which they find themselves. Surely, religion and humor, these two venerable expressions of the human imagination, can do as well.

Also, the following joke suggests that some assertive albeit nonaggressive action on humor's part is perhaps long overdue, and that if humor would stand up for itself a bit more, religion just might have to learn to respect it more:

A guy goes into a bar.

"Pour me a stiff one, Eddie. I just had another fight with the little woman."

"Oh, yeah?" says Eddie, "And how did this one end?"

"Well, when it was over, she came to me on her hands and knees."

"Really? Now that's a switch! What did she say?"

She said, "Come out from under the bed, you gutless weasel!"[101]

---

101. Tapper and Press, *A Guy Goes Into a Bar . . .*, 109.

4

Did Jesus Have a Sense of Humor?

In our discussion of empirical and theoretical studies of humor by Vasilis Saroglou and his colleagues in the preceding chapter, we saw that the early patristic writers tended to view humor negatively. In fact, Saroglou noted in his theoretical article that although contemporary authors have emphasized the "positive links between the comic and religion from a theological, religious, or spiritual point of view," a "deeper historical examination of the relationship between religion and the comic seems to justify the intuitive hypothesis of religion's suspicion of laughter and humor, and many scholars from different disciples have demonstrated this historical mistrust."[1] Then, alluding to Jesus' sayings about weeping and laughing in Luke 6:21 and 25, Saroglou suggests that "a social science scholar might be interested not in whether Jesus ever laughed, but why for two thousand years people thought he didn't."[2]

Another way to put the question is whether or not Jesus may be regarded as having the view of humor that the early patristic writers had. Or, to put the question more directly, did Jesus have a humorous attitude and manifest humorous personality characteristics or traits? The fact that the Christian tradition affirms that he is fully human (as well as fully divine) would suggest that he *did* have a humorous attitude and manifest humorous personality characteristics or traits. But, as we will see, the attribution of humorous qualities to Jesus has not been uniformly affirmed by those who consider themselves Jesus scholars and, in general, those who *do* affirm that he possessed these qualities have generally felt that these were not really central to who he was.

1. Saroglou, "Religion and Sense of Humor," 192.
2. Ibid.

This, of course, is not especially surprising, and the studies that we considered in the previous chapter help to explain why. We saw, for example, that religion is very much concerned with purposes and goals, while humor seems to be rather disinterested in these, or even deficient in this regard. It is virtually impossible to think of Jesus as *not* having any discernible purposes and goals. After all, we talk about his mission and have serious discussions about what his mission was and how successful he was in achieving it. The very notion that Jesus was a humorous man does not fit very well with this perception of him and with the discussions that this perception stimulates.

On the other hand, I believe that there can be some real value in asking whether Jesus would have affirmed or lamented the fact that the early patristic literature reflected a negative association between the Christian faith and humor. If he had read this literature, how would he have reacted to it? Would be have endorsed it? Or rejected it? Or perhaps found it amusing? To address this issue, I will make particular use in this chapter of an article titled "The Absence of Humor in Jesus," by Henry F. Harris, which was published in the *Methodist Quarterly Review* in 1908.[3] It would be easy to dismiss Harris' claim that Jesus was not humorous by suggesting that Harris had an unhappy childhood or an unhappy marriage, or that he was being reviewed for tenure at the time he wrote it, or by imagining that Jesus might reply with an article titled "The Absence of Humor in Harris." But I believe his article is worth taking seriously. Even if we eventually disagree with Harris, he helps us to clarify the theoretical grounds and evidence for our disagreement.

The Absence of Humor in Jesus

Harris begins his article with this observation: "If we are to regard the New Testament Scriptures as a complete revelation of the personality of Jesus, we are driven to the conclusion that he was almost totally devoid of humor, as understood in the modern sense."[4] Harris acknowledges that "an attempt has been made to read a humorous intent into the twenty-fourth verse of the twenty-third chapter of Matthew," but he contends that "modern scholarship has abundantly demonstrated that this was not

---

3. Harris, "Absence of Humor in Jesus." The only authorial identification provided in the article itself is that Harris resides in De Land, Florida.

4. Ibid., 460.

an original but a quoted apothegm, a part of the proverbial accumulation of a race, uncommonly rich in proverb."⁵

He is referring here to Jesus' allusion to "straining at gnats and swallowing camels" in his charge that the scribes and Pharisees are hypocrites: "Woe to you, scribes and Pharisees, hypocrites! For you tithe mint, dill, and cumin, and have neglected the weightier matters of the law: justice, mercy, and faith. It is these you ought to have practiced without neglecting the others. You blind guides! You strain out a gnat but swallow a camel!" (Matt 23:23–24 NRSV).⁶ Harris invokes the modern scholarship that was current at the time he was writing to claim that whatever humor there may be in the "You strain out a gnat but swallow a camel" proverb, there is no reason to believe that it was original with Jesus.

In an article on humor in the New Testament published seventy-years later, Lorenz Nieting cited the "straining a gnat and swallowing a camel" saying as an example of the fact that there is humor in exaggeration or hyperbole.⁷ This implies that Jesus used humor to draw attention to the hypocrisy of the scribes and Pharisees. But Harris is suggesting that Jesus borrowed this bit of proverbial wisdom and that it did not originate with him. Although his claim might imply that there was humor in the Jewish culture itself, Harris contends that this was not, in fact, the case. He says that the absence of humor in Jesus might have been foreseen from a variety of considerations:

> In the first place, the Jew is not humorous. The Old Testament is as serious as life, as weighty as judgment. And it is a notable fact that, while the Hebrew is so conspicuous in the history of great intellects (Gladstone is reported to have said that he could hardly recall a great man who had no strain of Jewish blood), yet the Hebrew nation has never produced a great humorist. There is no Jewish Shakespeare, no Jewish Cervantes. It is true that the scribes of the Talmud were masters of a certain insinuating and drastic irony, peculiarly sly and peculiarly incisive, yet there is no national masterpiece which is not serious.⁸

---

5. Ibid.
6. Ibid.
7. Nieting, "Humor in the New Testament," 168.
8. Harris, "Absence of Humor in Jesus," 460. The Gladstone to whom Harris makes reference here is William Ewart Gladstone. He was a British statesman and served for several terms as prime minister between 1868 and 1894.

Harris suggests that this fact is explicable on a variety of grounds. One is that "Jewish history has been predominantly tragic."[9] Another is that:

> The Hebrew genius is profoundly spiritual. If the world meant beauty to the Greek, and law to the Roman, it meant God to the Jew. And the spiritual temper does not readily combine with humor. Men in whom the religious instinct has been powerful—men like Paul, like Calvin, like Knox—have rarely been given to jest. On the contrary, a profound seriousness, which more often than not became solemnity, has generally characterized religious leadership. Intensity nearly always accompanies the religious temperament, and intensity is the very antithesis of humor. Humor tends to relax; intensity, as the word implies, to make tense.[10]

A third reason for the absence of humor among Jews is "the unexampled integrity and unity of the Jewish type—an integrity and unity which have resisted all dissolving and disintegrating forces of world-wide dispersion protracted over mighty periods of time."[11] In Harris' judgment, "this unity, this oneness, this hard compactness of type, is fatal to humor," for "humor rests not upon unity, but diversity; not upon fixity, but upon difference and contrast." In short, "essential seriousness of mood, of purpose, has been [the Jews'] hall-mark from the beginning."[12]

Readers who are aware of the role of Jewish comedians and of comedic films written and produced by Jews are likely to reject Harris' argument that Jesus' alleged lack of humor is due, at least in part, to his Jewish heritage. But, as I indicated above, I believe that in order to contest Harris' view that there is an absence of humor in Jesus, we need to take seriously the grounds on which he makes this claim. Interestingly enough, the reasons he has given for the absence of a humorous temperament among Jews are similar to the empirical evidence presented in chapter 3 of the incompatibility between religion and humor.

Next, Harris takes up the counterargument that "Jesus was not Jew, but archetypal Man," and therefore the points that he has made about Jews not being humorous are irrelevant to the question whether Jesus

---

9. Ibid.

10. Ibid., 460–61. Harris' suggestion that humor tends to relax is noteworthy in light of our discussion in chapter 1 of humor's support for the gospel of relaxation

11. Ibid., 461.

12. Ibid.

himself was humorous. Harris rejects this argument, noting that to say that Jesus "was unaffected by heredity, by environment, by race, is as rational as to say that he was unaffected by gravitation—no more and no less."[13] But if Jesus was affected by his Jewishness, then how are we to explain his universal appeal? Harris suggests that the answer to this question is obvious: all genius is universal. Otherwise, it is not genius: "If Homer had been Greek and nothing else, he would possess no interest for minds not Greek. Jesus was immeasurably more than a Jew, but he *was* a Jew, and his national temper emerges at every turn of the gospel narrative. So, on purely racial grounds, we should expect him to be devoid of humor."[14] Furthermore, "the national traits which are so conspicuous in the Jewish race as a whole are even more conspicuous in the character of Jesus," for Jesus "was a Jew of the Jews."[15] Harris explains:

> If the average Jew was intense, Jesus was far more so. An amazing illustration of his intensity is conveyed in the fact that he was not even conscious of physical hunger until he had fasted forty days and nights (see Luke 4: 2). If the average Jew was interested in religion—and we know that the whole social and political life of the Jew was only a variant of his religious life—Jesus was immensely more interested in it. It was his one theme. It absorbed all the activities of his life. It impelled him to utter self-sacrifice and to the death itself.[16]

Harris goes on to suggest that if Jesus exemplified the unity that is so much a part of the Jewish temperament, this very unity was "reinforced by another and special consideration," namely, the fact that he was possessed of a "fixed idea—the idea that he was born to be Messiah and Savior."[17] Harris notes that psychologists tell us that "nothing so tends to unify character as a fixed idea," and this was especially the case with Jesus:

> From the beginning he was impelled, by teaching from without and by his own nascent consciousness from within, to look upon himself as the One who should redeem Israel. All forces, personal, national and environmental, converged to produce in him a unity of temper and intelligence without parallel in history. It was this unity of character—will, emotion, and intelligence

13. Ibid.
14. Ibid.
15. Ibid.
16. Ibid., 461–62.
17. Ibid., 462.

all moving in perfect rhythm, not neutralizing each other as in the case of Hamlet—which explains, in part, the power of Jesus, humanly considered. And it was this collectedness, this concentration, this oneness of temper, which militated against the element of humor. For humor, which turns upon contrast, "the contrast between incongruities," does not arise out of unity, but out of difference and the sense of difference.[18]

In addition to the fact that Jesus was Jewish and exemplified the Jewish temperament, Harris offers another reason for the absence of humor in Jesus, and this is the fact that Jesus' personality was of the feminine rather than the masculine type. He notes that the biblical scholar Ernest Renan "declares that Jesus belonged to the feminine type,"[19] and adds that the editor of journal in which the article is being published "takes the

---

18. Ibid. Harris does not indicate his source for the phrase "the contrast between incongruities." It is noteworthy, however, that he invokes here one of the three main philosophical theories of humor, that of *incongruity*, noted in chapter 2, footnote 1. See Morreall, *Philosophy of Laughter and Humor*, 129–31. I assume that Harris would argue that the other two theories of humor—superiority or relief—would also be incongruent with Jesus' "oneness of temper."

19. Ibid. Harris does not cite his source for this statement that Renan declared that Jesus was of the feminine type. I have read Renan's *Life of Jesus*, published in 1863, and have not found anything in it to suggest that Renan believed Jesus was of the feminine type. What *does* come through in Renan's portrayal of Jesus is his view that in the later stages of his ministry Jesus' vision of the kingdom of God had taken on such an intensity that, as Renan puts it, "everything which was not the kingdom of God had absolutely disappeared," and family, friendship, and country "had no longer any meaning for him" (Renan, *Life of Jesus*, 165). He has reference to such declarations attributed to Jesus that "I have not come to bring peace, but a sword," and "I am come to set a man against his father, and a daughter against her mother, and a daughter-in-law against her mother-in-law" (Matt 10:34–35 NRSV: also Luke 12:51–53, NRSV). In Renan's view, Jesus' "intense and exalted form of morality" led to the loss of his own personal freedom, for he now belonged totally and irrevocably to his mission (ibid., 166). As a result, "he suffered great mental anguish and agitation," "the great vision of the kingdom of God glistening before his eyes bewildered him," "contact with the world pained and revolted him," and "his excessively impassioned temperament carried him incessantly beyond the bounds of human nature" (ibid., 166). Renan's portrayal of Jesus in the later stages of his ministry does not appear to be congruent with Harris' view that Jesus was of the feminine type. And although his portrayal of Jesus may seem to support, albeit indirectly, Harris' view that Jesus did not engage in humor, Renan *does* say that Jesus "laughed at all human systems, and his work, not being a work of the reason, that which he most imperiously required was 'faith'" (ibid., 166). It might be argued that such laughter was a form of humor, but, if so, humor was subordinate to faith, and Renan may therefore be viewed as a precursor to the theologians we discussed in chapter 3.

position that Jesus was psychologically bisexual." Thus, "both Renan and Dr. Alexander admit the presence of feminine elements," and, "indeed it would be impossible to overlook these elements":

> The self-effacement of Jesus, his tenderness, his tears, his love of children, furnish abundant evidence of traits more feminine than masculine. And to this testimony we may add the fact that he was—so far as the four Gospels show—without humor. For no doctrine of current psychology seems more generally conceded than that women, broadly considered without reference to special exceptions, are defective in the sense of humor.[20]

What is the explanation of this curious fact? Harris acknowledges that the answer to this question would require "a volume written by a trained specialist, and even then it would probably be tentative and provisional."[21] Meanwhile, the following suggestion may be offered:

> Man is physically positive and spiritually negative; woman is physically negative and spiritually positive. That there is a moral difference between men and women will emerge upon a comparison between the statistics of churches and the statistics of penitentiaries. But not only is woman more moral than man—she is more religious. It is said that religion in Italy today would fall into universal neglect except for the influence of women.[22]

The question then is "what bearing does the woman's sensitiveness to the appeal of religion have on 'her deficiency in the sense of the ludicrous?'" In Harris' view, the answer is obvious:

> Religion is a heavenward-tending and humor is an earthward-tending force. Humor is a sort of mischievous elf that ridicules and belittles. It has small reverence and less dignity. On the pages of a "funny" periodical it will present Mr. [William Jennings] Bryan with the body of a domestic animal, or clothe Mr. [Theodore] Roosevelt in the uncouth garb of a tramp. This is an extreme illustration, but a truth which might otherwise elude us sometimes stands clearly revealed in the exaggerations of caricature. Humor may be wholesome and sanative; it may serve admirably as a balance of the faculties; but there is no question that it is of the earth earthy. It does not readily join in chemical

---

20. Harris, "Absence of Humor in Jesus," 462.
21. Ibid., 463.
22. Ibid.

union with religion, despite much popular preaching to the contrary.²³

Harris notes that humor has "been known to destroy revivals," and that we "do not greatly care for humor in a sermon, and we could not tolerate it in a prayer."²⁴ He concludes:

> All the great emotions at their climax tend to pass beyond the merely humorous. And so women, who are rich in emotional and religious elements, have little relish for it. Few women take a fundamentally humorous view of a situation; fewer still, I imagine, think humorously when alone. Even with those women who are noted for saying "good things," one suspects the mirth to be largely histrionic, a playing to the galleries, a *mask* gladly laid aside when the lights are turned off. The essential woman, under the conventional, is as serious as the profound and intense emotions which are enwoven with her inmost self. And Christ, with his quivering sensibilities, his more than masculine fineness, seems to share this trait, as he shares so many others, with a sex that never in a single instance took part or lot against him.²⁵

This is not to deny that Christ was also masculine for "as the typal Human Being he was—necessarily—both."²⁶

A final explanation for the absence of humor in Jesus is that he "was clearly of the primitive type." Harris points out:

> The dilettante, forever refining upon his subtleties, the sophisticated and elaborately self-conscious intelligence that concerns itself with air-drawn casuistries and highly spiced epigrams—these were at an immeasurable remove from the Master's habitual mood. The nature of Jesus was big, simple, elemental. He talked only of things that were infinitely worthwhile, and he talked in the most direct way. He lived in the perpetual presence of the eternal and the universal. The ephemeral and conventional can hardly be said to have existed for him at all. And primitive men like him, who are as natural as the mountains and the sea—men like Aeschylus and Job, men like [William] Wordsworth and [Leo] Tolstoy in our own day—are nearly always humorless.

---

23. Ibid. He does not identify the preachers who have been employing humor in their sermons. We will return to this issue, however, in chapter 7.

24. Ibid.

25. Ibid., 463–64.

26. Ibid., 464.

> I think these primitive types thicken as we move backward into history; certainly humor becomes less conspicuous. Comparatively few specimens of antique wit have come down to us, and they are not poignantly amusing.[27]

Thus, Harris presents three arguments for an absence of humor in Jesus: his Jewish identity, his feminine nature, and his primitive nature. As with Harris' claim that the absence of humor in Jesus is due to his Jewish heredity, one could argue that women are not as humorless as he suggests—that, in fact, one may fail to perceive that Jesus is humorous precisely because his humor is of the more feminine type.[28] One could also contend that there are forms of humor that are not incongruent with the primitive type. After all, Harris characterizes humor in this passage as subtle and sophisticated, but there are, in fact, forms of humor that are simple and unsophisticated. Is it not possible that one can be of the primitive type and also engage in humor?

Finally, Harris suggests that the study of the character of Christ in relation to humor should also include the study of the character of Christ in relation to pathos. He notes that some have argued that humor and pathos spring from a common root. He agrees that intellectually they have much in common, but they differ emotionally. An incongruous headdress on the bald pate of a clown is humorous, but the same headdress on a poor and ailing child moves one to pity: "So in the case of Christ we may readily suppose that his outlook on life would be so profoundly serious and tender that humor would constantly tend to be arrested by pity, by reverence, by any and all of the finer feelings."[29] And this would also be true of the great paradoxes in the gospels. They "contain all the *mental* elements of humor, involving, as they clearly do, the contrast of incongruities; but they are not amusing, for the reason that they are saturated with *emotion* that transcends the merely humorous."[30]

---

27. Ibid.

28. It is noteworthy in this connection that Erik H. Erikson notes in his essay on the Galilean sayings of Jesus that one "cannot help noticing, on Jesus' part, an unobtrusive integration of maternal and paternal tenderness" in the episode to which the Gospel of Mark refers in which the disciples rebuked some parents for bringing their children to Jesus. Jesus said to them, "Let the children come to me, do not hinder them; for to such belongs the kingdom of God," and then "took them in his arms and blessed them, laying his hands upon them" (Mark 10:14–16). See Erikson, "Galilean Sayings and the Sense of 'I,'" 348.

29. Harris, "Absence of Humor in Jesus," 465.

30. Ibid.

Harris concludes the article with this question: Does the absence of humor in Jesus suggest a limitation in his character or temperament? In his view, the answer is clearly no:

> Nature delights in paradox, and what is usually felt to be defective in the non-humorous temperament, turns out to be a quality of strength in the case of Jesus. Take, for instance, the tendency to extremeness which is so apt to rise in the absence of a sense of humor. If Jesus was extreme, it was the extremeness of truth. It is well for mere men, exposed to manifold error, to be moderate in statement and opinion, to move warily and with due deliberation. But a god, to whom the truth is "an open scroll," has no need of such mental caution. Christ gives us the extreme of ethical law because he perceives the absolute ethical truth. "He makes no compromise; he builds no halfway house"; and, as a result, the Sermon on the Mount always "keeps in advance of the most progressive age." If Christ had stated anything less extreme than the absolute truth, he could not have been the universal Teacher whose doctrine is alterable by no accident of time or place or circumstance.[31]

Finally, then, "it is not too much to say that the lack of humor in Jesus is a side-proof of his divinity; for the shifting contrasts upon which humor depends must ever tend to disappear before that vision which beholds the fundamental unity that underlies all contrast."[32]

Taking Harris Seriously

I have presented Harris' article in some detail because I believe it needs to be taken seriously (!). On the one hand, it would be relatively easy to challenge many of his assertions and arguments. For example, the argument that Jews do not exhibit much humor because their history has been predominantly tragic is rather easy to challenge, as one could just as well argue that a predominantly tragic history would foster a humorous attitude toward life in this world.[33] It is also worth noting that Freud's *Jokes and Their Relation to the Unconscious* was published three years

---

31. Ibid., 466. Harris does not identify the author of the quoted material.

32. Ibid., 467.

33. See, for example, the chapter "Jewish Jokes and the Acceptance of Absurdity" in Cohen, *Jokes*, 45–68.

before Harris' article was published and that it clearly reflects his Jewish identity.[34]

Similarly, Harris' argument that women (with a few notable exceptions) lack a sense of humor is rather easy to dispute. To be sure, the empirical studies cited in chapter 2 do indicate that there are gender differences as far as humor is concerned, and that men have a tendency to employ humor more than women do. For instance, in their study of the effect of religion on humor creation, Saroglou and Jaspard found that after exposure to a humor video the men's score on humor creation was especially high.[35] Also, in their study of sick humor and religion, Saroglou and Anciaux found that among the humor styles studied (social, coping, hostile, earthy, self-defeating, and competent), essentially the same negative correlations between religion and humor were true of both women and men, except that for men, both religiosity and spirituality were positively associated with self-defeating humor. They guess that this may reflect a tendency for religious men to be insecure in their attachments.[36] On the other hand, they found that married couples who identified themselves as religious reflected similar ways of being amused, ways that reflect specific values with respect to order (earthy humor), respect of others (hostile humor), and seriousness in dealing with life problems (social and coping humor) and existential questions (macabre humor).[37] It is also noteworthy that Vilaythong et al. found no differences between men and women as far as humor's effect on hope is concerned.[38]

Thus, if Harris appeals to Jesus' femininity to support his view that Jesus was not a humorous man, the empirical studies would seem to suggest that he could just as well have argued that because Jesus is a religious man, he is less likely than nonreligious men to employ humor, or, at any rate, he will be more circumspect in his employment of humor. Being religious is the critical variable here, and Harris could well have cited examples of women who enjoy humor every bit as much as any man enjoys humor.

Also, although humor and laughter are not synonymous, Robert Provine reports in his book *Laughter* on his own study of speakers and

---

34. See on this point Oring, *Jokes of Sigmund Freud*; also Reik, *Jewish Wit*.
35. Saroglou and Jaspard, "Does Religion Affect Humor Creation?," 40.
36. Saroglou and Anciaux, "Liking Sick Humor," 264.
37. Ibid.
38. Vilaythong et al., "Humor and Hope," 86.

audiences, and indicates that he found that women tend to laugh more than men do.[39] This finding prompted one female colleague of Provine's to say, "Oh, my goodness, the stereotype of the giggling female has been confirmed," and prompted another female colleague to observe that, after all, women have more to laugh at than men do. On the other hand, Provine found that although women are the leading laughers, men are the best laugh-getters. He cites a study by Hugh Foot and Anthony Chapman that showed that among children viewing cartoons, girls laughed more often with boys than with girls, and girls reciprocated boys' laughter more often than boys reciprocated girls' laughter.[40]

An especially noteworthy example of women's tendency to laugh more than men do is the familiar story recounted in the book of Genesis relating to the birth of Isaac, the son of Abraham and Sarah. We are told that when the Lord initially promised Abraham that he would give him a son by Sarah, "Abraham fell on his face and laughed, and said to himself, 'Can a child be born to a man who is a hundred years old? Can Sarah, who is ninety years old, bear a child?'" (Genesis 17:17 NRSV).

Later, it was Sarah's turn to laugh. Three men happen to have appeared near the entrance to Abraham's tent, and he offered them food that his wife Sarah prepared. He stood by them under the tree while they ate. Then they said to him, "Where is your wife Sarah?" He replied, "There in the tent" (Genesis 18:9 NRSV). Then one of the men said, "I will surely return to you in due season, and your wife Sarah shall have a son" (v. 10). Sarah was listening at the tent entrance behind the man. The narrator notes that "Abraham and Sarah were old, advanced in age; it had ceased to be with Sarah after the manner of women" (v. 11). In other words, she was too old to bear a child: "So Sarah laughed to herself, saying, 'After I have grown old, and my husband is old, shall I have pleasure?'" (v. 12). Whereupon the Lord said to Abraham: "Why did Sarah laugh, and say, 'Shall I indeed bear a child, now that I am old?' Is anything too wonderful for the LORD? At the set time I will return to you, in due season, and Sarah shall have a son" (vv. 13–14). Sarah denied that she had laughed but the Lord said, "Oh yes, you did laugh" (v. 15).

When their son Isaac was born Sarah said, "God has brought laughter for me; for everyone who hears will laugh with me" (Genesis 21:6 NRSV). She added, "Who would ever have said to Abraham that Sarah

---

39. Provine, *Laughter,* 27–28.
40. Ibid., 28. See Foot and Chapman, "Social Responsiveness of Young Children."

would nurse children! Yet I have borne him a son in his old age" (v. 7). This story challenges Harris' view that women are lacking in humor and, because the story is biblical, it also calls into question his view that this is also true of the Jewish people.[41]

More difficult to challenge are Harris' arguments related to what type of man Jesus was and related to what characterizes divinity, but this is largely because there is considerable disagreement among biblical scholars as to Jesus' personality and among theologians as to what constitutes divinity. I do, however, believe that Harris makes an important point with regard to Jesus' essential unity, and I have suggested that Jesus impresses us as being "the self-reconciled one, as one who is not inwardly at war with himself."[42] On the other hand, I believe that Harris' assertion that humor "does not arise out of unity, but out of difference and the sense of difference" is not necessarily true, and I also believe that humor and truth are not necessarily in conflict with one another—that, in fact, humor can be used in the service of truth.

Moreover, although Harris offers examples of persons whose "spiritual temper does not readily combine with humor"—men like Paul, Calvin, and Knox—there are others whose spiritual temper seems to combine with humor quite readily. Martin Luther is one example. In the preface to his *The Wit of Martin Luther* Eric W. Gritsch describes the argument of his book.

The first chapter shows *how* humor became an integral part of Luther's work as a reformer. The second chapter *illustrates* his humor by means of examples of his work as an interpreter of the Bible, in his pastoral care, and in his encounter with mortality. The third chapter depicts *why* his anticipation of the Last Day made Luther not only serene but also free, and here Gritsch notes that in dealing with this question he came to realize "that Luther's humor in its eschatological setting is a mark of freedom in his life and work."[43] Luther has been acknowledged as a "theologian of the cross," but "his kind of humor also discloses a 'theol-

---

41. In my discussion of this biblical story in Capps, *Time to Laugh*, 81–84, I consider the view that the issue of doubtful paternity is an underlying theme of the story. See Bakan, *Duality of Human Existence*, 213–14. In other words, the joke is on Abraham himself. See also Olson's chapter "Why Did Sarah Laugh?" in *Laughter in a Time of Turmoil*, 53–75; and Martin, *Between Heaven and Mirth*, 102–7.

42. See Capps, *Erik Erikson's Verbal Portraits*, 101–33; also Capps, *Still Growing*, 163–65.

43. Gritsch, *Wit of Martin Luther*, ix.

ogy of freedom,' which should become the most attractive component of his enduring legacy."[44]

Also, although Harris identifies Paul as one who was not humorous because the religious instinct was especially powerful in him, Wilhelm C. Linss contends that there is "hidden humor" in Paul's epistles, most notably in his use of puns.[45] Although puns are said to be "the lowest form of humor," they *are* humor, and Linss makes a convincing case that "a few puns can be found in Paul's letters, although puns are not obvious in the English translation."[46] Linss also acknowledges that the examples he presents may or may not be intentionally humorous, for "just like beauty, the humor may be in the eye (or ear) of the beholder."[47]

However, Douglas Adams presents a stronger case for Paul's sense of humor in his book *The Prostitute in the Family Tree*.[48] He wonders how anyone could miss the humor of Paul when, for example, Paul has body parts talking to each other, as in his first letter to the Corinthians:

> If the foot would say, "Because I am not a hand, I do not belong to the body," that would not make it any less a part of the body. And if the ear would say, "Because I am not an eye, I do not belong to the body," that would not make it any less a part of the body. If the whole body were an eye, where would the hearing be? If the whole body were hearing, where would the sense of smell be? (1 Corinthians 12:15–17 NRSV).

Paul goes on to note that "God arranged the members in the body, each one of them, as he chose," and that there "are many members, but one body" (vs. 18, 20). Moreover,

> those members of the body that seem to be weaker are indispensable, and those members of the body that we think less honorable we clothe with greater honor, and our less respectable members are treated with greater respect; whereas our more respectable members do not need this. But God has so arranged

---

44. Ibid. See also my reflections on "Luther's 'Soft Spot' for the Sow" in my chapter "Humor—Remedy for Melancholia" in Capps, *Men and Their Religion*, 188–90, and my related parody of his hymn "A Mighty Fortress Is Our God" in Capps, *Time to Laugh*, 178–79. Erikson notes Luther's "soft spot" for the sow in *Young Man Luther*, 32–33.

45. Linss, "Hidden Humor of St. Paul."

46. Ibid., 195.

47. Ibid., 199.

48. Adams, *Prostitute in the Family Tree*.

the body, giving the greater honor to the inferior member, that there may be no dissension within the body, but the members may have the same care for one another (1 Corinthians 12:23–25 NRSV).

Adams suggests that our perception of the humor here increases when we see that the Christians in Corinth were behaving like the body parts in the lines of Paul's dialogue. He explains:

> Corinth was the wealthiest of Paul's churches, filled with many who considered themselves sophisticated leaders—like those body parts that are mostly on the head or the upper part of the body, such as the eye, ear, or hand. Each tried to lord it over the others. Paul's humor exposed the ways they were misbehaving. Many readers expect Paul to be solemn, so they miss the numerous comic elements in his epistles. Paul displays his humorous gifts especially in writing to the Corinthians, because their problems resulted from taking themselves too seriously.[49]

Adams clearly believes that the humor here is intentional and not merely in the eye or ear of the beholder. As he points out, one aspect of the humor is that Paul has the body parts talking to one another. Another is that Paul invites us to consider the "less respectable members" of the body, an invitation that is likely to prompt us to ask to which members is he referring, and to engage in our own proclivities for "low" humor. But, most important, Paul uses humor here to express a truth about the social body in general and the body of Christ in particular. Humor and truth are allies, not adversaries.

The Situational Humor of Jesus

The central point of Harris' article is that Jesus was not humorous. So although we can make the case that Luther and Paul were humorous persons, Harris could respond that this does not affect his central point that Jesus was not given to humor, and that this was due to the reasons that he has spelled out in his article.

On the other hand, various authors have written about the humor of Jesus. For example, Earl F. Palmer goes so far as to claim that "Jesus of Nazareth is the greatest humorist of all times."[50] He offers three reasons

49. Ibid., 79.
50. Palmer, *Humor of Jesus*, 25.

for this. The first is the breadth of what Jesus knows about reality. The second is the fact that Jesus is good to the core, and the greatest humor has always had its source in the good surprise of grace. The third is that Jesus is the most normal man we have ever met. As Palmer explains, "The best comedy does not come from the strange words of confusion but from the clear-headed words of a clear vision of reality. Confusion, whether it is cruel or drugged or silly is not really funny in the same robust way as is the humor of clear-headedness."[51]

Palmer goes on to identify eleven forms or expressions of humor in Jesus' repertoire of humor: the unexpected, repetition, justice, misunderstanding, exaggeration, irony, argument, love, joy, salty humor, and healing humor. Palmer's discussion of *exaggeration* is especially relevant to our discussion of Harris' views because Palmer draws attention to the humor in Jesus' charge that the scribes and Pharisees are hypocrites. Noting that "the exaggeration or hyperbole of the Bible is deeply rooted in Hebrew poetry and was well understood in the time of the first century," he suggests that "Jesus teaches and tells parables in this same rich tradition of the humor of exaggeration."[52] He explains that exaggeration enables one to see oneself "more clearly than if only the language of realism is used," and he adds that the humor in these exaggerated portrayals "lies in the exaggeration itself."[53] Thus,

> On one occasion Jesus challenged a group of Pharisees who prided themselves on their ability to offer precise definitions of the legal details of Sabbath law observance. Jesus said to them, "You strain at gnats and you swallow camels." This is a very humorous statement that exaggerates the special talents of the Pharisees as lawyers of the law. It oversimplifies their talents of precision and at the same time helps a Pharisee see the blind side of their interpretive skill. They discover themselves in the position of condemning Jesus for the healing act of love toward a paralyzed man who is walking away with his cot. The man had "labored" on the Sabbath but only because of the love that heals.[54]

51. Ibid.
52. Ibid., 64, 66.
53. Ibid., 66.

54. Ibid. Palmer's association between Jesus' "straining at gnats and swallowing a camel" comment and his healing of a paralyzed man is not, in fact, suggested in Matthew's account, for in Matthew the gnat-and-camel comment occurs in a series of charges against the hypocrisy of the scribes and Pharisees (Matt 23:13–36). But in

The issue, then, is not whether the "straining at gnats and swallowing a camel" saying was original with Jesus, but that he used the saying in such a way as to *exaggerate* the special talents of the Pharisees. By exaggerating what they considered their special talent, he suggested that they were overlooking something that was infinitely more important.

Palmer suggests that Jesus also used exaggeration when he said that it is easier for a camel to go through the eye of a needle than for a rich man to enter the kingdom of God (Mark 10:25).[55] Like the straining at gnats and swallowing a camel observation, this one also draws attention to the camel, and no doubt the hearer imagines a man swallowing a whole camel or a camel trying to squeeze its way through the eye of a needle and finds the picture inherently amusing. In any event, Jesus here uses the humor of incongruity, the suggestion that things are not what they appear to be. Thus, humor reveals a truth that might otherwise remain hidden and fail to come to light, and, as this example of Jesus' humor suggests, the truth may prove to be a truth about oneself. He calls this "the shock of recognition."[56] If so, it is the shock of self-recognition.

In *The Wit and Wisdom of Rabbi Jesus*, William E. Phipps also picks up on the gnat-and-camel saying, focusing especially on the camel. He writes: "More than once Jesus made hilarious humor out of the gangling camel, whose funny appearance is sometimes considered evidence of the Creator's humor."[57] He adds that Jesus' camel-and-needle hyperbole has its own amusing history of interpretation:

> Some apologists for the concentration of wealth in the hands of the elite have engaged their hermeneutical talents in assisting rich persons through the pearly gates. Literalists have dismissed the thought that Jesus would have spoken in a ridiculous manner. Since a length of twisted fiber is properly associated with needles, Calvin comments: 'The word *camel* denotes, I think, a rope used by sailors, rather than the animal so named.'"[58]

---

light of the fact that there are stories in other gospels about the Pharisees' criticism of Jesus for healing persons on the Sabbath (for example, Mark 3:1–6), this association seems entirely appropriate.

55. Palmer, *Humor of Jesus*, 66.
56. Palmer calls this "the shock of recognition" (ibid.).
57. Phipps, *Wit and Wisdom of Rabbi Jesus*, 89.
58. Ibid., 90. The Calvin citation is from his *Commentary of a Harmony of the Evangelists*, 2:401.

Thus, as Phipps points out, Calvin "imagined the possibility of a very thin rope and a huge needle!"[59]

While we might view Calvin's attempt to give a rational explanation for Jesus' allusion to the camel and the needle's eye as itself amusing, it may also support Harris' view that Calvin belongs in the category of men whose spiritual temper does not readily combine with humor.

But, in any case, Phipps also notes that William Barclay, in his popular commentary on the Gospel of Luke, suggested that there was a little gate beside the great gate into Jerusalem that, as Barclay put it, was "just wide and high enough for a man to get through," adding that the "little gate was called the needle's eye, and the picture is that of a camel trying to struggle through that little gate."[60] Phipps says that there is no historical basis for theory that Jesus was referring to an actual gate, but he notes that the idea gave modern-day capitalists the assurance that they could "squeeze through to heaven after giving away their huge moneybags!"[61]

Palmer also suggests that Jesus' critique of the Pharisees' emphasis on tithing and disregard of the larger issue of justice in Luke's Gospel is especially instructive:

> But woe to you Pharisees! For you tithe mint and rue and every herb, and neglect justice and the love of God; these you ought to have done, without neglecting the others. Woe to you Pharisees! For you love the best seat in the synagogues and salutations in the marketplaces. Woe to you! For you are like graves which are not seen, and men walk over them without knowing it. (Luke 11:42–44)

For persons who are accustomed to sitting in the best seats in the synagogues and receiving salutations in the marketplace, the idea that they are graves that others walk over without realizing it would undoubtedly be met with considerable resistance. But this does not mean that it isn't true.

Our focus here on exaggeration merely scratches the surface of Palmer's presentation of the humor of Jesus. But I believe that it makes a persuasive argument for the claim that Jesus was intentionally humorous, that it is not simply a matter of our seeing humor in statements of his that he did not intend to be humorous. It also illustrates the fact that Jesus'

---

59. Phipps, *Wit and Wisdom of Rabbi Jesus*, 90.
60. Ibid., 90.
61. Ibid. The citation is in Barclay, *Gospel of Luke*, 238.

humor relates to a concrete situation. Jesus is not a stand-up comedian who tells one joke after another. Rather, he sees the potential humor in a given situation, owing largely to the fact that there is something incongruous about it.

Douglas Adams also makes a persuasive case that Jesus was a humorist. In his chapter on the "wound-healing humor" of Jesus' parables he discusses the parables of the Prodigal Son (Luke 15:11–32) and the Marriage Feast (Matthew 22:1–14). In his chapter on the "mind-boggling" humor of Jesus' parables, he discusses the parables of the Mustard Seed (Mark 4:30–32), the Good Samaritan (Luke 10:30–35), and the Friend at Midnight (Luke 11:5–8). In his chapter on "the cutting-edge satire" of Jesus' parables he considers the parables of the Talents (Matthew 15:14–30), the Unjust Manager (Luke 16:1–8), the Unjust Judge (Luke 18:2–5), the Hidden Treasure (Matthew 13:44), and the Laborers in the Vineyard (Matthew 20:1–15).[62] Adams also considers the "clowning humor" of Jesus' miracle at the marriage at Cana (John 2:1–11) and several of the healing stories.[63] I will not discuss Adams' interpretations of these stories in detail but simply note his view that they are inherently humorous because they focus on the imperfections, incongruities, and foibles of humans, both individually and collectively. At the same time, the stories convey the idea—even conviction—that the situations they portray are not hopeless.[64]

Adams also makes the point that we miss the humor in many of these stories because we do not know the context in which they are written. To address this problem, he either supplies information that helps us to see the humor in the original story or provides analogies based on similar situations in our own context. He also creates classroom exercises that bring out the humor in the parables and miracle stories.

An especially important theme in Adams' book, one that has direct bearing on the suggestion that humor is an ally—not an adversary—of the truth, is that biblical stories are like the stories that grandparents tell. He begins chapter 1 with this question:

> Remember the stories your parents told you about what it was like when they were growing up and how hard they worked?

62. Adams, *Prostitute in the Family Tree*, 12–24, 25–42, 43–58.
63. Ibid., 59–77.
64. This conclusion is supported by Vilaythong et al., "Humor and Hope," which, as noted in chapter 3, shows that persons who were exposed to a humorous video experienced an increase in their state of hope.

Now remember the stories your grandparents told you about what your parents *really* did when they were growing up. Both parents and grandparents tell stories, but the content varies: Parents tend to clean up their stories; grandparents tell stories that are more truthful and have many rough edges. Parental stories are solemn and can kill by prescribing an ideal we cannot fulfill, but grandparent stories are humorous and give hope and life by sharing a reality similar to our own. Biblical stories are like grandparent stories. Jesus, Paul, and the Hebrew scriptures tell stories that include rough edges—unethical or ambiguous characters, unresolved or surprising endings—and so we laugh and know that we and others may live through the rough times in our lives, too.[65]

I would especially note here that in addition to being "truthful," these stories are "life-giving" because they share a reality similar to our own. Moreover, the suggestion that they are life-giving brings to mind Jesus' assurance to his disciples that "if I go to prepare a place for you, I will come again and take you to myself, so that where I am, you may be also" (John 14:3 NRSV). When Thomas said, "Lord, we do not know where you are going. How can we know the way?" Jesus responded, "I am the way, the truth, *and the life*" (v. 6, italics added). Humor is an ally of truth, but this is because it is identified with life itself. This, of course, recalls the scene of Sarah, who was old enough to be a grandmother, laughing to herself and saying, "After I have grown old, and my husband is old, shall I have pleasure?" (Genesis 18:12). Well, maybe not. But perhaps the pleasure is in the humor itself—in the imagining of the two of them, at their age, conceiving a child. And here it is likely that Abraham, true to his male identity, would be the laugh getter.

---

65. Adams, *Prostitute in the Family Tree*, 1.

5

Putting Humor to Work: The Laborers in the Vineyard

We saw in chapter 4 that Jesus' use of humor was situational, that it typically drew attention to the incongruities that were apparent or discernible in a given situation. As a case in point, we focused on Jesus' critique of the scribes and Pharisees for attending to the minutia of tithing and ignoring the issue of justice. In this chapter we will focus on his parable of the Laborers in the Vineyard (Matthew 20:1–16), a parable that centers on anxiety and stress in the workplace. Since this was a story that Jesus told, it may not describe or portray an event that actually happened. Nonetheless, it focuses on a real-life issue, that of inequities in the workplace, an issue that is as relevant today as it was in Jesus' day.

Both Earl F. Palmer and Douglas Adams, the two authors we discussed in the preceding chapter, suggest that this parable is an example of Jesus' penchant for humor. Palmer discusses it in his chapter on the humor of the unexpected. He begins the chapter with the observation that

> the humor of the unexpected discovery of incongruity is the most common cause of humor. Little children hide behind a door and say "boo"; we laugh because they thought we thought they were someone else and they surprised us and sometimes they really do. There are many instances of the humorously unexpected surprise in New Testament accounts and they were the sources of laughter then as now. We either laugh or catch our breath when we expect to find one thing and something different happens that we were not expecting; if the unexpected is

frightening and dangerous we shudder; if it is a welcome surprise we laugh.[1]

Jesus' turning of the water into wine at the marriage of Cana is an example of the welcome surprise.[2]

Palmer suggests that Jesus also makes use of parables "that are humorous through an unexpected turn in the story so that the humorous surprise takes up a major part of the story line of the parables."[3] He cites the parable of the Laborers in the Vineyard as illustrative:

> The parable of the all day workers tells a story of those who earned the agreed upon wage for their all day work. But the surprise in the parable is that the eleventh hour workers received the same full day pay because of the generosity of the employer. There is a bittersweet humor in this parable: The laughter belongs to the one hour workers who could not imagine such a windfall of good fortune after they had spent most of a day worried about how they could earn enough money to feed their families and then by surprise near the end of the day they are employed and paid as if they had a job all day.[4]

To be sure, "the all day workers complained but that is human nature and we who know ourselves expected this complaint. Nevertheless, nothing takes away from the wonderful and improbable humor of an employer either so rich or so generous that he paid everyone the same. It was not necessary and he did it because he wanted to."[5]

Thus, Palmer sees humor in the employer's behavior, i.e., in the fact that he paid everyone the same. He concludes that the "whole scene, complaints and all, is very funny because we could not have expected something so good, so contrary to ordinary experience, to happen right in front of our eyes."[6]

Douglas Adams considers the parable in his chapter on the cutting-edge satire of Jesus' parables.[7] The chapter centers on the parables of the Talents (Matthew 25:14–30), the Unjust Manager (Luke 16:1–8), the

1. Palmer, *Humor of Jesus*, 41.
2. Ibid., 41–42.
3. Ibid., 42.
4. Ibid.
5. Ibid.
6. Ibid.
7. Adams, *Prostitute in the Family Tree*, 43–58.

Unjust Judge (Luke 18:2–5), the Hidden Treasure (Matthew 13:44), and the Laborers in the Vineyard (Matthew 20:1–15). Adams is especially concerned with the issues of justice that these parables raise, and he takes particular note of the fact that the humor in some of these stories is in the fact that unethical behavior is considered commendable.[8]

He notes that the parables of the Hidden Treasure and the Laborers in the Vineyard suggest that "those with wealth have not necessarily earned it ethically and may not deserve it."[9] In the former parable "the one who ends up with the land containing buried treasure has acted unethically; for in that day one had an obligation to report to the owner of land any valuables on it before one bought it so the owner received a fair price," while in the latter parable "many of the laborers in the vineyard receive a day's wage for far less than a day's work." [10] Adams suggests that this situation may be inherently amusing, but he notes that

> there is further humor in the vineyard parable in the discussion between the master and those he hires at the end of the day, and that humor makes clear that they were undeserving. It is already happy hour when they show up in the marketplace. They were not there earlier or he would have hired them then; for example, those he saw standing idle in the marketplace in the morning he hired (v. 3), as he did throughout the day. So near the end of the day (the eleventh hour), when he went out and found others standing, his question to them has a satiric edge to it: "Why are you standing here idle all day?" (v.6). Rather than say they just arrived, they kiss the satire and lie, responding, "Because no one has hired us" (v.7). Of course no one hired them earlier in the day. They were not there to hire.[11]

Thus, both Palmer and Adams find humor in the story, but their grounds for doing so are quite different. For Palmer, the humor is in the fact that the men who came later got paid a full day's wage. For Adams, the humor is in the fact that they claimed they had been available all day for work and that they failed to recognize that the landowner knew that they had come for work at the last moment. Palmer and Adams share in common their perception that the parable's humor relates to the men who received a full day's pay for working an hour. The men who complain

8. See on this point Capps, "Pastoral Images."
9. Adams, *Prostitute in the Family Tree*, 48.
10. Ibid.
11. Ibid., 48–49.

about this inequity are not, for Palmer or Adams, the focus of the parable's humor. In effect, they are the straight men.

However, in the following discussion of the parable, I will be suggesting that there are humorous potentialities in the conversation that takes place between the landowner and the men who complain. I will also be suggesting that if the disgruntled workers and the defensive landowner could have seen the humor in the situation, they could have relaxed and allowed their "army" of nerves to take a much needed rest,[12] and the outcome would have been very different.

"Are You Envious Because I am Generous?"

The parable of the Laborers in the Vineyard is in the Gospel of Matthew. No other gospel, not even the Gospel of Thomas, has it. Here is the parable:

> The kingdom of heaven is like a landowner who went out early in the morning to hire laborers for his vineyard. After agreeing with the laborers for the usual daily wage, he sent them into his vineyard. When he went out about nine o'clock, he saw others standing idle in the marketplace; and he said to them, "You also go into the vineyard, and I will pay you whatever is right." So they went. When he went out again about noon and about three o'clock, he did the same. And about five o'clock he went out and found others standing around; and he said to them, "Why are you standing here idle all day?" They said to him, "Because no one has hired us." He said to them, "You also go into the vineyard." When evening came, the owner of the vineyard said to his manager, "Call the laborers and give them their pay, beginning with the last and then going to the first." When those hired about five o'clock came, each of them received the usual daily wage. Now, when the first came, they thought they would receive more; but each of them also received the usual daily wage. And when they received it, they grumbled against the landowner, saying, "These last worked only one hour, and you have made them equal to us who have borne the burden of the day and the scorching heat." But he replied to one of them, "Friend, I am doing you no wrong; did you not agree with me for the usual daily wage? Take whatever belongs to you and go;

---

12. For the reference to an "army," see the introduction for quotation from William James, who in turn quotes Dr. Clouston.

I chose to give to this last the same as I give to you. Am I not allowed to do what I choose with what belongs to me? Or are you envious because I am generous?" So the last shall be first, and the first will be last. (Matthew 20:1–15 NRSV)

Note that in this translation the landowner suggests that the complainant may be envious because he is generous. In the RSV translation he says, "Or do you begrudge my generosity?" I will return to this comment later, but for the moment I would simply like to note that "begrudging" and "envy" have rather different meanings and implications. Begrudging the landowner's generosity implies that the complainant resents the fact that he, the landowner, chose to be generous toward the other workers. Envying the landowner's generosity implies that the complainant resents the fact that he is not in a position to be similarly generous. Both, then, reflect feelings of resentment, but the resentment has a different basis, with the one expressing a sense of hurt or indignation that the landowner has been generous at what seems to be one's own expense, and the other expressing a sense of hurt or indignation that the landowner is in the position to be generous but one is not in this position oneself. At this point, I will not try to settle the question whether one of these forms of resentment was more likely than the other, but I will, as indicated, return to this issue when I consider the possibility that the landowner and the complaining workers could have turned to humor to reconcile their differences.

At this juncture, I want to look more closely at what is going on in the parable, and, to initiate this exploration, the insights of Richard Q. Ford in *The Parables of Jesus* will prove to be especially helpful.[13]

The Voicelessness of the Laborers

In his introduction to *The Parables of Jesus* Ford indicates that the book is "by a clinical psychologist long interested in responding to these brief, enigmatic stories with the particular ways of listening practiced by psychotherapists."[14] He discusses the parable which he names "Laborers and a Landowner" in a chapter in which he also discusses the interchange

---

13. Ford, *Parables of Jesus*. At the time he wrote the book, he was in private practice in Williamstown, Massachusetts. See also Kuhlman, *Humor and Psychotherapy*.

14. Ford, *Parables of Jesus*, 1.

between the father and elder brother in the parable of the Prodigal Son, which he names "Two Sons and a Father."

Ford's discussion of the two parables begins with the following observation concerning the contemporary listener to the parable: "Listeners familiar with these stories' Gospel contexts may have difficulty trusting the full range of their feelings. Because they have learned to assume that the beneficiaries of the superiors' generosity—the late-coming workers and the returning younger son—represent late-coming Christians, such listeners may not readily allow into awareness their sympathies for the hard-working early laborers and the hard-working elder son."[15] He notes that the elder son's anger and the early laborers' resentment "are founded on a widely accepted premise," namely, that "because I have worked harder and more faithfully, I should be given more."[16] The element of comparison here is central. One reasons, "If I work at the same task longer or more effectively than others, I deserve 'more' (and 'more' is always relative)."[17] But the father and the landowner do not accept this argument, for "each insists that the complainers have already received all that is coming to them."[18] In other words, there are no grounds for providing them a bonus.

Ford believes that some listeners will find "that their uncomfortable feelings persist," for is it not possible that the elder brother and the early workers have reason to be upset? Then, however, they may mistrust this nagging doubt because "the complaint of the subordinates seems to challenge the generosity of the superiors."[19] The listeners ask, "How can one question generosity, particularly when its providers have been faithful to their promises?"[20]

At this point, Ford begins to focus on each of the two parables individually. I will not discuss what he says about the parable of "The Father and Two Sons" but instead will focus on his interpretation of the parable of "The Laborers and the Landowner." He begins with the observation that the parable may well be exploring a pervasive conflict present in first-century Roman-occupied Jewish Palestine, namely, that

15. Ibid., 109.
16. Ibid.
17. Ibid., 110.
18. Ibid.
19. Ibid.
20. Ibid.

this small, crossroads country had for centuries been mediating between two contending cultural perspectives: the Greco-Roman norm of civilized custom and the Hebraic norm of divine justice. Whereas the former likely had the allegiance of the landed aristocracy, who had been steadily expropriating peasant land and forcing landowning peasants into the marginal underclass of day laborers, the latter, especially because it incorporated the concept that the land belongs to God, probably remained far more attractive to the vulnerable peasants.

While noting that this conflict is not made explicit in the parable itself, Ford nonetheless points out that the landowner focuses on "rights" rather than an appeal to "justice." That is, he tells the early workers that he will pay them "whatever is right" and responds to the worker who has complained that he is doing him "no wrong," that he has paid the complaining worker what they had "agreed" to. Ford notes, however, that the parable itself moves between these two very different understandings, of "what is right" (the Hellenistic norm) and "what is just" (the Hebraic norm), and does so largely because the landowner himself is conflicted. His early morning agreement with the laborers seems to reflect this very ambiguity, as his use of the word "right" may be construed either as "what is right according to custom" or "what is just in the eyes of God." However, by evening he "claims to be limiting himself merely to what is lawful" and "is no longer appealing, albeit ambiguously, to what might be understood as God's ways; he has now limited himself to customary legal obligations."[21]

On the other hand, he "cannot seem to free himself from his ambivalent desire to fit into the Hebraic norm," for his assertion that he is doing the early laborer "no wrong" *could* mean that he is doing him "no injustice," so we may have here at least "the echo of his earlier seeming promise to be just."[22] But is it anything more than a mere echo? For, after all, his earlier assurance that he will pay the early laborers "what is just" seems to be contradicted by his late-evening query, "Am I not allowed to do what I choose with what belongs to me?" Ford suggests that what seems to be central here is "the conflicted effort of the landowner, possessed both with unchecked power and with the desire to appear just, to pursue self-interest under the guise of apparent rectitude."[23]

21. Ibid., 116.
22. Ibid.
23. Ibid., 117.

Moreover, it is only his own definition of what constitutes the customary wage—without any input from the laborers—that becomes the basis for any later decision about what might be perceived as generosity. The owner's assertion that the laborers collaborated in setting the day's wages—"Did you not agree with me for the usual daily wage?"—"represents either self-deception or else a deliberate insult," for he knows full well that in light of the obvious unemployment of day laborers—as reflected in the fact that with each return to the marketplace throughout the day he found workers standing around idly—"none of these laborers can bargain with him."[24] Although he can appeal to the fact that there is a "customary daily wage," it is "insulated from any criteria of divine justice" and "open to no outside challenge."[25] Yet "he chooses to describe himself as someone entering into agreement with persons capable of independent bargaining, not as someone able to dominate a class of laborers wholly vulnerable to his self-interest."[26]

Ford points out that there is a great deal of dissimulation in this self-description, for

> in a world of unequally distributed resources and subsistence daily wages, the landowner in fact cannot realize his ambition to "pay what is just" out of what "belongs" to him until much more of what belongs to his landowning class belongs to the day-laborer class. If one believes that in his desire to be good the landowner is aspiring to justice, then at issue that evening may not be a decision about the worth of twelve hours of labor but rather a judgment about hundreds of years of land-grabbing. Because the underlying inequalities on which he depends would not permit it, the landowner's generosity cannot produce substantive change. To maintain his position, this aristocrat must continue to pay his laborers less than subsistence wages.[27]

Ford concludes his interpretation of the parable by drawing a contrast between the "voicelessness" of the early laborers and the "too-insistent voice" of the landowner. Although the early workers sense that something is wrong they are unable to articulate the problem. They "have awareness sufficient only to accept the superior's definition of what is 'lawful' or 'customary,'" for, because they have never experienced "a

24. Ibid.
25. Ibid.
26. Ibid.
27. Ibid., 117–18.

framework of justice, they lack the resources to imagine its contours."[28] Such work "falls to the listener," and, in this regard, contemporary listeners "may have a hard time estimating the sufficiency of the customary wage of a denarius a day but they should have no difficulty judging which party in this landowner-laborer twosome actually determined how much that customary wage would be—and how that party might rationalize a less-than-equitable amount."[29]

The contemporary listener may also suspect that the early workers' contention that if the late arrivals received a denarius for one hour's work then surely twelve hours' work should be worth more than a denarius functions "as a large distraction."[30] Why? Because what may be "both central and hidden is how the landowner (all the time making less than subsistence wages his benchmark) chooses to call upon both laborers and listeners alike to recognize him as someone who is generous and even someone who is just."[31] To be sure, if one fails to notice "his prior position of total control over the essential definitions, the landowner indeed appears to be generous," and yet, "oppressed peoples the world over are endlessly familiar with the difference between what is held out to them as lawful and what they themselves perceive to be just."[32] Thus, in Ford's view, "the anger of the early laborers may be located not only in their response to perceived inequity but also in their inarticulate reaction to the landowner's unacknowledged arrogance."[33] While they may not be able to articulate what is wrong here, they "are acutely sensitive to the way in which this aristocrat unilaterally defines who deserves what—and especially to how he dares, relying on such prejudiced definitions, to declare himself 'good.'"[34]

---

28. Ibid., 118.

29. Ibid.

30. Ibid.

31. Ibid.

32. Ibid. Ford's distinction here between what is held out to a person as lawful and what one perceives to be just is illustrated by a joke I heard when I was a young boy. A wealthy man disembarked from a taxi and handed the driver the exact fare. The driver, expecting a generous tip, frowned as he examined the money. Noticing his frown, the wealthy man said, "It's correct, isn't it?" to which the driver replied, "Yes, sir, it's correct, but it isn't right."

33. Ibid.

34. Ibid., 118–19.

As for the "too-insistent voice" of the landowner, Ford notes that the landowner seems to have "a need to portray himself as good."[35] Ford wonders why the landowner is "not content merely to exploit?"[36] Why, for example, does he spend so much energy going not once but several times to the marketplace? Why doesn't he send his manager? And why is he so interested in defending his actions to his day laborers? Why not let his manager deal with them? Ford wonders if the landowner's careful calculation of his generosity is a sign of his self-doubt, and suggests that he goes "a long way out of his way—too far, in my judgment—in order to make his case."[37] So what is going on here? Ford puts it this way: "I believe the landowner fails to estimate his labor needs efficiently because he has another goal in mind. At the start of the day he knows full well what he hopes to accomplish at its end: he intends to demonstrate his goodness. This wealthy man goes himself four times to the marketplace not only in search of labor but also in search of honor."[38]

Thus, the longing for honor may account for the landowner's reversal of the customary order in which laborers are paid. Agreeing with William Herzog's view that the owner's intent with this reversal is "to humiliate the early workers," Ford adds that this "need to shame others (he could have given everyone a proportionate bonus) is evidence of anxiety about shamefulness in himself."[39] To be sure, the landowner does not openly declare his desire for honor. Instead, "he crafts a drama designed to put blame on his victims and in the process elevate himself. By demeaning the worth of their only possession, their labor, he deliberately humiliates the early workers. He then counters their predictably angry response with a prepared appeal to his generosity."[40] He "expends considerable energy trying to convince these same laborers that he is a decent person,"[41] but, in Ford's view, he protests too much. He tells them that he will pay them what is right and that he has done them no injustice, and then, "using as evidence a generosity funded by parasitism, he arrogantly

---

35. Ibid., 119.

36. Ibid.

37. Ibid.

38. In point of fact, he went out to the marketplace *five* times—early morning, nine o'clock, noon, three o'clock, and five o'clock. This, of course, does not negatively affect Ford's argument.

39. Ibid. See Herzog, *Parables as Subversive Speech*.

40. Ibid., 119–20.

41. Ibid., 120.

tells these impoverished workers, 'I am good.'"[42] Thus, "the owner, by a careful engineering of his subordinate's response, enables himself to exit from this drama reassured of his own rectitude. He leaves, moreover, convinced that any anger in his laborers represents merely their envy of his sudden generosity—and could not possibly be the result of his chronic stinginess."[43] Ford, however, believes that "the landowner, by the evidence of his insistent efforts, will remain uncertain of his honor," and that his very immersion in a religious culture traditionally focused on justice places him in a dilemma, for "how can he participate in exploiting others and still go about believing himself to be an honorable man?"[44]

Ford concludes this chapter on the two parables with a suggestion that has bearing on the question of what Jesus intended the parable to mean or convey to his own listeners, namely, that "these parables may be proposing that the kingdom of God, or the reign of God, or the intent of God, or the longing of God (however one terms this core element of Jesus' teaching), may be found in that opening up of space between the misunderstandings of two persons—or of two social classes, or of two nations—where some possibility of creative reconciliation might be grasped."[45] And if so, "the work of the listener may be to imagine how, in spite of these polarizing and infuriating impasses, each based on the seemingly beneficent use of wealth, both parties might find ways to speak more honestly to the other."[46]

In the concluding chapter of the book—"How Are These Stories Told—And Heard?"—Ford suggests that the purpose of Jesus' parables was "to evoke in the hearer both how things are and how God yearns for them to be."[47] In other words, "God entrusts to the listener the way things are and waits, with hope, for the listener to discern how they are meant to be. At the center of this powerfully ironic vision, at the heart of the rule of God on earth, God is dependent. God relies on the hearer both to discover what is wrong and to reach for its corrective."[48] Ford adds that the seven parables presented in his book embody this vision in their very

42. Ibid.
43. Ibid., 120–21.
44. Ibid., 120.
45. Ibid., 121.
46. Ibid.
47. Ibid., 122.
48. Ibid.

structure, and he observes that it is this embodiment that, more than anything else, "identifies them as coming from a single creative genius."[49] This creative genius is reflected in the fact that when "engaging the balanced misperceptions that have enveloped the two parable protagonists, the only one separate enough from their entangled histories, the only one able to imagine a different outcome, is the listener."[50] Thus, "these parables entrust their outcomes to those outside their boundaries; the listener alone is empowered to determine not only what has happened but what will happen."[51]

In this view, it makes little sense to say that a character in the story—the father in the "Two Sons and a Father" parable or the landowner in the "Laborers and a Landowner"—is "a figure for God."[52] Nor would it be accurate to say that what happens in the story is an illustration of how it is in the kingdom of God. Rather, the parable depicts a human situation and asks the listener to identify what is wrong with this picture. But it does not tell the listener what would make it right. And, interestingly enough, neither does Ford. His analysis of "The Laborers and a Landowner," for example, is largely diagnostic. It makes a convincing case for the inarticulateness of the laborers and the too-insistent voice of the landowner, but it does not address the issue of how, as he himself puts it, "both parties might find ways to speak more honestly to the other."[53] Ford leaves this task to the listener and more specifically to the listener's imagination.

However, in the concluding chapter he says a bit more about how this might occur: Supposing that in your previous hearings of the story, you found yourself taking sides. For example, in the case of the landowner and early laborers, you sided with the landowner *or* you sided with the laborer whom the landowner chooses to address, calling him "Friend." But now, what if you instead assumed "a new position of listening that leads to greater complexity"? You would perceive the dynamics that Ford has brought out in his analysis of the parable and imagine "a gradually developing give and take between the parable participants."[54] You would ask, "What changes would enable these two persons to hear

49. Ibid.
50. Ibid.
51. Ibid.
52. Ibid., 118.
53. Ibid., 121.
54. Ibid. 131.

each other differently?" This very question may enable you to imagine how *they* might listen to one another and also invite a similar imaginative reflection on how *you* might change in order to become a better listener.[55]

In this regard, Ford suggests that "the parable form with imposing irony represents God's empire as approaching the listener as a vulnerable child."[56] He explains:

> Each listener is free to take the story in a wide array of directions. The narrative neither overwhelms nor resists; rather it waits and evokes, open and accepting. No part of it is so commanding as to compel a specific response. But once the listener chooses to attend, the parable requires choice. To attend is to decide among options. I perceive these parables as offering the listener a chance to do much of the work. In so doing, I see their author as doing the larger portion of the work As any parent or teacher—or psychotherapist—knows, rather than provide one, it is far more difficult to wait expectantly for a developing answer.[57]

In the following pages of this chapter I will offer my own response to the parable, realizing that it is simply one of many options. I will, however, have in mind Earl Palmer and Doug Adams' recognition that there is humor in this parable, and that it centers especially on the workers who worked an hour but received a full day's pay. To my listening ears, the greater potential for humor is in the interchange between the landowner and the workers who worked all day. To make my case, I need to bring psychoanalysis into the discussion and, more particularly, Sigmund Freud.

Generosity and Envy

Although Richard Ford has psychoanalytic leanings, his interpretation of the parable of "The Laborers and a Landowner" is not overtly psychoanalytic.[58] He cites several psychoanalysts in the book itself, but he makes no references to psychoanalytic authors in his discussion of this parable.

---

55. Ibid., 132.
56. Ibid.
57. Ibid.
58. Ford's psychoanalytic leanings are reflected in Blatt and Ford, *Therapeutic Change*, which is written from an object-relations perspective.

This, of course, does not mean that his interpretation of the parable is not psychoanalytically informed, for as the foregoing discussion indicates, he draws on various psychoanalytic concepts, especially in his analysis of the landowner's behavior. I believe, however, that Freud's writings on humor provide insights into how the disputing parties may begin to listen to one another and even, perhaps, resolve their differences.[59]

To set the stage for this discussion, I want to return to the fact, as noted earlier, that the landowner's concluding question to the complaining worker has been translated in two rather different ways: "Do you begrudge my generosity?" (RSV) and "Are you envious because I am generous?" (NRSV).

As I grew up on the Revised Standard Version, I simply assumed that the basic issue here was that the workers did, in fact, begrudge the landowner his generosity and did so because they naturally and justifiably believed that they were its victims. In fact, it was not until I read Richard Ford's reflections on the parable that I was able to see that the issue here might be one of envy.[60] For in a social context in which some persons are wealthy and getting wealthier and other persons are at best living at a subsistence level, the freedom to act generously toward others *is* likely to be an *enviable* position to be in—not only because it means that one possesses financial resources that exceed one's own needs and desires, but also because acting generously is likely to contribute to the esteem in which one is held by others and to enhance one's own sense of self-esteem. The person who lives on subsistence wages will never experience the good feelings that often accompany expressions of generosity.

A valuable clue to why the landowner may have felt that he was the object of the early workers' envy is provided, rather unexpectedly, by the

---

59. Freud, *Jokes and Their Relation to the Unconscious*; and Freud, "Humor."

60. I had written about envy in Capps, *Deadly Sins and Saving Virtues*, in which I assign the traditional deadly sins—gluttony, anger, greed, envy, pride, lust, apathy (commonly referred to as sloth), and melancholy (the sin later removed from the original list of eight deadly sins)—to Erik Erikson's stages of the life cycle, thus providing a dialectic between the deadly sins and the virtues that he had proposed for each of the eight stages of the life cycle. See Erikson, *Insight and Responsibility*, 109–57. In this dialectic, envy corresponds to the school age (approximately five to twelve years of age) and interacts with the virtue of competence. It would be possible to interpret the conflict between the landowner and the complaining workers as reflecting this stage of the life cycle, as this stage involves the psychodynamic of industry vs. inferiority. In light of the emphasis in this book on stress, anxiety, tension, and worry, it is noteworthy that Lance Webb, in *Conquering the Seven Deadly Sins*, adds a chapter on "Anxiety and Worry" to chapters on the traditional seven deadly sins.

translation of the landowner's question in the King James Version. In this version he says nothing about their begrudging his generosity or being envious of it, but instead says, "Is thine eye evil, because I am good?" (v. 15). What, we might ask, does the other man's eye have to do with it? But in his book on the historical Jesus, John Dominic Crossan cites David Gilmore's observation that belief in the evil eye is "one of the oldest continuous religious constructs in the Mediterranean area."[61] In his essay on "The 'Uncanny'" Freud identified dread of the evil eye as attributed envy:

> Whoever possesses something that is at once valuable and fragile is afraid of other people's envy, in so far as he projects on to them the envy he would have felt in their place. A feeling like this betrays itself by a look even though it is not put into words; and when a man is prominent owing to noticeable, and particularly owing to unattractive, attributes, other people are ready to believe that his envy is rising to a more than usual degree of intensity and that this intensity will convert it into effective action. What is feared is thus a secret intention of doing harm, and certain signs are taken to mean that that intention has the necessary power at its command.[62]

Thus, in suggesting that the other man possesses the evil eye, the landowner is probably thinking that the other man and his cohorts are prepared to take physical action against him.

At first glance, the landowner's suggestion that he was the envy of the laborers because he was able to be generous may not seem very plausible. They had not, after all, said anything that would lead the listener to

---

61. Gilmore, "Anthropology in the Mediterranean Area," 198. Cited in Crossan, *Historical Jesus*, 7.

62. Freud, "'Uncanny,'" 147. I discuss the attribution of the "evil eye" to Jews by non-Jews in late nineteenth- and early twentieth-century Europe in Capps, *Jesus: A Psychological Biography*, 208–10, and note its role in European anti-Semitic attitudes. I also note that in the time of Jesus Jews would have attributed the evil eye to other Jews, especially to those who were lower in social status, and I suggest that in a culture where belief in the evil eye was pervasive, the incidence of blindness should not surprise us. Suggesting that blindness was a first-century form of conversion disorder, I suggest that it served as an anxious defense, as though the blind person reasons, "If I cannot see the evil eye of others, I protect myself from their evil intentions." Also, a blind person would be considered incapable of visiting evil on another individual, and may, therefore, become the object of genuine sympathy. I noted, therefore, that in addition to the fact that a secondary gain from blindness was removal from onerous or degrading labor, there were also secondary gains associated with the ubiquity of the belief in the evil eye (ibid., 210). See also Capps, *Jesus the Village Psychiatrist*, 73–77.

feel that they wished that they, and not he, were the ones who had acted generously toward the workers who came later in the day. But Freud's commentary on the evil eye and the vulnerability of those who feel that they are the envy of others helps us to see the situation from the landowner's point of view and to understand why he thought the other men were envious of him in this regard.

In seeing the situation in this way, one does not need to question, much less reject, Ford's view that the laborers were essentially voiceless and that the landowner had total control over how a day's wages would be defined,[63] that the landowner was engaging in a calculated crafting of a drama "designed to put blame on his victims and in the process elevate himself," and that "by a careful engineering of his subordinate's response" he was able "to exit from the drama reassured of his own rectitude."[64] But we can view these calculations and careful engineering as prompted, at least in part, by his feelings of vulnerability due to what he believed to be the envious feelings of the laborers toward him. Members of the lower social classes could—and did—destroy the sources of the wealth belonging to members of the higher social classes. The chance to work in his vineyard might be the laborers' only means of supporting themselves (albeit at a barely subsistence level, if that); but frustrated with their lives and seeing no hope for a better future, they might decide to take direct physical action against him. Or, because the other grateful men may still be around to defend the landowner against physical attack, they might restrain themselves for the moment and then, later, enter the vineyard at night and steal the fruit or even set fire to the vines. If they did, would he have the power to stop them?

Men of Honor

It is noteworthy, however, that the dispute that Jesus as storyteller imagines is between men who view themselves as men of honor.[65] After all, the early laborers appeal to the fact that they worked all day, through the scorching heat of the midday, and their complaint is not in reference

---

63. Ford, *Parables of Jesus*, 118.

64. Ibid., 119–20.

65. Crossan, *Historical Jesus*, 9–15, discusses the honor-and-shame ideology in Mediterranean societies. See also my discussion of this ideology in *Jesus: A Psychological Biography*, 98–103. I also discuss the religion of honor in *Men and Their Religion*, chs. 2, 5; and in Dykstra et al., *Losers, Loners, and Rebels*, chs. 6–7.

to all of the other laborers, but to those who worked "only an hour" (v. 12). Similarly, the landowner appeals to the fact that he did not, after all, cheat any of the workers or give any of them *less* than was their due. So perhaps the fundamental problem here is that they truly want to be men of honor but feel that the social world into which they have been thrust is conspiring against them.

Ford emphasizes the landowner's total control over the laborers (and thus refers to the laborers as "victims"), but there is also a sense in which the landowner has relatively little personal control in a society in which there is rampant unemployment and a social-class structure riddled with inequities. While we would not expect the laborers to have any sympathies for him, perhaps we—the listeners—can hear his own plea for understanding in the very awkwardness of his projection onto the laborers of the envy he would have felt in their place. His apparent need to demean them in order to maintain his own sense of honor may be a function of this very projection. But, in any case, Ford's contention that these men need to get beyond their current impasse is absolutely crucial. The question is how this might happen. I believe that Freud's discussion of beggar jokes in *Jokes and Their Relation to the Unconscious* points the way.[66]

Beggar Jokes

The beggar jokes are in Freud's chapter on the purposes of jokes. He begins this chapter with a comment on German poet and essayist Heinrich Heine's analogy, which he had mentioned at the end of the preceding chapter, between the church and commercial enterprises. Heine had suggested that a Catholic priest is like an employee in a wholesale business, and a Protestant minister is like a retail merchant.[67] Freud confesses that

---

66. Freud, *Jokes and Their Relation to the Unconscious*, 134–35.

67. In a later chapter Freud notes that Heine was Jewish but that he converted to Christianity at the age of twenty-seven. He changed his first name from Harry to Heinrich when he was baptized (ibid., 173). Freud suggests that there is a bit of self-parody in Heine's creation of a comic character named Hirsch, a Hamburg lottery agent, extractor of corns, professional appraiser, and valet of Baron Christoforo Gumpelion, who changed his own name to Hyacinth. Heine explains that there was an advantage to changing it from Hirsch to Hyacinth since he already had an *H* on his signet ring and therefore did not need to have a new ring cut (ibid., 172). It is also worth noting that Heine's witticism about a Catholic priest and a Protestant minister is virtually begging for a third—a rabbi—to transform it into a full-fledged joke. See Tapper and

he was aware of an inhibition "which was trying to induce me not to make use of the analogy."[68] He explains:

> I told myself that among my readers there would probably be a few who felt respect not only for religion but for its governors and assistants. Such readers would merely be indignant about the analogy and would get into an emotional state which would deprive them of all interest in deciding whether the analogy had the appearance of being a joke on its own account or as a result of something extra added to it.[69]

In other words, they would focus on the content of the analogy and not on the problem with which Freud was concerned in his analysis of how jokes work.

I mention Freud's awareness of this inhibition relating to Catholic and Protestant clerics because I suspect that he experienced a similar inhibition regarding the beggar jokes, as these jokes are clearly Jewish jokes, and he would have been aware that some of his Jewish readers would object to his use of Jewish jokes that may cast Jews in a rather bad light, especially at a time when Germany and Austria were experiencing a revival of anti-Semitism.[70] Freud notes that the jokes that he relates in this chapter "have grown up on the soil of Jewish popular life" and "are stories created by Jews and directed against Jewish characteristics."[71] The jokes are about marriage brokers and beggars.[72] I will only discuss the beggar jokes because they are more directly relevant to the economic issues raised by the parable of the Laborers in the Vineyard or (to use Ford's title) "The Laborers and a Landowner."

Earlier, Freud suggested that there are two types of jokes—innocent and tendentious—a distinction based on whether or not a joke has "an aim in itself." Innocent jokes do not have an aim. Tendentious jokes do, and they are of two types: *obscene* (serving the purpose of exposure) and *hostile* (serving the purpose of aggressiveness, satire, or defense).[73] The

---

Press, *A Minister, a Priest, and a Rabbi*. See also Capps, *Laughter Ever After*, ch. 5.

68. Freud, *Jokes and Their Relation to the Unconscious*, 106.

69. Ibid.

70. See Gilman, *Freud, Race, and Gender*; and Gilman, *The Case of Sigmund Freud*.

71. Freud, *Jokes and Their Relation to the Unconscious*, 133.

72. In *Jokes of Sigmund Freud* Orring discusses the personal relevance of marriage-broker jokes to Freud's prolonged, four-year engagement to Martha Bernays and of beggar jokes to his reliance on wealthy benefactors while he was a medical student.

73. Freud, *Jokes and Their Relation to the Unconscious*, 114–15. See also the earlier

beggar jokes are presented in the section of the chapter that examines jokes that serve a *hostile* purpose.

Freud starts this section with the observation that from the beginning of human existence "hostile impulses against our fellow men have been subject to the same restrictions, the same progressive repression, as our sexual urges."[74] We have not gotten to the point in our evolution where we are able "to love our enemies or to offer our left cheek after being struck on the right."[75] Furthermore, "all moral rules for the restriction of active hatred give the clearest evidence to this day that they were originally framed for a small society of fellow clansmen."[76] Thus, to the extent that we are able to feel that we are members of one people "we allow ourselves to disregard most of these restrictions in relation to a foreign people."[77] On the other hand, "within our own circle we have made some advances in the control of hostile impulses."[78] For example, "brutal hostility, forbidden by law, has been replaced by verbal invective, and a better knowledge of the interlinking of human impulses is more and more robbing us of the capacity for feeling angry with a fellow man who gets in our way."[79] Thus, even though "as children we are still endowed with a powerful inherited disposition to hostility, we are later taught by a higher personal civilization that it is an unworthy thing to use abusive language, and even where fighting has in itself remained permissible, the number of things which may not be employed as methods of fighting has extraordinarily increased."[80]

However, a consequence of our having been taught to renounce the expression of hostility by deeds—often, a third person whose own interest is in preserving personal security restrains the two potential combatants—is that we have developed a new form of invective whose aim is to enlist this third person against our enemy. And this is where jokes come in: "By making our enemy small, inferior, despicable or comic, we achieve in a roundabout way the enjoyment of overcoming him—to

---

discussion in chapter 3 of tendentious jokes.
74. Ibid., 121.
75. Ibid., 121–22.
76. Ibid., 122.
77. Ibid.
78. Ibid.
79. Ibid.
80. Ibid.

which the third person, who has made no efforts, bears witness by his laughter."⁸¹ Thus, the joke allows us "to exploit something ridiculous in our enemy which we could not, on account of obstacles in the way, bring forward openly or consciously."⁸² It "evades restrictions and opens sources of pleasure that have become inaccessible."⁸³ Furthermore, by offering pleasure it bribes the hearer "into taking sides with us without any very close investigation, just as on other occasions we ourselves have often been bribed by an innocent joke into overestimating the substance of a statement expressed jokingly."⁸⁴

Freud notes that in the natural course of our lives, we have assumed both roles, and this fact brings him to the jokes about beggars.⁸⁵ He prefaces his discussion of these jokes with the observation that "jokes made about Jews by foreigners are for the most part brutal comic stories in which a joke is made unnecessary by the fact that Jews are regarded by foreigners as comic figures."⁸⁶ Jewish jokes that originate among Jews admit this comic aspect, but in addition, Jews "know their real faults as well as the connection between them and their good qualities, and the share which the subject has in the person found fault with creates the subjective determinant (usually so hard to arrive at) of the joke-work."⁸⁷ By "subjective determinant" Freud means that which is in the mind of the person who makes the joke. He adds that he does not know whether "there are many other instances of a people making fun to such a degree of its own character."⁸⁸

Especially noteworthy here is that although Jewish jokes focus on the awareness that Jews have real faults, there is a connection between these faults and their good qualities. This connection—and their awareness of it—is directly relevant to the parable because both parties to the dispute—the landowner and the early workers—impress the listener as having "good qualities"—the former for their work ethic and the latter for his desire to be generous toward the unemployed. The problem is that

81. Ibid.
82. Ibid., 122–23.
83. Ibid., 123.
84. Ibid.
85. The Yiddish word for "beggar" is *Schnorrer*, and this is the word that Freud uses throughout his discussion of these jokes.
86. Freud, *Jokes and Their Relation to the Unconscious*, 133.
87. Ibid.
88. Ibid.

"real faults" accompany these "good qualities." And this is what the beggar jokes are designed to reveal but also to make light of.

Freud introduces these beggar jokes—there are four of them—as an "interesting group of jokes" that portrays "the relation of poor and rich Jews to one another," and he adds that "their heroes are the *Schnorrer* [beggar] and the charitable householder or the Baron."[89] Here's the first one:

> A *Schnorrer*, who was allowed as a guest into the same house every Sunday, appeared one day in the company of an unknown young man who gave signs of being about to sit down to table. "Who is this?" asked the householder. "He's been my son-in-law," was the reply, "since last week. I've promised him his board for the first year."[90]

Noting that the purpose of these stories is always the same, Freud suggests that this purpose emerges most clearly in the next one:

> The *Schnorrer* begged the Baron for some money for a journey to Ostend; his doctor had recommended sea-bathing for his troubles. The Baron thought Ostend was a particularly expensive resort; a cheaper one would do equally well. The *Schnorrer*, however, rejected the proposal with the words: "Herr Baron, I consider nothing too expensive for my health."[91]

Freud explains what is going on in this joke: "The Baron evidently wants to save his money, but the *Schnorrer* answers as though the Baron's money was his own, which he may then quite well value less than his health."[92] Thus, "we are expected to laugh at the impertinence of the demand."[93] Freud notes, however, that "it is rarely that these jokes are not equipped with a façade to mislead the understanding," and in this particular joke, the "truth that lies behind [it] is that the *Schnorrer*, who in his thoughts treats the rich man's money as his own, has actually, according to the sacred ordinances of the Jews, almost a right to make this

---

89. Ibid., 134. Interestingly enough, the landowner is called a "householder" in the King James Version translation of the parable.
90. Ibid.
91. Ibid.
92. Ibid.
93. Ibid.

confusion."[94] Thus, "the indignation raised by this joke is of course directed against a Law which is highly oppressive even to pious people."[95]

Freud's reference to the "sacred ordinances" is probably an allusion to the teachings of Rabbi Moses ben Maimonides, the twelfth-century rabbi, physician, and philosopher. But these ordinances are rooted more deeply in Jewish history, and would have been in the minds of the original listeners to Jesus' parable about the landowner and the vineyard workers. As Julie Salamon notes, Maimonides was very explicit about what wealthy persons were expected to do for the poor. He wrote: "You are commanded to clothe the poor man and buy him furniture. If he isn't married, you are supposed to help him find a wife," and "if the poor person is a woman, you are supposed to marry her off."[96] Salamon notes that Maimonides' "ever-expanding template for order bespeaks an overwhelming desire for fairness and good will," and although he understood "that quantifying morality might be impossible," this "didn't stop him from trying."[97] By the time he "is finished offering instructions on how the poor should be treated, charity has gone well beyond the tithe to become an intrinsic part of life."[98]

Given these sacred ordinances, it is understandable that the beggar acts as though the baron's money is virtually his own. It is also understandable that even "pious people" would at least secretly find these ordinances infuriating, especially in a social environment where the traditional two-class system in which the rich and poor were clearly differentiated was being replaced with a three-class system in which this differentiation was much less apparent. These jokes were especially popular among middle-class Jews who resented the obligation to be generous toward persons whom they considered only a little worse off than themselves.

The third joke reflects the same theme, but it adds a new wrinkle, namely, that the beggar is doing the rich man a favor by accepting his charity:

94. Ibid., 134–35.
95. Ibid., 135.
96. Salamon, *Rambam's Ladder*, 40–41.
97. Ibid., 41.

98. Ibid., 41–42. Speaking of tithing, there is an old joke that I rather like about a preacher who declares from the pulpit, "You ought to give a tenth of all that you get." Whereupon a congregant, catching the spirit of the occasion, declares: "But a tenth isn't enough. I say, let's raise it to a twentieth!" (Lupton, *Treasury of Modern Humor*, 281).

> A *Schnorrer* on his way up a rich man's staircase met a fellow-member of his profession, who advised him to go no further. "Don't go up today," he said, "the Baron is in a bad mood today; he's giving nobody more than one florin." "I'll go up all the same," said the first *Schnorrer*. "Why should I give him a florin? Does he give *me* anything?"⁹⁹

Freud notes that this joke employs the technique of absurdity "since it makes the *Schnorrer* assert that the Baron gives him nothing at the very moment at which he is preparing to beg him for a gift."¹⁰⁰ The absurdity, however, "is only apparent," for it "is almost true that the rich man gives him nothing, since he is obliged by the Law to give him alms and should, strictly speaking, be grateful to him for giving him an opportunity for beneficence."¹⁰¹ Freud suggests that in this joke the "ordinary, middle-class view of charity is in conflict . . . with the religious one."¹⁰²

If this joke reflects a subjective state that is "in conflict" with the religious view of charity (based on "the sacred ordinances"), the fourth and final joke that Freud presents is in "open rebellion" against this view. It is the story of the Baron who, "deeply moved by a *Schnorrer's* tale of woe, rang for his servants: 'Throw him out! He's breaking my heart!'"¹⁰³ Freud suggests that this joke (like the one preceding it) makes an "open revelation of its purpose," and it is only in the fact that it focuses on an "individual case" that it differs from a complaint that is no longer a joke—namely, if one is a Jew, there is no real advantage in being a rich man because "other people's misery makes it impossible to enjoy one's own happiness."¹⁰⁴

---

99. Freud, *Jokes and Their Relation to the Unconscious*, 135.
100. Ibid.
101. Ibid.
102. Ibid.
103. Ibid.
104. Ibid. Freud focuses on beggar jokes that reflect conflicts within the Jewish community. The following beggar joke has more to do with the fact that Jews are generally a minority group within a given society or culture: Two beggars are sitting on a park bench in Mexico City. One is holding a crucifix and the other a Star of David. Both are holding hats to collect contributions. People walk by and lift their noses at the beggar with the Star of David, and then drop money in the hat held by the beggar with the crucifix. Soon the hat of the beggar with the crucifix is filled, and the hat of the beggar with the Star of David is still empty. A priest watches and then approaches the two beggars. He turns to the beggar with the Star of David and says, "Young man, don't you realize that this is a Catholic country? You'll never get any contributions in this country holding a Star of David." The beggar with the Star of David turns to the

In *Jewish Wit* Theodor Reik, a member of Freud's early circle, presents the third and fourth of these jokes in his discussion of "the sacred duty of charity." He notes that the "cynical attitude in these Jewish jokes is not always shown only by the beggar," that it "sometimes emerges surprisingly in the person who is irritatingly importuned by the Schnorrer."[105] Then he relates the following joke: "One Schnorrer complains to a rich man that he has not eaten for three days. The millionaire says, 'Sometimes one has to force oneself.'"[106] This joke loses its association with the sacred duty of charity when it gets assimilated into the genre of Jewish mother jokes: "A down-and-out walked up to a Jewish mother and said, 'Lady, I haven't eaten in three days.' 'Force yourself,' she said."[107]

The Comforting Side of the Superego

Freud's structural division of the mind into the three components of id, ego, and superego was presented in its mature form in *The Ego and the Id*,[108] although many of its essential elements are prefigured in earlier writings. His discussion of beggar jokes in *Jokes and Their Relation to the Unconscious* may be viewed as giving examples of how the ego finds ways to circumvent the restrictions that are imposed by the superego.

However, in his essay "Humor," written two decades after his book on jokes, Freud makes the rather surprising suggestion that humor operates under the aegis or sponsorship of the superego. As we will see, this suggestion has bearing on the parable of the Workers in the Vineyard and, more specifically, on how the early workers and the landowner may use humor to resolve their differences.

In his essay "Humor," Freud discusses the characteristics of humor, and he suggests that humor, like wit and the comic, "has in it a *liberating* element."[109] But unlike these "other two ways of deriving pleasure from

---

beggar with the crucifix and says, "Moishe, can you imagine, this guy is trying to tell us how to run our business?"
Tapper and Press, *Minister, a Priest, and a Rabbi*, 244.
105. Reik, *Jewish Wit*, 76.
106. Ibid.
107. Tibballs, *Mammoth Book of Humor*, 175. See also Capps, "Bad-Enough Mother," which suggests that Rebekah, the mother of Jacob and Esau, may be viewed as the prototypical Jewish mother.
108. Freud, *Ego and the Id*.
109. Freud, "Humor," 265.

intellectual activity," humor also has "something fine and elevating."[110] Freud explains that the "fine" thing about humor is "the triumph of narcissism, the ego's victorious assertion of its own invulnerability"; its refusal "to be hurt by the arrows of reality or to be compelled to suffer"; and its insistence "that it is impervious to wounds dealt by the outside world, in fact, that these are merely occasions for affording it pleasure."[111] In this sense, humor "is not resigned; it is rebellious."[112] But what is "elevating" about humor is that its refusal to suffer conveys a sense of "dignity which is wholly lacking, for instance, in wit, for the aim of wit is either simply to afford gratification, or, in so doing, to provide an outlet for aggressive tendencies."[113] Moreover, humor does all this "without quitting the ground of mental sanity, as happens when other means to the same end are adopted."[114]

How are these positive effects of humor possible? Freud suggests that we have the superego to thank for this achievement. He explains it this way: In his book on jokes he had suggested that when one person adopts a humorous attitude toward another, he or she is, in effect, "adopting towards the other an attitude of an adult towards a child, recognizing and smiling at the triviality of the interests and sufferings which seem to the child so big."[115] Thus, "the humorist acquires his superiority by assuming the role of the grown-up" while reducing "the other people to the position of children."[116] But now, in his later article on humor, he wants to suggest that there is another aspect of humor, one that is probably the original and certainly the more important of the two. This is when a person "adopts a humorous attitude towards himself in order to ward off possible suffering."[117] In a sense, he treats himself like a child and at the same time plays the part of the superior adult in relation to this child.

This is where the superego comes in. Freud notes that the ego and the superego are sometimes impossible to differentiate from each other, but in other situations they can be sharply differentiated. Self-directed

---

110. Ibid.
111. Ibid.
112. Ibid.
113. Ibid.
114. Ibid., 266. Freud also mentions intoxication in this regard.
115. Ibid.
116. Ibid.
117. Ibid., 267.

humor is an instance of the latter. By recognizing that genetically the superego "inherits the parental function," often holding the ego in strict subordination and treating it as the parents treated the child in his early years, we "obtain a dynamic explanation of the humorous attitude."[118] In effect, the humorous attitude involves removing the accent from one's own ego and transferring it to one's superego. To the superego, thus inflated, "the ego can appear tiny and all its interests trivial, and with this fresh distribution of energy it may be an easy matter for it to suppress the potential reactions of the ego."[119]

To be sure, the superego is ordinarily "a stern master," and it goes against its basic nature "that it should wink at affording the ego a little gratification."[120] Nor does it normally suspend reality and serve an illusion. Yet, this is precisely what it does in bringing about the humorous attitude. By means of humor, it says to the ego, "Look here! This is all that this seemingly dangerous world amounts to. Child's play—the very thing to jest about!"[121]

Freud concludes that in light of the fact that the superego "speaks such kindly words of comfort to the intimidated ego," we realize "that we have still very much to learn about the nature of that energy."[122] But one thing is clear: If the superego "does try to comfort the ego by humor and to protect it from suffering, this does not conflict with its derivation from the parental function."[123] So although "it is not everyone who is capable of the humorous attitude," and "there are many people who have not even the capacity for deriving pleasure from humor when it is presented to them by others," it is "a rare and precious gift" as it reduces suffering and provides pleasure; and, not incidentally, it reveals a side of the superego that would otherwise be hidden from view.[124]

118. Ibid., 266.
119. Ibid., 267.
120. Ibid., 268.
121. Ibid.
122. Ibid.
123. Ibid., 269.

124. Ibid., 268–69. In light of the fact that Freud wrote a book on jokes and an essay on humor, it is perhaps worth noting that psychoanalysis has itself been the object of numerous jokes, some friendly and some not so friendly. One that I rather like is the suggestion that psychoanalysis is easier for a man than for a woman, because when it is time to go back to childhood, he is already there: see Becker, *Prairie Home Companion Pretty Good Joke Book,* 177. Also, a joke that is relevant to the emphasis in this book on anxiety and related emotions is the one about the psychoanalyst who

Humor and the Possibility of Creative Reconciliation

How might this exploration of Freud's reflections on beggar jokes and on the psychodynamics of humor assist us as listeners to the parable of the Laborers in the Vineyard, especially in "imagining a different outcome,"[125] one in which the landowner and the early laborer whom he addresses as "Friend" find an amicable way to resolve their dispute? What seems especially helpful in this regard is Freud's emphasis on the situation in humor in which one adopts a humorous attitude towards himself in order to ward off possible suffering; and, we may add, that in doing so one affords oneself some genuine pleasure, pleasure that is not, however, achieved at another's expense.

The beggar jokes seem especially useful in this regard as far as the landowner is concerned. It is clear that for the landowner the "sacred ordinances"—what Ford calls "the Hebraic norm of divine justice"[126]—are oppressive burdens. His repeated trips to the marketplace, his carefully crafted drama designed to demean the early workers and elevate himself, his protestation that he has done the early workers no injustice—all of this, as Ford has shown, points to his ambivalences relating to these sacred ordinances.

I believe, therefore, that he needs to give himself a break, and this means, practically speaking, that he needs to discover the more indulgent and thus comforting side of the superego as reflected, for example, in the joke that Freud tells about the Baron who rang for his servants and told them to throw the *Schnorrer* out because "he's breaking my heart!" Or the joke that Theodore Reik relates about the millionaire who tells the *Schnorrer* who says he hasn't eaten for three days to "force yourself."[127]

Ford is certainly right in his observation that if one believes that in his desire to be good the landowner is aspiring to justice, "then at issue that evening may not be a decision about the worth of twelve hours of labor but rather a judgment about hundreds of years of land-grabbing."[128] But Freud is also right when he notes that the Jewish jokes he relates in his chapter on the purposes of jokes reflect the Jews' awareness of the

---

maintains that he doesn't have to worry as long as other people do, see Rovin, *1001 More Great Jokes*, 251.

125. Ford, *Parables of Jesus*, 122.
126. Ibid., 115.
127. Reik, *Jewish Wit*, 76.
128. Ford, *Parables of Jesus*, 117.

connection between their real faults and their good qualities.[129] It would do the landowner and the workers whom he employs a world of good if he, the landowner, could express in some form of self-directed humor his evident if unacknowledged complaint that there is really no advantage in being a rich man because the misery of others "makes it impossible to enjoy one's own happiness."[130] If he truly wants to be a generous man, he might consider the fact that humor is itself "a rare and precious gift."[131]

Regarding the early workers, they too seem equally burdened by a sense of their own superiority—as workers—to the other laborers. They tell the landowner that, unlike those who came to work late in the day, they had to bear "the burden of the day and the scorching heat" (Matthew 20:12). I see no reason to minimize this burden. Twelve hours in the vineyard was certainly hard work. On the other hand, the fact that they knew they would receive a full day's pay at the end of the day would ease the burden. And even if we agree with Douglas Adams' satirical interpretation of the conversation between the landowner and the men who worked for only an hour, there were other men who were "standing idle" over the course of the day, and theirs is hardly an enviable situation either, for they needed work to maintain a subsistence level for themselves and those dependent upon them.

If the superegos of both the landowner and the laborer he addresses as "Friend" would cut them both some slack, this might well be reflected in the way they talk to each other. Admittedly, this is a very big *if*. But Ford suggests that the parable invites the listener to imagine the *possible*.[132] I can imagine that this process might be engineered, as it were, by a third party, such as one of the early laborers who was intently listening to their conversation. When the landowner asks, "Do you begrudge—or envy—my generosity?" he might say to the gathering, "Funny, that's exactly what my wife said the other night when I caught her in bed with another guy!" This might prompt another laborer in the group to say, "No fooling?" and a third to say, "He's telling the truth. After all, I was there!" I would like to think that this bit of humor would make everyone laugh—including the landowner—and defuse the tension between them.

---

129. Freud, *Jokes and Their Relation to the Unconscious*, 133.
130. Ibid., 135.
131. Freud, "Humor," 268.
132. Ford, *Parables of Jesus*, 122.

This attempt at humor may not meet with everyone's approval.[133] For a Sunday morning sermon,[134] it might simply be best to raise the idea of a *possible* reconciling intervention and leave it to the listeners to imagine what it might be. But one thing seems clear: For reconciliation to occur, a joke is better than a witty rejoinder that simply raises the ante, such as responding to the landowner's "Do you begrudge—or envy—my generosity?" with "No more than you would begrudge—or envy—my youth, my good looks, or the fact that I have fathered three of your children!"

On the other hand, this allusion to the fathering of children invites the following concluding observation, namely, that Freud's claim that the superego's role in making the humorous attitude possible "does not conflict with its derivation from the parental function" sheds light on Ford's reference to "the kingdom of God, or the reign of God, or the intent of God, or the longing of God (however one terms this core element of Jesus' teaching)."[135] We know from other sayings of Jesus that a distinctive feature of his understanding of God is that God is a father. So perhaps we can see that Jesus, in telling this story about the kingdom, also has a wink in his eye as he tells it, a wink that, as Freud puts it, affords the beleaguered ego "a little gratification."[136] If so, perhaps we may view this story about the kingdom of God as an invitation to the landowner to discover, through self-directed humor, the more comforting side of his own superego. Perhaps, then, the real message of the parable is that the *landowner* needs to treat *himself* more generously.[137]

In any event, my listening ear has advised me that readers of this chapter on work might themselves need a respite, so I will conclude this chapter with a couple of jokes that relate to the issue of work. Here's one:

---

133. We saw in chapter 4 that not only hostile but also sexual jokes are considered tendentious jokes, and tendentious jokes are most likely to be offensive to religious persons.

134. We will return to this issue in ch. 7 in our discussion of Phillips Brooks' critique of clergy who make wisecracks from the pulpit.

135. Freud, "Humor," 269; Ford, *Parables of Jesus*, 121.

136. Ibid., 268.

137. The discussion in this chapter of Jesus' parable of the Laborers in the Vineyard only scratches the surface of the role that humor plays in his parables. Other examples are the parables of the mustard seed, the lost sheep, and the lost coin. See Crossan, *Dark Interval*, 93–101. Also, for a contemporary version of the parable of the Laborers in the Vineyard, see Cohen, "One Company's New Minimum Wage"; and Cohen, "Company Copes with Backlash."

> Ever since he graduated from high school, Brian spent most of his waking hours lounging on the couch, watching sports programs, and drinking beer. One day, as he reached for another can, he tumbled off the sofa onto his head and had to be rushed to the hospital. After X-rays were taken, the doctor went right to Brian's bedside. "I'm sorry, but I have some bad news for you, young man. Your X-rays show that you've broken a vertebra in your neck. I'm afraid you'll never work again." "Thanks, Doc. Now what's the bad news?"[138]

Here's another:

> Several medical students, accompanied by a newspaper reporter who was interested in the students' reactions to their first professional encounter with mentally ill patients, were visiting a psychiatric ward. The attendant who was showing them around pointed out a patient who believed that he was God. The reporter, sensing a possible story, approached the patient and asked him if he really created the world in seven days. The patient, discerning the reporter's motives, replied, "I'm not in the mood to talk shop!"[139]

---

138. Greene, *Greatest Joke Book Ever*, 131.

139. Lupton, *Treasury of Modern Humor*, 463. I have revised the wording of this joke.

6

Gossip, Humor, and the Joking Community

The scenario presented in the conclusion of our consideration of the Laborers in the Vineyard parable imagines what Ted Cohen refers to in his book on jokes as "a joking community."[1] This community consists of the disgruntled workers and the landowner. Other workers, curious about how the landowner and the disgruntled workers air their differences, may be observers of what is going on between the landowner and the disgruntled workers, but they are not really a part of this community. And what makes it a community is the fact that one of the disgruntled workers puts a rather different spin on the landowner's question, "Do you envy my generosity?" by suggesting that the same question was posed to him by his wife when he found her in bed with another man.

In this chapter, I want to elaborate on this idea of the joking community and suggest that there were times when Jesus and his disciples were themselves such a community. Most of the time, they were engaged in serious business. They were involved in a ministry of healing as they traveled from one village to another. They were also involved in an educational ministry as they sought to teach the people they encountered a new way of understanding the Lord they had learned about as children or of how this Lord was active in their personal and collective lives. In this regard, they were challenging the teachings of the official religious leaders, referred to in the Gospels as the Pharisees and scribes. Thus, they were not a group of comedians whose purpose was to entertain the residents of the villages they visited on their journey.

---

1. Cohen, *Jokes*, 25–32. I will return to Cohen's reflections on the joking community later in this chapter.

But the very fact that they were engaged in serious work, work that was demanding, even exhausting, and full of the life stresses that we discussed in chapter 2, suggests that there must have been times when they found themselves in need of relaxation, and that humor played a role in helping them to meet this need.

The problem, of course, is that the Gospels were not written with this particular issue or theme in mind. So those who have wanted to make the case that humor played a role in Jesus' life and ministry have tended to focus on the question whether some of the things that he said publicly were intentionally humorous, and we have considered some of their proposals in this regard in chapter 4. Except for occasions when Jesus met with someone on a more private basis, such as his late evening conversation with Nicodemus (John 3:1–21) or his conversation with the Samaritan woman when his disciples had gone into the city to buy food (John 4:7–30), the disciples were among his regular listeners at these more public events. There were occasions when they were the object of his criticism, as when he rebuked them when they told the parents of children not to bother him by bringing their children to him so that he could bless their little ones. But, most of the time, they were simply there to listen, and as regular listeners they would have been in a privileged position to recognize when Jesus was being intentionally humorous.

These, though, were more public events, and if on these occasions his disciples saw the humor in his observations and comments, these would not have been situations in which the idea of "the joking community" would be applicable because the disciples were simply part of a larger crowd of listeners. Rather, such occasions would have occurred on more private occasions when Jesus and his disciples were alone—or mostly alone—together. We have evidence of such occasions in the gospel accounts of the disciples asking Jesus why he spoke in parables to the crowds who had gathered to hear him (Matthew 13:10; Mark 4:10; Luke 8:9) and of the fact that when they were together in private he would explain everything to them (Mark 5:33–34). The account of the last meal that Jesus experienced with his disciples also suggests that they were accustomed to having conversations together over their evening meals (Luke 22:1–37).

Of course, the last meal that Jesus experienced with his disciples was one of tension and profound anxiety, and it would be ludicrous to suggest that humor would have occurred on that particular evening. But it seems reasonable to suggest that if Jesus' sense of humor manifested itself in his public role, it would also have manifested itself, and perhaps to an even greater degree, when he and his disciples met more privately. Thus, on these occasions, or, at least on some of them, Jesus and his disciples formed "a joking community." But because the Gospels do not provide detailed accounts of these occasions, we can only imagine how humor manifested itself on during these times.

To give such imaginary scenarios a certain amount of credibility, I will discuss the subject of gossip in some detail.[2] The relevance and significance of the subject of gossip to our concern to make the case that Jesus and his disciples were, on occasion, a joking community will become clear as our discussion proceeds. But, in brief, I will be drawing on John Morreall's article on gossip and humor in which he suggests that gossip and humor have a lot in common and that when gossip is infused with the spirit of humor, "it tends to transcend the pettiness and viciousness that have given gossip such a bad name."[3] Thus, because gossip and humor have a great deal in common, we can make a stronger case for the claim that Jesus and his disciples formed "a joking community" if we first establish that the social world that they inhabited was itself "a gossiping community" and that the Gospels themselves reflect this fundamental fact.

Gossip and Localism

In an article published in 1971, Ernest L. Abel used contemporary psychological research on memory and rumor transmission to shed light on the role that oral transmission played in early Christianity.[4] He noted that we cannot assume that the same changes that have occurred in written transmission (as when Matthew and Luke alter narratives in the earlier Gospel of Mark) also occurred in the oral transmission that preceded the writing of the Gospel of Mark. Oral transmission follows certain rules, but they are not the same as the rules that govern written transmission. He drew on Gordon W. Allport and Leo Postman's studies of the psychology of rumor, which were carried out during World War II, to explain

---

2. I discussed the topic of gossip and pastoral counseling in Capps, *Living Stories*, 173–201.

3. Morreall, "Gossip and Humor," 56.

4. Abel, "Psychology of Memory and Rumor Transmission."

how the oral transmission process worked in the preliterary period of early Christianity.[5]

One of Allport and Postman's major findings was that as information is transmitted from one person (typically an eyewitness of an event) to another person, and as the second person transmits it to a third, the general form or outline of the story remains intact, but fewer words and few original details are preserved. On the other hand, they also found that this shortening process cannot go on indefinitely. It eventually stabilizes at some point at which the story can be faithfully reproduced by rote and is therefore no longer subject to further alteration or distortion. In contrast, Matthew and Luke expand on Mark's original narratives, adding new contexts and details and new associations between two previously unrelated narratives.[6]

Abel drew on Allport and Postman's study because he was interested in the spread of rumors, and this seemed to be an appropriate way of assessing the oral transmission process that occurred in the early years of community formation following the crucifixion of Jesus and appearances of the risen Christ. But as I thought about Abel's work, I began to wonder about the transmission process that occurred before the crucifixion, when Jesus, accompanied by his disciples, traveled from one village to another and word about his healings and teachings preceded them. I questioned whether *rumor* is the best word to describe or characterize this form of oral transmission. It seemed that the word *gossip* might be a better descriptive word. It was interesting in this connection that, in their preface, Allport and Postman used the two words interchangeably. The preface begins: "A large part of ordinary social conversation consists of rumor mongering. In our daily chitchat with friends we both take in and give out whole lungfuls of gossip—sometimes idle, sometimes not."[7] They go on to note that some "idle rumors are an unverified, casual type of discourse serving no purpose other than passing the time of day with a friend," but "most rumors, and most gossip too, are far from idle." In fact:

> They are profoundly purposive, serving important emotional ends. Just what these ends may be both teller and listener are

---

5. Allport and Postman, *Psychology of Rumor*.

6. It is possible that they were inspired to do this because they saw a similar example of the combining of two narratives in Mark's Gospel, namely, his combining the stories of Jairus' daughter and the woman who had been hemorrhaging for twelve years (Mark 5:21–43); see also Capps, *Jesus the Village Psychiatrist*, chap. 7.

7. Allport and Postman, *Psychology of Rumor*, vii.

usually unable to say. They know only that the tale seems important to them. In some mysterious way it seems to alleviate their intellectual uncertainty and personal anxiety.[8]

So far, the preface treats rumor and gossip as more or less interchangeable. However, in the second paragraph Allport and Postman make it clear that they are really interested in rumors, especially rumors spread in times of national crisis. They write:

> Although rumor spreading is at all times a social and psychological problem of major proportions, it is especially so in time of crisis. Whenever there is social strain, false report grows virulent. In wartime, rumors sap morale and menace national safety by spreading needless alarm and by raising extravagant hopes. They menace the security of military information and, most damaging of all, spread the virus of hostility and hate against loyal subgroups within the nation. In the years of postwar strain rumors are only slightly less destructive in their effect.[9]

They add that "the problem of wartime rumors" was the original catalyst for their undertaking of the experimental investigations reported in the book. From here on, the word "gossip" no longer appears in the book, and there is no mention of it in the index.

The very disappearance of *gossip* from their own discourse prompted me to wonder if this might be another way to think about the oral transmission processes in early Christianity. Could it be that initially, during the time that Jesus was a familiar presence in the villages of Galilee, the oral transmission was one largely of gossip, but that when Christian communities formed after his death and experienced conflict with other groups, rumors began to replace gossip and something like the atmosphere that Allport and Postman describe—the spreading of the virus of hostility and hate against loyal subgroups within the nation—began to emerge? This way of thinking would be supported by the fact that, although the two words are often used interchangeably, one of the dictionary definitions of *rumor* suggests that a rumor is an unconfirmed report, story, or statement in general circulation, while *gossip* is characterized as idle talk, especially about the private affairs of others.[10] If so, this suggests that gossip tends to be more local and less cosmopolitan, a

---

8. Ibid.
9. Ibid., vii–viii.
10. Agnes, ed., *Webster's New World College Dictionary*, 1254, 613.

distinction that Wade Clark Roof formulated to account for the fact that some individuals' religious commitments are oriented toward their "immediate social locale" and "the primary groups with which they interact, such as family, neighborhood cliques, and community organizations," whereas other individuals "have their commitments centered outside the residential community and tend to identify more with abstract, generalized groups."[11] It seems, then, that gossip is to localism what rumor is to cosmopolitanism. Because Jesus' ministry prior to his pilgrimage to Jerusalem was centered in the villages of Galilee and he avoided the larger cities of Galilee it makes sense to view his ministry as having taken place in gossip communities.[12]

Definitions of Gossip

But what does it mean to say that they were gossiping communities? And what are we implying about these communities when we say that they were gossiping communities? To answer these questions we need to consider the very meaning of the word *gossip*.[13] Etymologically, it actually means "god-related." In Old English, it was originally *god-sib*, which referred to a godparent of either gender. Then its meaning expanded to include any close friend, that is, someone belonging to the group from which godparents would naturally be chosen. This would be someone to whom one could reveal one's personal secrets, trusting them to keep these secrets to themselves. In time, however, the word underwent a process of degradation, perhaps because the trust that was placed in god-sibs proved misplaced. Benjamin Franklin points out, for example, that "Three may keep a secret, if two of them are dead."[14]

---

11. Roof, *Community and Commitment*, 41.

12. As I pointed out in Capps, *Jesus the Village Psychiatrist*, xx, "Jewish villagers in Galilee resented the cities of Sepphoris and Tiberias, a resentment stemming from the fact that the city dwellers were economically better off, that the villagers were heavily taxed and received little in return, that the lion's share of the food that the villagers produced ended up in the city markets, and that the cities had embraced Hellenistic political structures and cultural traditions, thus straying from traditional Jewish mores and values. If Jesus left the desert areas to John the Baptist, he also avoided the cities and focused his attention on the villages that lay some miles from the major cities but experienced the cities' very existence as a threat to their ways of life and chance to make a decent living."

13. Spacks, *Gossip*, 25–26, discusses of the etymology of the word *gossip*.

14. Franklin, *Poor Richard's Almanack*, 31. This, of course, was not a new insight.

In the eighteenth century, Samuel Johnson's dictionary added two meanings. One was that a gossip is a "tippling companion," and the other was that a gossip is "one who runs about tattling like women at a lying-in."[15] The "tippling companion" would apply to men, as a tippling companion would be a friend with whom one drinks in a tavern, something that women would not do. The third meaning adds the word "tattling," implying that private matters which ought to be kept to oneself are being told to others who should not be privy to this information. This meaning identifies women as gossips in the negative sense. With a "tippling companion," the talk is "just between us," and therefore not considered harmful to whoever may be the subject of conversation. But much harm can be done when one "runs about tattling as women at a lying-in," for this implies that no discretion or circumspection is being exercised in what is being communicated. It also appears to associate gossiping with disclosure of the identity of the father of a baby born out of wedlock. In his historical study of Plymouth, John Demos points out that midwives were expected by town authorities to get a woman to reveal the father's identity during the birth process—"when delivery was actually in progress and the girl's powers of resistance were presumed to be at their lowest ebb."[16] Such information would be used to punish the father and make him financially responsible for the child's maintenance. The midwife, then, became a "tattler," an "informer"; this was a role, however, that served the larger interests of the community.

The dictionary now defines a *gossip* as "a person who chatters or repeats idle talk and rumors, especially about the private affairs of others," and says that *gossip* is "(a) such talk or rumors; (b) chatter."[17] It defines *chatter* as "rapid, foolish talk."[18] Thus, the more positive connotations of the *gossip* as one in whom one may confide has been lost altogether and the "tippling companion" idea is absent as well. What remains, essentially, is *tattling*, which has three definitions: "(1) to talk idly; chatter, gossip; (2) to reveal other people's secrets; tell tales; and (3) to inform against

---

In fact, the book of Proverbs has this to say about gossipers: "A gossip goes about telling secrets, but one who is trustworthy in spirit keeps a confidence" (11:13). It also advises us to steer clear of the gossip: "A gossip reveals secrets; therefore do not associate with a babbler" (20:19).

15. See Spacks, *Gossip*, 26.
16. Demos, *Little Commonwealth*, 152.
17. Agnes, ed., *New World College Dictionary*, 613.
18. Ibid., 249.

someone."[19] Little wonder, then, that gossip is disparaged, for although it is merely "idle talk," such "idle talk" has implications of indiscretion and informing against another person. It also has connotations of disloyalty.[20]

The Problem of False Witness and Slander

The association of gossip with the local and its negative connotations are reflected in a couple of poems by anonymous authors titled "Gossiptown" and "Gossipy Ears."[21] The former suggests that the town is located on the shore of Falsehood Bay and that in the midst of the town is Telltale Park. The latter suggests that the gossipy tongue would not succeed in causing heart burnings and tears if it were not assisted by the misguided man who possesses two gossipy ears. These poems, which reflect town life in the United States in the early decades of the twentieth century, seem far removed from the village life in Galilee in the first century.

Yet the Gospel of Matthew suggests that gossip was an issue for Jesus and his contemporaries. Matthew tells us that the disciples of John the Baptist were saying negative things about Jesus because, unlike themselves and the Pharisees, Jesus' disciples did not fast (Matt 9:14–17). Matthew also reports that when the Pharisees complained to Jesus that his disciples transgressed the tradition of the elders for failing to wash their hands when they ate (Matt 15:1–2), Jesus responded not by defending his disciples but by lambasting his critics, who, in his view, had a lot of explaining to do for saying things that directly violate the commandments of God, including the command to honor your father and mother (Matt 15:4–5). Matthew goes on to note that Jesus called the people to him and said to them, "Listen and understand; it is not what goes into the mouth that defiles a person, but what comes out of the mouth that defiles" (Matt 15:10–11). In other words, it is what we say, not what we eat, that condemns us.

---

19. Ibid., 1466.

20. It is noteworthy that tattling is often associated with childhood and, specifically, either with a classmate who informs a teacher that another child has done something wrong, or with a sibling who informs a parent that a brother or sister has misbehaved.

21. McNeill, *Breakfast Club Family Album*, 10, 75. McNeill was host of *The Breakfast Club*, a morning variety radio show that ran from June 23, 1933, through December 27, 1968. It consisted of comedy performers, various vocal groups and soloists, sentimental verse, conversations with members of the studio audience, and a silent moment of prayer. See *Wikipedia*, "Don McNeill's Breakfast Club."

Continuing his narrative, Matthew reports that Jesus' disciples came to him and said, "Do you know that the Pharisees took offense when they heard what you said?" and that Jesus, perceiving that his disciples were not convinced that he was right, said to them:

> Do you not see that whatever goes into the mouth enters the stomach, and goes out into the sewer? But what comes out of the mouth proceeds from the heart, and this is what defiles. For out of the heart come evil intentions, murder, adultery, fornication, theft, false witness, slander. These are what defile a person; but to eat with unwashed hands does not defile. (Matt 15:17–20)

Here, Jesus includes false witness and slander among the "evil intentions" that defile a person, intentions that comprise murder, adultery, fornication, and theft.

Matthew also tells us that on another occasion Jesus declared that it is out of the abundance of the heart that the mouth speaks, and that "on the day of judgment you will have to give an account for every careless word you utter, for by your words you will be justified, and by your words you will be condemned" (Matt 12:34–37). No doubt Jesus has more than gossip in mind here, but gossip clearly has the connotation of "careless" words, especially as the word *gossip* implies a disregard for its potentially harmful effects on the lives of others.

These accounts indicate that gossip was common in Jesus' time and that Jesus himself considered careless and malicious talk—false witness and slander—a more serious offense against God than the violation of dietary laws, for such talk is the product of evil intentions. These warnings against careless and malicious talk were necessary because Upper Palestine was a largely rural society that relied almost exclusively on oral transmission of information—"the grapevine"—as a means of communication from village to village. There was not much of a written tradition that could challenge assertions and allegations made orally.

Gossip as a Form of Social Exchange

To explore gossip and its role in local communities further, I would now like to turn to writings on gossip by social psychologists, sociologists, and anthropologists who take the position that although gossip may be dismissed as "idle talk," it is actually an important form of social exchange. In their book on rumor and gossip, Ralph F. Rosnow and

Gary Alan Fine, sociologists at Temple University and the University of Minnesota, cite social anthropologist Max Gluckman's suggestion that gossip is primarily used by groups for the purpose of maintaining exclusivity or an established social hierarchy.[22] Gluckman identifies three such groups: professional groups (for instance, lawyers, educators, physicians) in which gossip is interwoven with technical terms and is practically indecipherable to the outsider; social groups that seek to preserve their exclusiveness by closing their doors to newcomers; and groups that have exclusivity thrust upon them, as, for example, an ethnic or minority group. In all three groups, gossip helps to preserve the unity of the group vis-à-vis the wider society, and it may also support a class system within the group that keeps individuals in their assigned places in the social order, especially in instances where those assigned to the lower positions have come into possessions which, in an earlier generation, would have qualified them for a higher social position. An insider's knowledge about the lives of others in the group is a source of power.[23]

In their own empirical study of gossip, Rosnow and Fine note that each social group has its own etiquette for gossiping:

> One who doesn't follow the rules is seen and treated as a deviant. In the medical community there is gossip that is considered proper and gossip that is considered improper; proper gossip is that indulged in by all M.D.s, which preserves the status of the profession; improper gossip aims at raising the teller's self-esteem at the expense of his professional peers. Thus, again, gossip is not merely *idle* talk, but talk with a social purpose. Like gamesmanship, or the art of winning games without cheating, the etiquette of what is proper and improper in gossiping is rigidly controlled.[24]

Rosnow and Fine point out that although gossiping can be a potent force for wreaking vengeance, not all gossip is negative or degrading of another. Gossip offers a means of passing time, and, as chitchat, helps to maintain the fluidity of communication patterns. It is also the repository of folklore within a given community, as stories about members of the community, living and dead are often recounted. Moreover, the very fact

---

22. Rosnow and Fine, *Rumor and Gossip*, 90. See Gluckman, "Gossip and Scandal."

23. Rosnow and Fine, *Rumor and Gossip*, 90–91. Another example of a social group that has exclusivity thrust upon it is the patient population in a mental hospital. See Goffman, *Asylum*; see also Capps, "Mortification of the Self."

24. Rosnow and Fine, *Rumor and Gossip*, 91.

that a story is told about another person, even one in which the subject is satirized, is often taken to be a sign of affection and respect. Gossip also serves the desire of gossipers to reaffirm their shared values, for talking about someone else who behaves in a manner judged to be offensive or wrong enables those who talk about this person to reaffirm their commitment to values that the person portrayed has violated.[25]

The fact that gossip is typically about persons who are not present leads to the natural assumption that gossip is mainly or even exclusively derogatory and unkind. However, Jack Levin and Arnold Arluke, sociologists at Northeastern University, conducted an empirical study in which a student would sit in the student lounge and overhear the conversations of other students.[26] They found that 27 percent of all student gossip was clearly negative, 27 percent was clearly positive, and the rest was mixed. Thus: "There is probably far less negative gossip than most people might have predicted, as gossip is so often associated with nasty talk only."[27] This finding is relevant to the fact that positive word about Jesus often preceded his arrival in a given town.

Levin and Arluke also point out that gossip serves an initiatory function. For some social groups, gossip is used to exclude others, but in other groups it is used to welcome new members. In a study of high-tech organizations in California's Silicon Valley, gossip was found to be helpful to newly hired employees in "learning the ropes" by providing information about what to expect from the boss. For example, "Will he come on to female employees?" or "Will he chew you out if you make a mistake?" Through gossip the newcomer also learns which coworkers should be avoided because their personalities are obnoxious, or because they never paid back loans. Conversely, newcomers were informed as to who was good to talk with when they had personal problems or who would stick up for them when work fell behind schedule. The study also found that employees exchanged stories about people that communicated, correctly or incorrectly, the likelihood of being promoted or fired. The authors conclude that "this kind of informal 'on-the-job training' is every bit as essential as the formal training in classrooms and apprenticeships."[28]

---

25. Ibid.
26. Levin and Arluke, *Gossip*, 19.
27. Ibid.
28. Ibid., 24.

Levin and Arluke also note that gossip has entertainment and relaxation value. Informal gatherings "convened for the purpose of playing cards, welcoming newcomers to the neighborhood, taking a break on the job, or eating dinner with friends often provide an excuse to gossip."[29] Typically, the manifest purpose for meeting takes a backseat to conversation: "A card game is transformed into a lively talk over drinks; several employees take their coffee breaks together to swap information about their new boss; over the dinner table, the members of a family discuss the sexual activities of a neighbor."[30]

Levin and Arluke acknowledge that even if gossip is shared with a new employee or a new neighbor, it is likely to serve the purposes of exclusivity more than inclusivity. Even the very act of sharing gossip with a new employee is not from a motive of being more inclusive, but to present this individual with an opportunity to become a part of the in-group. If the new employee responds to this implied invitation in a noncommittal manner, failing to express appropriate interest in or gratitude for the inside tips that have been offered, the new employee risks affronting the group and may well become the object of its ire, not to mention a new target for their gossip sessions. Thus, "gossip is used to maintain the dividing line between those who are part of the 'in group' and those who are not," and it often indicates "that the teller and the recipient share a degree of closeness or intimacy not necessarily shared with others."[31]

These and other social-scientific discussions of gossip emphasize that gossip plays an important role in social exchange. On the other hand, they do not consider it to be a very high form of social exchange. This is partly because these studies typically include gossip in a larger consideration of rumor, and rumor, especially in periods of national crisis, has much greater social impact than gossip. A false rumor can create havoc in a town, a city, or a nation, whereas the social effects of gossip occur within the workplace, the family, the school, or the church, and are therefore of lesser importance, even though they may be just as devastating for the persons involved. Furthermore, of the many forms of social exchange involving language, gossip is considered among the least valuable, precisely because the functions it serves in social interaction are not considered to be among the most important, and even when gossip

29. Ibid., 27.
30. Ibid.
31. Ibid., 24.

is not malicious or degrading to another person or persons, the fact that it supports exclusivity and is entertaining implies that it is more to be tolerated than highly valued in an egalitarian society. Also, if gossip has a negative effect, it is considered malicious, but if it doesn't have any effect, it is considered trivial. Thus, its potential for malice or triviality seems to outweigh its positive effects, such as its role in supporting and confirming the shared values of those who engage in it. Social-scientific studies have therefore avoided much of the pejorative tone of moralists who merely inveigh against gossip, but they have also, for the most part, considered gossip to be a relatively trivial form of communication.

Gossip as an Expression of Intimacy

However, if we take a more psychological view of gossip, we can see that despite its apparent triviality, it can play a very important role in the lives of the persons who engage in it. As we have seen, Arluke and Levin found that gossip can play a significant role in the initiation of new employees. But Patricia Meyer Spacks, a professor of English at Yale University when she wrote her book on gossip, shows that gossip can play an even deeper role in the personal lives of the persons who engage in gossip together.[32]

Spacks had come to an appreciative view of gossip through her work with novels, for novels often show that gossip plays a vital, even essential role in human interaction, and that this role is not always negative. Also, as a woman, she had an agenda that she readily acknowledges—that of contesting the devaluation of women that has been an integral part of the attribution of gossip to women and its corollary implication that when men talk privately together, they are engaged in serious conversation. However, the primary inspiration for her book originated in two personal experiences. One involved a close friend, a woman colleague. Spacks writes:

> Beleaguered though we both felt, trying to sustain families and careers, we met early every morning for half an hour of coffee and reinvigorating conversation. Sometimes a male colleague would come in, his expression conveying—or, so we fancied—contempt at our verbal trivialities as our talk moved from details of our own lives to speculation about others, or from discussion of novels to contemplation of friends' love affairs. Our

---

32. Spacks, *Gossip*.

husbands couldn't understand why, considering our frequently proclaimed, desperate need for more time, we counted these morning minutes sacred: only dire emergency interfered with them. Both married to unusually sensitive, understanding men, we felt shocked to discover their incomprehension of this essential part of our lives. But we couldn't explain to them; nor did we ever fully explain to ourselves.[33]

The other experience happened when Spacks went to China with a group of professional women, several of whom were social workers and psychiatrists with a special interest in adolescence. The group met with Chinese mental health workers and asked questions. One question they would ask concerned teenage pregnancy, and, over and over again, they would be told that it does not exist. Skeptical, they kept asking until someone provided an explanation. China had little adolescent pregnancy because a neighborhood of voluntary spies prevented it. Chinese men retired at age fifty-five, and women retired at age fifty. Life expectancy had risen to seventy-five years. This large population without paid work found various socially acceptable occupations, and one of these involved watching and discussing the activities of neighbors in order to inhibit deviations from established social conventions and values.[34]

This experience demonstrated the uses of gossip as an instrument of social control, to which Spacks reacted ambivalently; but what of those treasured daily conversations, which, in self-condemning moments, she and her friend referred to as gossip?

> If gossip could have useful public functions, it also appeared to have useful private ones. Yet the very word, to my ear, implied severe derogation. I looked it up in the dictionary, to discover that official definitions suggest triviality as a concomitant of gossip, but nothing worse. How had the word acquired such negative overtones? Why did my friend and I feel faint guilt about what we did every morning? Why were we so addicted to it? What was the relation between gossip as public and as private instrument? Such questions inspired my investigation. I started giving public lectures about gossip, and found that the subject elicited general interest. But almost every time I held forth, someone in the audience would suggest, helpfully, that I find another word to designate the kind of talk that preoccupied me—a term without such bad connotations. My mission began

33. Ibid., ix.
34. Ibid., x.

> to define itself as a rescue operation: to restore positive meaning to a word that had once held it, and to celebrate a set of values and assumptions particularly associated with women, as well as with gossip.[35]

Spacks readily acknowledges that much of gossip's narratives are generated out of trivia. But, quoting Reinhold Niebuhr, who was reported to have said that "surfaces are not superficial," she observes that gossip often delights by means of "an aesthetic of surfaces" which "dwell on specific personal particularities." Also, gossip suggests that the way in which people and their concerns matter "evolves from belief in the importance of the small particular."[36] If, then, the assumed triviality of gossip has constituted a major basis for attacking this activity, it might equally well supply a ground for defense, for "to make something out of nothing is gossip's 'special creativity.'"[37] Spacks' implied association of gossip with the divine act of creation ex nihilo is especially noteworthy, and the original Old English term *god-sib* (that is, a godparent of either sex) supports this association.

Spacks also notes that because gossip deals in small particulars, in local knowledge, the worldview that it expresses is not that of the dominant culture but rather "the beliefs of quiet sub-cultures."[38] As gossip "inhabits a space of intimacy, it builds on and implicitly articulates shared values of intimates."[39] The social-scientific discussions also say that gossip reflects the shared values of those who engage in it, but instead of viewing this feature of gossip as evidence of its "in-groupism," she emphasizes the fact that it is an expression of intimacy, especially between or among members of "quiet sub-cultures."

What, though, of the long-standing view that gossip is frivolous, malicious, or both? While Spacks recognizes that gossip may have a malicious intent, her conversations with her colleague seem not to have had any such purpose, and their husbands did not appear to view them in that way either. However, they did intimate that their wives' conversations were about trivial matters, and Spacks does not disagree. In fact, she contends that their very triviality—that they created something out

---

35. Ibid.
36. Ibid., 15.
37. Ibid.
38. Ibid.
39. Ibid.

of nothing—is what made their conversations valuable, and even, in a certain sense, important—important enough to warrant including these conversations in their daily schedule.

Gossip as Expression of Interpersonal and Social Bonding

Finally, then, Spacks agrees with the social scientists who view gossip as a form of social exchange, but she wants to go further and contend that gossip is an especially valuable form of social exchange, for "more insistently than other forms of conversation, gossip involves exchange not merely, not even mainly, of information, and not solely of understanding, but of point of view."[40] Moreover, it supports a *shared* point of view that, above all else, offers reassurance: "Participants assure one another of what they share."[41] In this regard, gossip "may involve a torrent of talk," but "its most vital claims remain silent," for "seldom does anyone articulate the bonding that it generates or intensifies."[42] Also, noting that social scientists explain how gossip consolidates and uses social power to influence status and opinion in a community, Spacks suggests that, on a more personal level, gossip "gets its power by the illusion of mastery gained through taking imaginative possession of another's experience."[43] She notes that people "use this pseudo-mastery for their own purposes," such as "to manipulate the subject's reputation, to generate feelings of superiority, to provide evidence for argument."[44] But one may also use it simply to feel that one is in the presence of the other and enjoying the other's company. Thus, "the sensibility that gossip helps to create is dual: a mode of feeling and of apprehending which rises, as it were, in the space between the talkers, enveloping both."[45] Thus, gossip is or at least has the potential to become an expression of intimacy.

40. Ibid., 21–22.
41. Ibid., 22.
42. Ibid.
43. Ibid.
44. Ibid., 23.
45. Ibid., 22. Spacks explores this sharing aspect of gossip further by drawing on the writings of psychoanalysts Erik Erikson and D. W. Winnicott on play to suggest that when two persons gossip they are playing together. See Erikson, *Toys and Reasons*; and Winnicott, "Location of Cultural Experience." Spacks, *Gossip*, 60–61, concludes from these references to Erikson and Winnicott that "if gossip belongs to the genre of

The bond that gossip creates between two persons also invites us to consider the possibility that it may be a binding influence or force in the community as a whole. Traditionally engaged in by those who lack power and influence in a given society, gossip is a form of dissent, a refusal to be dominated by those who hold the power. Nonetheless, it may be in the service of the larger community, whether the dominant culture realizes this fact or not. In support of this view that gossip may serve the community's best interests, Spacks cites the following comment by anthropologists Melville J. Herskovits and Francs S. Herskovits in their book *Trinidad Village*:

> Old and young delight in telling, and hearing told, all the little incidents that go on in the village. To the outsider the speed with which news spreads never ceases to be a source of amazement. Equally amazing was the celerity with which the story acquired a texture that made of the commonplace a thing of meaningful or ironic sequences, often going back to relatives long dead, or at the very least recalling to memory some comparable happening that led to the unforeseen climaxes. No story was too trivial to stir an active response from the community, and to set in motion the weaving backwards and forwards in time of tales of supernatural deeds, and of retribution. Repudiating the meagerness of his everyday world, the Tocoan [resident of a settlement in northeastern Trinidad] draws on tradition and wit to fill a canvas with more than life-size figures—and always there is the humorous detail, the grotesque situation, the incisive comment.[46]

Spacks adds that most social groups "demonstrate the same collective capacity to lend 'texture' to the commonplace by placing it in a context of past happenings literal or imagined—or literal touched by imagination."[47]

Such gossip interprets the community to itself. In this interpretive use, the force of gossip is relatively benign: unifying, reassuring, more often inclusive than exclusive, sometimes defensive but rarely aggressive. This is not to say that, even in this form, it may not have negative consequences, but the benefits of "good gossip" far outweigh the negative as "the

---

play, it harks back to—perhaps embodies an attempt to recapture—the primal experience of intimacy and trust," and, if so, "its subject matter, however trivial or malicious, facilitates not aggression or voyeurism but human association." See also Rudnytsky, ed., *Transitional Objects and Potential Spaces*.

46. Spacks, *Gossip*, 231; see Herskovits and Herskovits, *Trinidad Village*, 275.
47. Spacks, *Gossip*, 231

talk itself, as well as its results in lasting legend, unites its participants."[48] Also, gossip serves individual as well as communal ends as it incorporates individuals into the communal myth. To be sure, as Trinidad small talk reveals, gossip about "the half-surmised activities of other people often attribute petty motives." At the same time, it may "enlarge its characters' stature" by means of "often repeated stories and slowly elaborated speculation."[49] Thus, to be the subject of gossip is not necessarily a fate to be deplored. Just as gossip can affect one's reputation negatively, it can also transform an individual into an exemplar of the community's most deeply felt values and convictions about itself.

Spacks concludes that gossip, as a kind of myth making, differs from tradition in the temporal emphases of their material. Gossip deals with the present, while tradition concerns the past. Yet, "both involve the working of imagination on the material of experience; both embody verbal freedom."[50] For some, especially those who have little control over the allocation and distribution of the community's resources, such verbal freedom may be all the freedom that they enjoy in life. But this is not a specious form of freedom. It is real freedom, and one that the powerful in a community can do little about, for where two or three gather for talk, gossip is always possible. This is why those who are insecure in their power employ informants on the speech of others and impose heavy sanctions against gossip. Spacks emphasizes, however, that gossip in these circumstances, while subversive of those in power, may conserve the deeper values of the community, values that the powerful are flaunting for their own selfish ends. And this brings us back to Jesus and the community in which he lived and worked.[51]

From Gossip to Gossipels

As noted earlier, reports of Jesus' teachings and healings was spread from village to village by means of the village grapevine. The dictionary

---

48. Ibid. The phrase "good gossip" is also the title of a book edited by Robert F. Goodman and Aaron Ben-Ze'ev. Especially noteworthy are Ben-Ze'ev's "The Vindication of Gossip," De Sousa's "In Praise of Gossip," and Morreall's "Gossip and Humor."

49. Ibid., 231–232.

50. Ibid. 248.

51. The foregoing discussion of gossip is relevant to religious communities such as congregations, monastic communities, and the like; see Capps, *Living Stories*, ch. 5; see also Schweitzer "Gossip."

defines *grapevine* as "a secret means of spreading or receiving information; also, the spreading of news or gossip from one person to another."[52] Since the spreading process was rather informal and unstructured, the second of these two meanings is more accurate than the first, and this means that Jesus became known throughout the region as a consequence of the fact that its inhabitants engaged in gossip. There were, after all, no newspapers or other formal means of communication from one village to another. Thus, the spreading of his reputation as a teacher and healer is unimaginable apart from the role played by the gossiping community.[53]

Also, the very fact that gossip played a major role in spreading the word about Jesus means that particular emphasis was placed on happenings, for happenings are what gossiping privileges. As John W. Daniels points out in his article on gossip in the New Testament, the social discourse takes unscripted/unexpected actions, events, or speech and gossip emerges in "the attempt to (re)construct the event itself" and "either re-enforce or re-script the social reality in light of the event, given the new information gained from the multiple subjective experiences of it." He adds that "the multiple experiences and retellings of events are what constitute the 'generative event,' and in such a way that the event is only fully constituted and knowable 'in its collective experiencing, telling, and retelling.'"[54]

This is not, of course, to say that Jesus did not have seminal ideas. But these ideas are not presented in the form of a treatise or statement of belief. Rather, they are presented as statements or comments that he made when he was engaged in conversations with others, and these others were not a group of scholars or highly learned individuals but persons whom he would meet along the way, whether on roads that connected villages, or in fields, or in village houses. Thus, inasmuch as the gospel writers draw on the oral traditions that were passed down to them, an especially

---

52. Agnes, ed., *New World College Dictionary*, 618.

53. I have also noted in Capps, *Jesus: A Psychological Biography*, 35, that Jesus and his traveling companions would have been the source of information about what was happening in other villages. As peasant cultures rely on travelers to provide information about what is going on in neighboring villages and in the region as a whole, the villagers would have appreciated the opportunity to engage in conversation with Jesus and his disciples, especially because he and his disciples were not there to victimize the villagers, as were the bandits that roamed the countryside.

54. Daniels, "Gossip in the New Testament," 206; he is quoting here from Craffert, *Life of a Galilean Shaman*, 104. See also Daniels, *Gossiping Jesus*; and Daniels, "Gossip in John's Gospel and the Social Processing of Jesus' Identity."

significant feature of the Gospels is that they give such great importance to the seemingly trivial events and conversations that occurred in the daily life of Galilee's peasantry. In comparison with the political events of the time, the happenings they recount seem both commonplace and parochial.

To say that the Gospels are filled with seemingly trivial events and conversations is not, however, to disparage them. It all depends on one's point of view. What seems commonplace and unremarkable may, in fact, have profound revelatory power. No doubt some of Jesus' followers felt that he should be engaging in conversation with the political and cultural leaders of his day, that he was wasting his time on the insignificant persons he encountered along the way. But if he had done so, would he be remembered today? I doubt it. Instead, the stories that the gospel writers relate reflect the fact that Jesus was more than willing to engage in the kinds of conversations that qualify as gossip, and the fact that they relate these very stories reflects their skill in transferring these conversations to the written page.

Unfortunately, we have become so accustomed to thinking of the Gospels from the perspective of those who privilege ideas over happenings that we have become desensitized to the fact that they *are* the product of gossip: without gossip, no Gospels. We can open any gospel at any page and begin reading, and what we find ourselves reading is a series of happenings—all local—and loosely connected. Mark 2 begins, "When he returned to Capernaum after some days, it was reported that he was at home" (v. 1). This is both the form and subject matter of gossip. As this chapter in Mark continues, happenings are far more important than ideas, and the narrative is a string of happenings, in no particular order, with only the semblance of connectedness. The absence of connectedness, the sense that the conversation is random, is also a characteristic of gossip.

And yet the narrator achieves something important in telling us about a day in the life of Jesus. In the first place, he establishes that *surfaces are not superficial.* Much gossip delights by its aesthetics of surfaces, its dwelling on specific personal particulars. We err, therefore, in trying to make these stories about Jesus deeper and more profound than they are, or when we try to generalize from one or two of these stories to make a larger point. Gossip works because it does not share the dominant culture's desire to assimilate the small particulars into a larger schema of meaning, for when this happens, the particulars are no longer entertaining in their own right, and we lose the pleasure of creating the impression that the story that *I* am about to tell has a connection with the one *you* just related. The dominant culture despises non sequiturs. Gossip thrives on them.

Second, like gossip, a gospel *gets its power by the illusion of mastery gained through taking possession of another's experience.* By taking a story that was handed down to him by others and adding various local touches about which only someone who was there could have known, the gospel writer presents himself as an insider, and thus as an intimate of Jesus. And in telling it as one who was actually present, the writer draws us into the story as well and makes us feel as though we, if not intimates of Jesus, are at least eyewitnesses of what is going on or taking place.

There is power in this freedom to enter imaginatively into the life of another, to take possession of the very experience of Jesus, and thereby make oneself an intimate of his. The gospel stories of Jesus entering the house of a villager for a meal are especially significant in this regard, as they present him in intimate surroundings and create a more conversational Jesus. They appeal to the reader's or listener's desire to be among Jesus' intimates, to be at table with him, to hear his voice, and to know him as a personal friend and confidante. To take possession of his experience is not for the purpose of cutting Jesus down to size but in order to experience the *empowerment* that comes with being an intimate of his. In short, the line between gossip and gospel is a very fine one. To say this is not to disparage the gospel but to elevate gossip, especially its belief that intimacy may happen on the very surfaces of life. As Reinhold Niebuhr points out, the surfaces (which are the situational locus of gossip) are not superficial. And this brings us back to the issue with which we began this chapter—the idea that a segment of society that values gossip is altogether likely to make ample room for humor.

Gossip and Humor

One of the essays in Robert F. Goodman and Aaron Ze'ev's *Good Gossip* is John Morreall's "Gossip and Humor."[55] Morreall was a member of the

---

55. Morreall, "Gossip and Humor." It is interesting to note that in *The Psychology of Rumor* Allport and Postman consider the role of humor in rumor. They suggest that "many stories that spread *like* rumors are frank products of imagination, intended to arouse not credulity but laughter," and point out that "in the manner in which they circulate and in the function they serve, jokes and rumors are often surprisingly similar" (191–92).

philosophy department at Rochester Institute of Technology at the time he wrote this essay. He begins his essay on gossip and humor with the observation that humor and gossip were traditionally neglected by academics and for many of the same reasons, but that in more recent years, humor has come into its own as an academic topic, so perhaps there is hope for gossip as well. He identifies the reasons for this neglect:

> Two of the most important traditional objections to humor are that it is frivolous and that it is mean-spirited or even hostile. These objections apply also to gossip. A third objection to humor that it is irrational—more precisely, that it is cognitively irresponsible—has a counterpart in objections to gossip. In gossiping, we spread stories without caring about the evidence for their truth, and this epistemic irresponsibility can be seen as a kind of irrationality.[56]

He suggests, however, that even as he has previously argued that these traditional objections to humor do not stand up as general objections to it, the same may be said about gossip.

Morreall goes on to note that the formal features of humor—"its use of surprise, its hypothetical exploration of topics, and its social features, particularly its playfulness and its fostering of intimacy, make the comparison of humor and gossip especially interesting."[57] Furthermore, "when gossip is dominated by a spirit of humor, it tends to transcend the pettiness and viciousness that have given gossip such a bad name for so long."[58]

He identifies three similarities that link gossip and conversational humor: First, both gossip and conversational humor are *sources of pleasure*. One of the pleasures of gossip is its being the source of information, while one of the pleasures of humor is its making people laugh. Second, both gossip and humor usually take narrative form, and the idea in both cases is to present an *entertaining narrative*. In this regard, even as individuals have reputations as good or poor tellers of funny stories and jokes, so individuals can be known as good or poor gossips. Third, conversational humor and gossip primarily *please the imagination*, making both of them candidates for aesthetic experience: "Not truth value, but entertainment value—their ability to delight, shock, amuse, or move

---

56. Morreall, "Gossip and Humor," 56.
57. Ibid.
58. Ibid.

us—is paramount."⁵⁹ In much humor, especially fictional jokes, the issue of truth doesn't even arise. But, in point of fact, the distinction between fiction and reality offers no hard distinction between humor and gossip because much humor is based on real, not fictional events, and even when funny stories are fictional they are often presented as real.⁶⁰ The same is true of gossip: "Suppose we are discussing our friend Bob's secret affair with his boss, Rhonda. One of us says, 'What if Bob accidentally ran into his wife at the ski lodge some weekend when he's there with Rhonda' and off our gossip goes with possible scenarios. We're not saying that he did or will do any of the things we are imagining—we're simply entertaining these ideas for the pleasure they bring."⁶¹ Morreall concludes: "Given all these similarities between humor and gossip, it's no surprise that they often overlap. There is humorous gossip and gossipy humor."⁶²

As noted, Morreall believes that when gossip is infused with the spirit of humor, "it tends to transcend the pettiness and viciousness that have given gossip such a bad name."⁶³ For this reason, he devotes several pages to the role of humor in gossip and introduces the most comprehensive theory of humor—the incongruity theory.⁶⁴ According to this theory, amusement is the enjoyment of experiencing or thinking about something that somehow clashes with our conceptual patterns and their related expectations. If the doorbell rings and we get up to answer it, we expect that there will be at least one person standing there who wants to speak to us. If we open the door and find that there is no one there, or that a goat is standing there, or that there is a person who stands there and

59. Ibid., 57.

60. For example, in *Jokes and Their Relation to the Unconscious* Freud cites Mark Twain's account of how his brother was employed on a great road-making enterprise. According to Twain, the premature explosion of a mine blew his brother up into the air and he came down at place that was at a considerable distance from where he had been working. Freud suggests that our feelings of sympathy for Twain's brother vanish when Twain goes on to say that his brother had a half-day's wages deducted for being "absent from his place of employment" (*Jokes and Their Relation to the Unconscious*, 286). Twain may have had a brother who worked in road construction, but even if this was the case, we have no reason to believe that the rest of the story is true. In fact, if it were, it would cease to be funny.

61. Morreall, "Gossip and Humor," 57.

62. Ibid.

63. Ibid., 56.

64. As I noted in chapter 2, footnote 1, Morreall identifies three major theories of humor: superiority, incongruity, and relief. See Morreall, "A New Theory of Laughter," 129–31.

says nothing, these experiences are incongruous. If one enjoys this incongruity, such enjoyment is amusement. Jokes work by leading us down one mental track and then at the punch line force us into another track. Of course, not all incongruity is enjoyable—the goat may cause us to laugh (and perhaps to wonder how it managed to ring the doorbell), but finding no one there could make us puzzled or even angry as we assume that someone was playing a practical joke on us. So, to enjoy having our conceptual patterns and expectations violated, the incongruity should not present a serious threat to us nor evoke other major practical concerns.

Morreall suggests that the experience of incongruity is as central to gossip as it is to humor. Suppose, for example, that our neighbor Lydia has just been arrested for shoplifting and we are going to describe this event in a conversation. The funniest and probably the most conversationally successful way to present it would be to make the event, and her general situation, as incongruous as we can. We might emphasize the incongruity of her attempt to seem innocent when it was clear to everyone that she was guilty; or note the incongruity between her shoplifting and the moral principles she preaches to her children; or highlight the incongruity due to the fact that the shoplifting occurred in a hardware store and the objects that were recovered from her purse included a screwdriver, a package of screws, and carpenter's glue. Thus, in gossiping about Lydia being arrested for shoplifting, it is natural to make her and what she did seem funny. So, too, with Bob's affair—our speculations about what would happen if his wife shows up at the ski lodge some weekend when he is there with Rhonda are very likely to take a humorous turn.[65]

Morreall believes that a good part of the pleasure in these instances is based on "the community feeling produced by humor," and that "gossip and humor foster intimacy and solidarity."[66] As we have seen, Spacks makes a similar point about gossip creating a sense of community, solidarity, and intimacy. These feelings of solidarity and intimacy may, of

---

65. Taking a humorous view of Lydia's predicament may, of course, reveal our insensitivity to her plight, especially if her shoplifting is a function of a mental or emotional illness. This may also be true of the creation of a scenario in which Bob's wife encounters the two of them at a ski lodge. Conceivably, Bob's wife already knows about her husband's affair and has accepted it, but it is also possible that she knows about it and is deeply hurt by it, or has no knowledge about it—in which case, imagining the ski lodge scenario reveals our own insensitivity to her pain, victimization, or both. The point of these examples, though, is simply to illustrate the role of incongruity in the tendency of gossip to take a humorous turn.

66. Morreall, "Gossip and Humor," 62.

course, occur at the expense of other persons, whether Bob's wife, Lydia herself, or an especially close friend of theirs. But when gossip reflects the playfulness of humor, it is less likely to be threatening to others and is more likely to enable us to make comments about another person that would otherwise seem heavy-handed. When we criticize someone with a touch of humor, for example, we are saying that we can see the problem in perspective and thus appreciate that it is not the end of the world.

Morreall acknowledges that gossip can be small-minded, nasty, or even malicious. He contends, however, that a notable feature of such cases is their lack of humor. In his view, the best kind of humor—aesthetically and morally—has these four aspects: (1) it is *playful* (those gossiping are in the conversation for the surprising news and ideas that will emerge, for the witty banter, for the entertainment); (2) it is *self-reflective* (those gossiping are aware of the lightness, superficiality, and sensationalism of the conversation, of the lack of evidence for much of what they are saying, and of the fact that self-awareness contributes to the fun); (3) it is *universalizing* (it sees the faults and problems of the people being gossiped about as faults and problems that any of us might fall into); and (4) it is *gentle* (because it sees problems and mistakes as universal, it is relatively nonjudgmental in its treatment of individuals, even when they have major shortcomings).[67]

The kind of playful, self-reflective, universalizing, and gentle humor that Morreall has in mind here is not found in all or perhaps even most gossip, "but it occurs often enough to show that there is nothing inherently vicious about gossip."[68] In fact, gossip "can express some of our most valuable human traits, especially the interest we take in each other's lives and the delight we take in entertaining one another."[69]

The Joking Community

For Morreall, as for Spacks, gossip is often an expression of intimacy. He adds, however, that this may also be true of joking conversations. Thus, intimacy is itself a common bond between gossip, on the one hand, and humor, on the other. In light of this common bond, I would now like to circle back around to the topic with which I began this chapter, namely,

67. Ibid., 64.
68. Ibid.
69. Ibid.

the idea that Jesus and his disciples formed, on various occasions, a joking community. To explore this topic further, I now wish to bring Ted Cohen into the conversation. Cohen was a member of the philosophy department at the University of Chicago when he wrote his book on jokes.[70]

Cohen notes that the conditions that underlie jokes and make then amusing or even funny are not normally expressed in jokes themselves. These conditions—for example, a stereotype of a particular ethnic or professional group—need not be believed by the persons sharing the joke, but they do need to be known to them in order for the joke to work. Otherwise, the person to whom the joke is told will respond, "I don't get it," and the joke teller will need to explain it, thereby ruining the pleasure of telling the joke. For example, one doesn't want to have to explain that the condition underlying a joke about the most expensive heart transplants being those that use a lawyer's heart is that lawyers have a reputation for exhibiting sympathy or concern for others, and hence their hearts are as good as new.[71]

The very fact that the underlying conditions of the joke go unsaid leads Cohen to suggest that "a deep satisfaction in successful joke transactions is the sense held mutually by teller and hearer that they are joined in feeling."[72] This means that the teller of the joke begins "with an implicit acknowledgment of a shared background, a background of awareness that you both are already in possession of and bring to the joke," and this is "the foundation of the intimacy that will develop if your joke succeeds, and the hearer then also joins you in a shared response to the joke."[73] Thus, if you have to explain or make a direct reference to the conditions that the joke assumes, you are probably telling the joke to the wrong hearers and setting yourself up for a deflating reaction. And when this happens, the joke teller has no reason to condemn the hearer, to claim, for example, that the hearer is a humorless clod: "All you can say of the fellow who doesn't laugh at your joke . . . is that *he is not like you*, at least, not in regard to the dynamics of your joke."[74]

On the other hand, the fact that the hearer did not laugh at your joke is not an insignificant fact, for what has happened in this case is the

---

70. Cohen, *Jokes*.
71. Ibid., 12–32. See also Capps, *Laughter Ever After*, 67–70.
72. Ibid., 25.
73. Ibid., 28.
74. Ibid., 26 (italics original).

failure of "the effort to achieve an intimacy between teller and hearer," a failure "to join one another in a community of appreciation."[75] Thus, on the plus side, when the hearer does join you in a shared response to the joke, the intimacy that results is "the shared sense of those in a *community*."[76] This intimacy has two constituents. One is a shared set of beliefs, dispositions, prejudices, preferences, and so forth—a shared outlook on the world, or at least part of such an outlook. The other is a shared feeling—a shared response to something. Both may be cultivated without jokes, but jokes exemplify the second constituent—shared feeling—by means of the first—shared beliefs and so on—and this, Cohen suggests, "is a very curious and wonderful fact about jokes."[77]

Cohen acknowledges that he may be overvaluing the intimacy made available through joke telling. Still, he is confident that this is an intimacy that we should not underestimate: "When we laugh at the same thing, this is a very special occasion. It is already noteworthy that we laugh at all, at anything, and that we laugh all alone. That we do it *together* is the satisfaction of a deep human longing, the realization of a desperate hope. It is the hope that we are enough like one another to sense one another, to be able to live together."[78] Thus, humor that contributes to our sense of intimacy with another contributes thereby to our sense of hopefulness, our sense that our situation is promising and that we have grounds for expecting that our desires will be fulfilled.[79]

Finally, as with our earlier discussion of gossip, it is noteworthy that Cohen recognizes the importance of moral considerations in joke telling. In his concluding chapter, "Taste, Morality, and the Propriety of Joking," he provides several examples of "asymmetrical" jokes, that is, jokes where the teller and hearer do not share the relevant background, such as adults urging a child to tell a joke that the child does not understand and ethnic jokes told in settings in which shared beliefs and feelings are absent. He also cautions against joke telling "when it is a kind of avoidance," where, for example, a joke about death is used to avoid rather than to deal with the reality of death. Moreover, he contends that it is inappropriate to accuse a person who considers a joke offensive of lacking a sense of humor

75. Ibid.
76 Ibid., 28 (italics original).
77. Ibid.
78. Ibid., 29 (italics original).
79. For a further discussion of the relationship of humor and hope see Capps, *At Home in the World*, xviii–xix, 62, and 69.

but, by the same token, he believes that it is wrong to claim that an offensive joke is inherently unfunny.[80] In the final analysis, however, Cohen's discussion of the moral considerations relating to jokes suggests that the issue of offensiveness plays a significant, perhaps determinative role as far as the intimacy that jokes may effect is concerned. And for him the issue of intimacy is primary.

The Art of Becoming an Intimate of Jesus

The relationship that Morreall has drawn between gossip on the one hand and humor on the other supports, at least in theory, the view that when Jesus and his disciples were alone together, they not only engaged in gossip but also in humor. No doubt there were many occasions when it would have been difficult if not impossible to separate the gossip from the humor, for, as we have seen, gossip is often infused with the spirit of humor, and when this is the case, it is less likely to be small-minded, nasty, or malicious, and more likely to be playful, self-reflective, universalizing, and gentle. I would like to believe that this was characteristic of the gossip in which Jesus and his disciples engaged, and the fact that Jesus is reported to have been critical of slander and false witness suggests that he would not have countenanced, much less encouraged, small-minded, nasty, or malicious gossip.

To lend support, however circumstantial, to this belief, I would like to return to the episode with which the chapter began, namely, Matthew's account of the Pharisees and scribes' complaint to Jesus that his disciples violated the tradition of the elders for failing to wash their hands before they took their meals (Matt 15:1–2). As Matthew tells it, Jesus responded by accusing the Pharisees and scribes of far worse transgressions, transgressions that involved saying things that directly violated the commandments of God. Then he called the people to him and said, "Listen and understand: it is not what goes into the mouth that defiles a person, but it is what comes out of the mouth that defiles" (Matt 15:10–11).

Matthew goes on to say that his disciples came to him later and told him that the Pharisees were offended by what he had said, and that Jesus, perceiving that his own disciples were not entirely persuaded, asked them: "Do you not see that whatever goes into the mouth enters the stomach,

---

80. Ibid., 82–84. See also Capps, *Time to Laugh*, 72–76.

and goes out the sewer? But what comes out of the mouth proceeds from the heart, and this is what defiles" (Matt 15:17-18).

Now, let us suppose that this conversation between Jesus and his disciples occurred when they were eating and drinking together. And let us also suppose that Jesus intended that his disciples would find his comment about food entering the stomach and going out the sewer amusing. They might ask themselves: What does he mean by "the sewer"? Is he speaking literally or metaphorically? Is he referring to a first-century equivalent of a drain pipe? Or is he referring to human physiology and, more specifically, to the anus? And let us also suppose that we are sitting there and listening to their conversation. Knowing that it was not our place to speak out loud, we take out our pencils and begin taking notes on what they are saying with the possible intention of sharing what we have heard with others.

I can imagine that I would begin doodling on a pad of paper and that I would draw a mouth with an arrow indicating that some food is entering it and passing down through the stomach, into the rectum, dropping out of the anus and finding its way to some sort of primitive sewer. I would also have an arrow indicating that some offensive words are moving upwards from the heart into the throat and then come blasting out of the mouth. I'd find myself thinking that the words spitting out are far more disgusting than the food dropping out.

And then, observing the trajectories of the two arrows, one going inside and the other going outside, my mind would probably have wandered a bit, and I may well have recalled George A. Strong's parody of Henry Wadsworth Longfellow's epic poem *The Song of Hiawatha*.[81] In Longfellow's version, Hiawatha, a great Native American chief thought to have lived in the sixteenth century, had a pair of magic mittens that enabled him to crush large boulders into hand-size rocks, which he flung at Mudjekeewis, the "immortal Father," in an attempt to kill him. The

---

81. Strong, "Modern Hiawatha." This parody is published in Gardner, *Martin Gardner's Favorite Poetic Parodies*, 91–92. It is also published in Baker, *Norton Book of Light Verse*, as written by an anonymous poet under the title "What Hiawatha Probably Did," 67–68. For Longfellow's original poem, see Longfellow, *Favorite Poems of Henry Wadsworth Longfellow*, 149–298. Longfellow was born in Portland, Maine, in 1807 and died in Cambridge, Massachusetts, in 1882. He was educated at Bowdoin College and taught there until 1836 when he became a professor of modern languages at Harvard. *The Song of Hiawatha* was published in 1855, by which time Longfellow had resigned his Harvard professorship and was writing poems that especially focused on America's aboriginal past.

attempt did not succeed, but in the parody by George Strong he was more successful. Here is Strong's parody:

What Hiawatha Probably Did

He slew the noble Mudjekeewis
With his skin he made him mittens;
Made them with the fur-side inside;
Made them with the skin-side outside.
He to keep the warm-side inside,
Put the cold side, skin-side, outside;
He, to keep the cold-side outside,
Put the warm side, fur-side, inside:—
That's why he put the cold side outside,
Why he put the warm side inside,
Why he turned them inside outside.

Thinking of Strong's repeated use of the inside/outside dynamic, I would have proceeded to write this poem:

What Jesus Probably Said

Sin works from the inside–outside,
And not, my friends, from outside–inside.
For outside–inside ends up outside,
While inside–outside just stays inside,
And this is sin's unhappy downside.
But that's why I came thereside–hereside,
To turn this matter rightside–upside,
And make the devil take the hindside.
So now, if this be on the clear-side,
It's time, my friends, to bottoms-upside.

    This bit of poetic license takes for granted that Jesus and his disciples are "tippling companions," the second definition of gossip noted earlier. It also assumes that Jesus and his disciples are a joking community, and that they were able to take the serious issues that had come up during the day and take a rather lighthearted view of them when evening came and they were relaxing together. Finally, the poem may even express the poet's bid for unofficial inclusion in their joking community. Others may say that this is not the way to do it, or that there are better ways to do it. No doubt this is true, but given the setting and the spirit that pervades the room, I don't really worry about it. In fact, I feel rather relaxed about it.

I stay a while longer and then, as darkness descends, I get up from where I am sitting, gather my pad and paper and walk over to the door and go outside. As I begin walking home, and reflect on the fact that I have taken imaginative possession of the shared experience of Jesus and his disciples, I find myself recalling his invitation to those who are stressed out and anxious: "Come unto me, all who labor and are heavy laden, and I will give you rest. Take my yoke upon you, and learn from me, for I am gentle, and lowly in heart, and you will find rest for your souls. For my yoke is easy, and my burden is light" (Matthew 11:28–30 RSV). There are no better words to express what William James refers to as "the gospel of relaxation."[82] And perhaps I can be forgiven for thinking that there might be some significance in the fact that *yoke* rhymes with *joke* and for thinking that there is something to be said for *local yokels*.

---

82. James, "Gospel of Relaxation."

7

Why the Long Face?

In chapters 1 and 2 we focused on the role that humor may play in helping persons deal with anxiety and the stresses of life. In our discussion of anxiety, we found that humor can be a very helpful resource in dealing with anxiety, but we discovered that worry can also help us to cope with anxiety. Here, in chapter 7, I want to return to the issue of worry and suggest that in Jesus' vision of the kingdom of God there is nothing to worry about, and because this is so, the kingdom of God exemplifies the gospel of relaxation. To provide a context for our reflections on his vision of the kingdom of God, I will begin with a personal story.

Joyce Kilmer's "Trees"

I grew up in Omaha, Nebraska. Every spring our elementary school would observe Arbor Day, which is a tree-planting day observed throughout the United States, but we were told by our teachers that in our state it was special because the founder of Arbor Day, Julius Sterling Morton, was a Nebraskan. On this day our class would walk to a field that adjoined the school and we would plant a sapling. Our teacher would point out trees that we or other classes had planted in previous years. After we planted the sapling we recited a poem titled "Trees" by Joyce Kilmer.[1] We did not know anything about the poet other than the poet's name, and no doubt we assumed that a poet named Joyce was a woman.

Many years later, when my wife and son and I had moved to Princeton, New Jersey, we were driving to New York City and we stopped at a

---

1. Kilmer, *Trees and Other Poems*, 19.

rest area that was named after Joyce Kilmer. Seeing the name Joyce Kilmer at the rest stop brought back memories of our tree-planting ceremony in Omaha, Nebraska, and this led me to do some rather informal research on the poet who wrote "Trees."

Joyce Kilmer was born in New Brunswick, New Jersey, in 1886 and he was named after the rector Alfred Joyce of Christ (Episcopal) Church, which his parents attended.[2] With no living brothers or sisters, Joyce was especially close to his mother. His father, Frederick, a chemist, was director of the scientific labs at Johnson & Johnson, the renowned medical supply firm. He graduated from Rutgers College in 1904 and received his BA degree from Columbia University in 1906. He married Aline Murray the same year and began teaching Latin at Morristown High School. He soon concluded that he was not cut out to be a teacher and began working in New York as an editor of a journal for horsemen. Then he took a job as a retail salesman at Scribner's bookstore, and before long he was writing reviews for the *New York Times Review of Books*. Later he became literary editor of the *Churchman* and served for several years as corresponding secretary for The Poetry Society of America and poetry editor of the *Literary Digest*. In 1913, due in part to the fact that his daughter Rose was stricken with infantile paralysis, he and his wife, Aline, along with their children, became Roman Catholics. Shortly after the United States entered World War I in April 1917, Kilmer enlisted in the army and was killed in France in 1918 when he was involved in an intelligence mission.[3]

His poem "Trees" was published in *Poetry* magazine in August 1913. Various musical renditions of the poem began to appear in the

---

2. A. K. Kilmer, *Memories of My Son Sergeant Joyce Kilmer*, 1. I have wondered if his name, which was clearly chosen by his mother, may also have reflected a certain disappointment that she had not given birth to a daughter. In any event, here's a relevant joke: Every year, Saint Peter conducted a tour down on earth. "This year," he told the Virgin Mary, "I'm going to survey all your shrines and compare them to the shrines I've seen in previous years." He took his tour and visited shrines around the world before he came back to heaven and reported to Mary, "I've got great news! There are more people at your shrines than anyone else's. But I noticed one thing—every single statue portrayed you with a sad expression on your face. Why is that?" Mary said, "You might not understand my feelings." Saint Peter replied, "Now, Mary, I've had many people tell me their innermost feelings—can't you open up to me?" Mary hesitated then said, "Well, you see, Peter . . . I really wanted a girl," Alexander et al., *Prairie Home Companion Pretty Good Joke Book* (5th ed.), 135.

3. Smaridge, *Pen and Bayonet*; Holliday, ed., *Joyce Kilmer*.

1920s.[4] The poem was dedicated to Mrs. Henry Mills Alden, his wife's stepmother. Here is the poem:

Trees

I think that I shall never see
A poem lovely as a tree.

A tree whose hungry mouth is prest
Against the earth's sweet flowing breast;

A tree that looks to God all day
And lifts her leafy arms to pray;

A tree that may in Summer wear
A nest of robins in her hair;

Upon whose bosom snow has lain;
Who intimately lives with rain.

Poems are made by fools like me,
But only God can make a tree.

Joan Shelley Rubin, a professor of history at the University of Rochester, notes that this was one of several poems about nature that were included in high school textbooks on poetry in the late 1920s and early 1930s.[5] She adds, however, that a 1938 anthology of poetry for college students by Cleanth Brooks Jr. and Robert Penn Warren included a "devastating inspection" of the poem. They "took apart each of the poet's metaphors—the tree's roots are a human's mouth, the branches are 'leafy arms,' the tree is a 'sucking babe,' a 'girl with jewels in her hair'—to indict Kilmer for failing to think clearly about the 'implications' of his imagery."[6] The poem soon became an object of parody and, thanks to

---

4. The most popular was one by Oscar Rasbach, written in 1922. Various vocalists performed it, including Ernestine Schumann-Heink, Paul Robeson, John Charles Thomas, and Nelson Eddy. See *Wikipedia*, "Joyce Kilmer."

5. Rubin, *Songs of Ourselves*, 124. See, for example, Carhart and McGhee, *Magic Casements*, 57.

6. Ibid., 158. See Brooks and Warren, *Understanding Poetry*.

Brooks and Warren, "an object lesson in the pitfalls of imprecision in poetic imagery."[7]

But Rubin defends the poem, noting that part of its appeal has been its uncomplicated diction and easily felt rhythm, which has helped readers to find it beautiful and to take it to heart.[8] Also, Kilmer's suggestion at the beginning of the poem—"I think that I shall never see / A poem lovely as a tree"—"counterposes human artifice to the natural world, suggesting that no assemblage of words can substitute for the direct experience of life."[9] And yet, as Rubin also notes, there is a deep irony in his "deprecation of himself as a 'fool' while he simultaneously demonstrates the power of the verbal to transmit sensory perception," for if only God can make a tree, "only poets can help readers to understand that fact."[10]

Several years before I read Rubin's discussion of Kilmer's "Trees" and discovered that there has been considerable controversy concerning its metaphorical language, I wrote the following parody of the poem.

My Tree

I think I'll never cease to see
A poem barking up a tree.

My tree is eighteen inches round
And firmly rooted in the ground.

Its branches spread from here to there,
And leaves are growing everywhere.

Its limbs the robins sit a-top
And let their droppings ploppy-plop

---

7. Rubin, *Songs of Ourselves*, 336.
8. Ibid.
9. Ibid.
10. Ibid., 337–38. A book of poems by Aline Kilmer, Joyce Kilmer's wife, titled *Candles That Burn* was published the year after his death and was dedicated to his memory. In her poem "The Windy Night," written after his death, she recalls how he loved to hear the wind "like brazen trumpets in the night" and to listen to the "silver lances of the rain, / And see the birches' cavalry / Go sweeping past the window pane." Thus, she also makes a metaphorical association of trees with humans, but suggests in her poem that the trees in this case display a "martial panoply" (Kilmer, *Candles That Burn*, 33).

> Upon my neighbors walking by
> Who think it's manna from the sky.
>
> Poems are written by fools like me,
> On paper made from such a tree.

In his poem, Kilmer views the tree as an infant suckling at the breast of Mother Earth, then growing up to be a lovely young woman with a nest of robins in her hair. In contrast, my poem provides a rather pedestrian description of the size of the tree, and notes the fact that it is rooted in the ground and that the robins' droppings fall into the hair of people who walk underneath. Also, whereas his poem concludes with a reference to divine creation, my poem merely observes that trees are the source of the paper on which poems are written. In other words, Kilmer's poem (as Brooks and Warren were only too happy to point out) works with metaphor, while mine invites the suspicion that the poet hasn't the foggiest notion of what a metaphor is, much less how to use it.[11]

The Healing of the Blind Man

In light of the fact that in his late teens Kilmer began serving as a lay reader in the church that he and his parents attended and gave serious thought to becoming an Episcopal priest, we may assume that he was familiar with the story of Jesus' healing of the blind man. Here is Mark's account:

> They came to Bethsaida. Some people brought a blind man to him and begged him to touch him. He took the blind man by the hand and led him out of the village; and when he had put saliva on his eyes and laid his hands on him, he asked him, "Can you see anything?" And he man looked up and said, "I can see people, but they look like trees, walking." Then Jesus laid his hands on his eyes again; and he looked intently and his sight was restored, and he saw everything clearly. Then he sent him away to his home, saying, "Do not even go into the village" (Mark 8:22–26).

In this story we have, in effect, the metaphorical association of humans and trees. So Kilmer's "Trees" is in very good company.

---

11. See also Capps, "Trees and Us."

But why did Jesus take the blind man out of the village in order to heal him? And why did he advise the man not to return to the village nearby? In *Jesus the Village Psychiatrist* I suggested that Jesus attributed the man's blindness to the fact that he was living in this particular village, and that his blindness may have been due to the fact that he was looking at someone he shouldn't be looking at, such as a woman who was morally or socially unavailable to him.[12] If this was so, returning to the village could result in a relapse.

Let us assume, then, that Jesus and his disciples are having a meal together later that day, and his disciples have some questions for him concerning his healing of the blind man. Those who are more interested in the physiological features of the man's blindness may ask Jesus what he makes of the fact that when the man initially gained his sight other men looked like walking trees, while those who are more interested in the psychosocial features of the man's blindness may want to know why Jesus advised the man to go home and not return to the village.

Supposing, though, that after these issues are fully discussed, one of the disciples observes that there is a larger issue here, namely, the fact that some villages provide better living conditions than others. And let us suppose that Jesus responds by noting that this is an interesting observation, and that after they discuss various Galilean villages, Jesus tells his friends that he has foreknowledge—after all, he *is* the son of God—of the fact that a few American poets will be writing about this issue in the late nineteenth century. He mentions several of these poems and then suggests that someone read one of them to the group.[13] It is a poem titled "The Town of Don't-You-Worry," by Rev. I. J. Bartlett. Peter graciously volunteers to read it.[14]

---

12. Capps, *Jesus the Village Psychiatrist*, 70.

13. Others were "The Town of Nogood," by W. E. Penny and "It Isn't the Town, It's You," by R. W. Glover, the latter of which inspired "It Isn't the Church—It's You," by an unknown poet, in Felleman, *Best Loved Poems of the American People*, 93, 104–5.

14. In Felleman, *Best Loved Poems of the American People*, 103. In Felleman's book Bartlett is identified by his first and middle initial only. But a blog titled "Lynn's Waffles" has an October 21, 2014, comment about her recent purchase of an old poetry book, and her discovery that inside the book there was a piece of folded paper with Bartlett's poem penciled in full with the poet's name. The first and second names are initials only, but he is identified as Rev. I. J. Bartlett. Her research efforts led to her discovery that the poem was published in two New Jersey newspapers in 1916–1917 and that both indicate that the poem was originally published in the *Christian Herald*.

The Town of Don't-You-Worry

There's a town called Don't-You-Worry,
On the banks of River Smile:
Where the Cheer-Up and Be-Happy
Blossom sweetly all the while.
Where the Never-Grumble flower
Blooms beside the fragrant Try,
And the Ne'er-Give-Up and Patience
Point their faces to the sky.
In the valley of Contentment,
In the province of I-Will,
You will find this lovely city,
At the foot of No-Fret Hill.
There are thoroughfares delightful
In this very charming town,
And on every hand are shade trees
Named the Very-Seldom-Frown.
Rustic benches quite enticing
You'll find scattered here and there;
And to each a vine is clinging
Called the Frequent-Earnest-Prayer.
Everybody there is happy
And is singing all the while,
In the town of Don't-You-Worry,
On the banks of River Smile.

When Peter finished reading the poem, the others agreed that this sounds like a nice town to live in, but they wondered where in the world one would ever find a town like that. Whereupon Jesus said to them: "May I remind you of what I've been saying about the kingdom of God, that because it is no place, it can be anyplace." Andrew replied, "You mean, it could be here, now, in this room, as we sit and talk with one another?" Jesus answered, "Yes, but it often appears on the wings of humor." Whereupon James, the brother of John, told the following joke:

> A ventriloquist is doing a show in an out-of-the-way place and as part of his act he makes several jokes about the town and its residents. The audience finds these jokes offensive and insulting.

Finally a man in the audience who can't take it anymore stands up. He shouts, "Hey! You on stage! You've been making fun of us all night! We ain't stupid, you know!" The ventriloquist responds, "Hey, relax, they're just jokes!" "I'm not talking to you," the man shouts back, "but to that little smart-ass sitting on your knee!"[15]

The other disciples laughed and Jesus smiled.

We might suppose that a joke about ventriloquists wouldn't make much sense to first-century Galileans. But we should keep in mind the fact that the disciples would have known the story of how Moses raised several objections to God's proposal that he go to Pharaoh and ask him to free the people of Israel. One of these objections was that he was not "eloquent," that he "was slow of speech and of tongue" (Exod 4:10, RSV). God replied that he would be with Moses' mouth and would teach him what to say, to which Moses replied, "Oh, my Lord, send, I pray, some other person." Whereupon God became angry and asked:

> Is there not Aaron, your brother, the Levite? I know that he can speak well; and behold, he is coming out to meet you, and when he sees you he will be glad in his heart. And you shall speak to him and put the words in his mouth; and I will be with your mouth and his mouth, and will teach you what you shall do. He shall speak for you to the people and he shall be a mouth for you, and you shall be to him as God. (Exodus 4:14–16, RSV)

No doubt, it is something of a stretch to draw a parallel between the story of how Aaron became Moses' mouthpiece and the ventriloquist joke, but, as James, the brother of John, perceived, this joke raises the question of what, after all, is out-of-the-way, especially as far as the kingdom of God is concerned? As Jesus had said, "Because it is no place, it can be anyplace, and you will know you are there because you know—and feel it in your heart—that you have no reason to worry." We might say that James' joke was not as out of place as it might appear to have been.

But Jesus' suggestion that the kingdom of God is a place where you have no reason to worry raises another question: What if you know that there is no reason to worry, but you can't help yourself, for worry has become a habit? It should come as no surprise that Jesus had thought of this dilemma. As Matthew 6:25–34 tells us, Jesus once told his listeners

---

15. Greene, *Greatest Joke Book Ever*, 292–93. I have slightly revised the wording of this joke.

not to worry about their life, especially about the things they feel they need, like food and clothing. As far as food is concerned, he suggested that they look at the birds that fly in the air and consider the fact that they neither sow nor reap nor gather into barns, and yet "your heavenly Father feeds them." As far as clothes are concerned, he suggested that they consider the lilies that grow in the fields and neither toil nor spin, and reflect on the fact that they are better clothed than King Solomon ever was. So why worry about what you will eat or what you will wear? After all, your heavenly Father knows that you need these things, so there is no cause for worry. Jesus also points out that worriers tend to think about the future and what will happen to them as time goes on, and he asks, "What good does that do? Will it make the future any better?" And, furthermore, can you add a single hour to your span of life by worrying? He concludes with a concrete suggestion, one that is designed to counteract the worry habit: Focus your thoughts and your emotions on the present, and don't try to anticipate what may go wrong tomorrow or the next several days.

In effect, Jesus has made a compelling case for the gospel of relaxation, and has offered a very concrete suggestion for how to experience it. And he has done so by encouraging his listeners to consider the birds in the air and the lilies in the field. There is no doubt that his intentions here are serious, that he is deeply concerned that those who have come out to hear him are anxious, stressed out, worried about a host of things, and about their lives in general. But there is also a certain lightheartedness and humor in the manner in which he makes his point. Perhaps the most obvious illustration of his humorous touch is the comparison he makes between a lily and King Solomon. Solomon was evidently noteworthy for the grandeur of his dress. But when you come right down to it, which of them—King Solomon or the lily—is the more beautifully clothed? Jesus casts his vote for the lily. No doubt the majority of his listeners would agree.

As for his allusion to the birds of the air, he invites his listeners to envision a scene in which a group of birds get together in the springtime and sow some seeds—let's imagine that they are turtledoves and that they have a hankering for beans—and several months later they come back to reap what they have sown and carry their bags of beans a few hundred yards and deposit them in a barn that they have constructed.[16] And let's

---

16. The prophet Jeremiah mentions four species of birds: storks, turtledoves, swallows, and cranes (8:7). I chose the turtledoves because they are noted for their plaintive cooing and the affection that the mates are traditionally thought of as showing toward

imagine that as we watch them struggle with their bags of beans we begin to wonder, what has gotten into them? Is it a demon perhaps? No doubt there will be listeners who do not find this scenario amusing. But I suspect that some of them, especially the children, whose imaginations have not been educated out of them, will think it is rather funny.[17]

As for me, I would probably be thinking that Jesus could also have mentioned in this context that foxes have holes (Matthew 8:20), and this reference to animals would have brought to mind one of my favorite proverbs: "He who meddles in a quarrel not his own is like one who takes a passing dog by the ears" (Proverbs 26:17). Better to stay out of it and follow the dog to find what he is sniffing out. This proverb, I might be thinking, is also relevant to the gospel of relaxation, as it suggests that some issues simply aren't worth getting ourselves worked up about. But more directly relevant is another one of my favorite proverbs: "Better is a dry morsel with quiet than a houseful of feasting with strife" (Proverbs 17:1). One could, of course, say that even better would be a nice big meal in a quiet atmosphere, but this proverb supports the point that Jesus is making here: that you can live on less than you think you can, and this being the case, you can spare yourself a lot of unnecessary anxiety, stress, and, above all, worry.

Finally, it is noteworthy that like Joyce Kilmer, Rev. Bartlett wrote about trees, and, specifically, the shade trees named "the Very-Seldom-Frown." In effect, he invites us to look at ourselves in the mirror to see whether our forehead displays a frown or our mouth displays a smile, and consider the fact that we can't have it both ways; and that we might also want to consider the fact that when we are relaxed it is hard *not* to smile. I would simply add that when I see a frown, this often helps: "A horse goes into a bar. The bartender looks at him and says, "Why the long face?"[18]

---

each other. See Agnes, ed., *Webster's New World College Dictionary*, 1545. See also Lior Kislev's website on "Birding Tours and Bird-watching in Israel" which notes that even as Israel has been a migratory region as far as humans are concerned, so, too, it attracts many migratory birds on a seasonal basis.

17. See Wolfenstein, *Children's Humor*; see also Capps, "Riddles and Jokes"; and Capps, *Erik Erikson's Verbal Portraits*; see also Capps and Capps, *You've Got to Be Kidding!*

18. Tapper and Press, *Guy Goes Into a Bar...*, 72.

Conclusion

Rev. Bartlett's "The Town of Don't-You-Worry" was written and published in the second decade of the twentieth century. Fifty years earlier a young minister who was serving a church in Philadelphia wrote a poem about another town. His name is Phillips Brooks. He was born in Boston in 1835, did his undergraduate work at Harvard, spent a year (as did Joyce Kilmer) teaching school, and then began training to become a minister at Virginia Theological Seminary. When he graduated in 1859, he accepted a pastoral position at the Church of the Advent in Philadelphia. Three years later he accepted a position at Holy Trinity Church in Philadelphia. During this time he was a very outspoken critic of slavery. When the Civil War came to an end, it was evident to his parishioners that his involvement in mobilizing the Philadelphia clergy in support of the war against slavery and his heavy workload in the parish had taken their toll, and that he needed a rest. Recognizing this, the parish gave him a year's leave of absence in 1865 with full salary.[19]

He began his sabbatical with some brief theological study in Germany (enough to convince him that he lacked the necessary background and technical skills to be a scholar); then after touring several other parts of Europe, he went to the Holy Land. While there he wrote a poem titled "O Little Town of Bethlehem."[20] When he returned to Philadelphia to resume his pastoral duties, he shared his poem with the church organist, Lewis H. Redner, who composed the music for the poem. It soon became a very popular Christmas hymn.

The poem focuses on a little town that would not be considered worth a nineteenth-century tourist's time and expense to visit were it not for the fact that it was the birthplace of Jesus. For Brooks, it was as though the birth was taking place again:

> O little town of Bethlehem,
> How still we see thee lie!
> Above thy deep and dreamless sleep
> The silent stars go by:
> Yet in thy dark streets shineth
> The everlasting Light;
> The hopes and fears of all the years
> Are met in thee tonight.

19. See Capps, *Young Clergy*, 37–57.
20. Ernest, *Family Album of Favorite Poems*, 518.

These hopes and fears were associated with the conclusion of the Civil War—a very hopeful sign—but also the fears aroused by the fact that President Lincoln had been assassinated and the reconstruction was being badly handled by his successor, President Andrew Johnson. They were also associated with more personal matters relating to the fact that although his career was off to a very promising start, he was involved in a personal relationship that was not going well and various occupational opportunities had left him in a quandary.

The poem does not go on to ask for clarity of vision or divine guidance. It only asks the Holy Child of Bethlehem to "descend to us," to "be born in us" and "abide with us." It is as if this child who was born of Mary can be born of others too, and that in this rebirth these others may also come to life again. And perhaps we are not reading too much into the poem if we take the poet to be suggesting that the child (himself) who had been born some thirty years before will remind the older man of truths about himself that he used to know but has subsequently forgotten. Perhaps, then, Bethlehem is the town where, in contemplating the birth of the Holy Child, one has the experience of self-rediscovery.

This, however, is a book on humor, and, more specifically, on our desire and need to be humored. So I would like to conclude with Brooks' reflections in his lectures at Yale Divinity School twelve years later on the place of humor in preaching. In his lecture on "The Preacher Himself" he discusses the "necessary qualities" of the preacher and then discusses the elements of personal power that make one a successful preacher. Here he mentions the importance of personal character, a freedom from self-consciousness, and genuine respect for the people to whom one preaches. Then he comes to an element that he hesitates to name lest it be misunderstood, but he settles on the word "gravity," by which he

> means simply that grave and serious way of looking at life which, while it never repels the true lightheartedness of pure and trustful hearts, welcomes into a manifest sympathy the souls of those who are oppressed and burdened, anxious and full of questions which for the time at least have banished all laughter from their faces.[21]

He says that he is aware of "mock gravity," and that he is as disgusted by it as anybody, and adds that "the abuse and satire that have

---

21. Brooks, *Lectures on Preaching*, 54.

been heaped upon it are legitimate enough, though somewhat cheap."[22] On the other hand, he feels that there is "another creature who ought to share with the clerical prig the contempt of Christian people," and says that he is referring to "the clerical jester in all the varieties of his unpleasant existence."[23] This character

> lays his hands on the most sacred things and leaves defilement upon all he touches. He is full of Bible jokes. He talks about the Church's sacred symbols in the language of stale jests that have come down from generations of feeble clerical jesters before him ... There are passages in the Bible which are soiled forever by the touches which the ministers who delight in cheap and easy jokes have left upon them.[24]

In his earlier discussion of the power that a preacher derives from the genuine respect he has for those to whom he preaches, Brooks cites the counterexample of the medieval preacher who, when discoursing on the necessary cooperation of the clergy and the laity, took as his text Job 1:14: "The oxen were ploughing and the asses feeding beside them."[25] We may assume that this is an example of what Brooks has in mind in his reference to "generations of feeble clerical jesters" who have forever soiled various biblical passages.

Declaring that there is nothing that stirs one's indignation more than this behavior of ministers, he suggests that

> what is simply stupid everywhere else becomes terrible here. The buffoonery which merely tries me when I hear it from a gang of laborers digging a ditch beside my door angers and frightens me when it comes from the lips of the captain who holds the helm or the surgeon on whose skill my life depends. You will not misunderstand me, I am sure. The gravity of which I speak is not inconsistent with the keenest perception of the ludicrous side of things. It is more than consistent with—it is even necessary—to humor. Humor involves the perception of the true proportions of life. It is one of the most helpful qualities that the preacher can possess. It is one of the most helpful qualities that the preacher can possess. There is no extravagance which deforms the pulpit which would not be modified and

22. Ibid.
23. Ibid., 55.
24. Ibid., 56.
25. Ibid., 53.

repressed, often entirely obliterated, if the minister had a true sense of humor. It has softened the bitterness of controversy a thousand times. You cannot encourage it too much.[26]

He advises his listeners to read books "which have in them the truest humor, for the truest humor is the bloom of the highest life," and cites, in particular, the writings of English novelists George Eliot (the pseudonym of Mary Ann Evans), William Makepeace Thackeray, and especially William Shakespeare because they "will help you to keep from extravagances without fading into insipidity" and "preserve your gravity while they save you from pompous solemnity."[27] He cautions, however, that "humor is something very different from frivolity," adding:

> People sometimes ask whether it is right to make people laugh in church by something that you say from the pulpit,—as if laughter were always one invariable thing; as if there were not a smile which swept across a great congregation like the breath of a May morning, making it fruitful for whatever good thing might be sowed in it, and another laughter that was like the crackling of thorns under a pot. The smile that is stirred by true humor and the smile that comes from the mere tickling of the fancy are as different from one another as the tears that sorrow forces from the soul are from the tears that you compel a man to shed by pinching him.[28]

Brooks goes on to identify one more source of personal power that makes one an effective preacher, and this is courage. Noting that courage is the indispensable requisite of true ministry, he suggests that

> The timid minister is as bad as the timid surgeon. Courage is good everywhere, but it is necessary here. If you are afraid of others and a slave to their opinion, go and do something else. Go and make shoes to fit them. Go even and paint pictures which you know are bad but which suit their bad taste. But do not keep on all your life preaching sermons which shall say not what God sent you to declare, but what they hire you to say. Be courageous. Be independent. Only remember where the true courage and independence comes from. Courage in the ministry is, I think, one of those qualities which cannot be healthily acquired if it is sought for directly. It must come as health comes

---

26. Ibid., 56–57.
27. Ibid., 57.
28. Ibid.

> in the body, as the result of the seeking for other things.... Jesus himself was bold before others out of the infinite love which He felt for them.[29]

If, as Brooks suggests, the truest humor is the bloom of the highest life, and if, as Saint Paul declared, love as the highest gift of all (1 Corinthians 12:31, 13:13), it would seem that Jesus' ability to engage in genuine humor is an expression of his infinite love for us. And this means that he is not about the tickling of our fancy. He is about the replacing of the frowns on our faces with smiles of peace, contentment, and the sense that we are infinitely loved.

---

29. Ibid., 59.

Epilogue

I have been emphasizing throughout this book that humor can play a valuable role in countering stress and anxiety and supporting the gospel of relaxation. Since relaxation works best when the body and mind relax together, it can be rather disconcerting when one is unable to sleep because one's mind is working on various issues and problems. In chapter 4 we considered Freud's writings on humor but did not have anything to say about dreams, the topic for which he is best known.[1] This is not the place to discuss the fact that in his classic work on dreams Freud discussed anxiety-dreams, but it is worth noting that this very discussion indicates that it is quite common for persons to take their anxieties to bed with them.

I would like to comment here on a dream of my own that addressed a long-standing anxiety of mine and essentially resolved the anxiety by means of displacement. I need not go into a discussion of displacement in order to convey how this worked; it suffices to say that Freud identifies various forms and expressions of displacement in dreams, and that what essentially occurs in such displacement that strong and troubling emotions are detached from their real causes and attached to another, often trivial, one.[2] The relevance of this dream to the topic of humor is that the dream struck me as being humorous, both during the dreaming itself and when I reflected on the dream after waking up. Here is the dream:

> I was walking down a road and came to another road. The sign on the road said that it was Tyrus Road. It occurred to me that Tyrus Cobb was a well known baseball player when I was growing up and that he was especially noted for his prowess in stealing bases. The fact that he was a base stealer caused me to wonder if this dream was up to something, that it was, as it were,

1. Freud, *Interpretation of Dreams*.
2. Rennison, *Freud and Psychoanalysis*, 85.

playing a game. In any event, I began walking down Tyrus Road and after I had passed several houses, a dog came out of one of them and began walking beside me. I didn't greet the dog, much less reach down to pet him. But we walked a hundred yards or so together. Then, I began to worry that the dog might not be able to find his way home so I suggested to him that he probably ought to be turning back. The house from which he had emerged was still visible. He looked at me rather plaintively, then looked at the house, and said, "Sometimes the ones who make the decisions are not the wisest ones." Whereupon, he began walking, quite slowly, back to house, and I continued on down Tyrus Road. And then I woke up.

The reason I refer to this as an anxiety dream is that I developed a fear of dogs in my childhood. As I had never been directly attacked by a dog, I could not attribute this fear to any specific event. But I began carrying newspapers when I was eight or nine years old and sometimes dogs would bark at me and occasionally run toward me as though they might want to attack me, but they never did. Then it occurred to me that this fear of dogs had something to do with the fact that I was a small child during World War II As I noted in chapter 7, I grew up in Omaha, Nebraska, and I had an uncle who served in the United States Army in France, and returned with serious injuries due to the fact that the military vehicle in which he was riding went into a ditch. As a child I heard about warfare occurring on Omaha Beach, which is, of course, located in France, but I believe that the Omaha Beach that was being referred to was local. Also, I heard about the "dogfights" that were taking place between German and Allied fighter planes but failed to realize that they involved airplanes, not actual dogs, and that these fights were not occurring in our local neighborhood. While these associations may seem a bit far-fetched, and, admittedly, they were my attempt to make sense of the fact that I had a great fear of dogs, this fear had continued into my adulthood even though I was well aware of the fact that it was irrational.

But then I had the dream in which the dog walked alongside of me and we shared a few moments together, neither of us mistrusting the other. I recall how reluctant I was to suggest that he turn back and how reluctant he was to do so. We had become companions. And then, when he spoke, I sensed that he, and not I, was the anxious one, as there was something about living in the house that made him uneasy. His comment—"Sometimes the ones who make the decisions are not the wisest ones"—suggested that there were persons in the house who were making poor decisions or exercising poor judgment, and that he was not in a position to do anything about it. He did not say that he himself was the victim of their poor judgment, and it is entirely conceivable that he was simply observing that there were other humans in the house who *were* the victims of their poor judgment.

What I realized when I woke up and thought about the dream was that my anxiety in the presence of dogs had been, as it were, displaced onto the dog himself, that he was the anxious one. Given my long-standing fear of dogs, this was a new experience for me, and although I knew that a dog who barks at a human may be doing so because the human is making the dog anxious, I had not considered the possibility that a dog might want to take me into his confidence with the hope that I would at least be sympathetic even if I could not do anything to ameliorate the situation. Admittedly, the dog was a figment of my imagination, so it wasn't as if a real dog spoke these words to me and did so in the hope that I would sympathize with him and his situation.

Yet, this dream has made a significant difference in my life, especially because it has liberated me from the anxiety that I have carried with me since childhood, an anxiety related to the fact that there was a war going on and I was too young to comprehend it. It has also contributed to my conviction that humor is a tremendously important resource in dealing with our anxieties. The dream was not overtly humorous—the dog did not tell a joke, and neither did I. In fact, the power of his comment to me was in the seriousness with which he said it. There was a tone of gravity in his voice. On the other hand, there is certainly something incongruous about a dog speaking in English and making a comment about wisdom that was itself wise. In fact, it occurred to me that I have probably said something similar in a variety of situations and contexts, but the wisdom of this observation comes through when it is spoken by a dog and not by me.

But now it is time to conclude this book and to do so with a joke about another talking dog:

> A man tried to sell his dog to a neighbor. "This is a talking dog," said the man, "and he's yours for five bucks." "I don't believe you," the neighbor replied, "There's no such thing as a talking dog." Just then, the dog looked up dolefully and said, "Please buy me, sir. This man has been cruel to me. He never takes me for a walk, he buys me the cheapest dog food and he makes me

sleep in the garage. He doesn't realize what a special dog I am. I swam the Atlantic two years ago, and went to the North Pole the year before that." "You're right!" exclaimed the neighbor. "This dog can talk. So why are you selling him so cheap?" The owner replied: "Because I'm sick of his lies."[3]

---

3. Tibballs, *Mammoth Book of Humor*, 113.

References

Abel, Ernest. "The Psychology of Memory and Rumor Transmission and Their Bearing on Theories of Oral Transmission in Early Christianity." *Journal of Religion* 51 (1971) 270–81.
Adams, Douglas. *The Prostitute in the Family Tree: Discovering Humor and Irony in the Bible*. Louisville: Westminster John Knox, 1997.
Agnes, Michael, ed. *Webster's New World College Dictionary*. Foster City, CA: IDG, 2001.
Alexander, Jeff et al. *A Prairie Home Companion Pretty Good Joke Book*. 5th ed. Minneapolis: HighBridge, 2009.
Allport, Gordon W., and Leo Postman. *The Psychology of Rumor*. New York: Holt, 1947.
Anderson, Paul N. *The Riddles of the Fourth Gospel: An Introduction to John*. Minneapolis: Fortress, 2011.
Apte, Mahadev L. *Humor and Laughter: An Anthropological Approach*. Ithaca, NY: Cornell University Press, 1985.
Bakan, David. *The Duality of Human Existence: An Essay on Psychology and Religion*. Chicago: Rand McNally, 1966.
Baker, Russell, ed. *The Norton Book of Light Verse*. New York: Norton, 1986.
Barclay, William. *The Gospel of Luke*. The Daily Study Bible Series. Philadelphia: Westminster, 1956.
Bartlett, I. J. "The Town of Don't-You-Worry." In *The Best Loved Poems of the American People*, selected by Hazel Felleman, 103. Garden City, NY: Doubleday, 1936.
Basil, Saint, Bishop of Caesarea. "The Long Rules." In *Ascetical Works*. Translated by Monica Wagner, 223–337. Fathers of the Church 9. Washington, DC: Fathers of the Church, 1950.
Beck, Aaron T., and Gary Emery, with Ruth L. Greenberg. *Anxiety Disorders and Phobias: A Cognitive Perspective*. New York: Basic Books, 1985.
Becker, Brian et al. *A Prairie Home Companion Pretty Good Joke Book*. 3rd ed. Minneapolis: HighBridge, 2003.
Beers, Mark H. et al., eds. *The Merck Manual of Medical Information*. 2nd ed. White House Station, NJ: Merck Research Laboratories, 2003.
Beit-Hallahmi, Benjamin, and Michael Argyle. *The Psychology of Religious Behaviour, Belief, and Experience*. London: Routledge, 1997.
Ben-Ze'ev, Aaron. "The Vindication of Gossip." In *Good Gossip*, edited by Robert F. Goodman and Aaron Ben-Ze'ev, 11–24. Lawrence: University Press of Kansas, 1994.
Berger, Peter L. *Redeeming Laughter: The Comic Dimension of the Human Experience*. Berlin: de Gruyter, 1997.

References

———. *A Rumor of Angels: Modern Society and the Rediscovery of the Supernatural.* Garden City, NY: Doubleday, 1969.

Berlyne, D. E. "Laughter, Humor, and Play." In *The Individual in a Social Context*, 795–852. The Handbook of Social Psychology 3. Edited by Gardner Lindzey. Reading, MA: Addison-Wesley, 1969.

Bizi, Smadar et al. "Humor and Coping with Stress: A Test under Real-Life Conditions." *Personality and Individual Differences* 9 (1988) 951–56.

Blatt, S. J., and Richard Q. Ford, in collaboration with William H. Berman et al. *Therapeutic Change: An Object Relations Perspective.* Applied Clinical Psychology. The Language of Science. New York: Plenum, 1994.

Bradley, Margaret M., and Peter J. Lang. "Measuring Emotion: The Self-Assessment Manikin and the Semantic Differential." *Journal of Behavioral Therapy and Experimental Psychiatry* 25 (1994) 49–59.

Brooks, Cleanth, and Robert Penn Warren. *Understanding Poetry: An Anthology for College Students.* New York: Holt, 1938.

Brooks, Michael. *Thirteen Things That Don't Make Sense: The Most Baffling Scientific Mysteries of Our Time.* New York: Doubleday, 2008.

Brooks, Phillips. *Lectures on Preaching, Delivered Before the Divinity School of Yale College.* New York: Dutton, 1877.

Calvin, John. *Commentary on a Harmony of the Evangelists.* Grand Rapids: Eerdmans, 1949.

Campiche, Roland J., ed. *Cultures Jeunes et Religions en Europe.* Sciences humaines et religions. Paris: Cerf, 1997.

Capps, Donald. *Agents of Hope: A Pastoral Psychology.* 1995. Reprinted, Eugene, OR: Wipf & Stock, 2001.

———. *At Home in the World: A Study in Psychoanalysis, Religion, and Art.* Eugene, OR: Cascade Books, 2013.

———. "The Bad-Enough Mother." *Journal of Pastoral Care & Counseling* 59 (2005) 289–92.

———. *Deadly Sins and Saving Virtues.* 1987. Reprinted, Eugene, OR: Wipf & Stock, 2000.

———. *Erik Erikson's Verbal Portraits: Luther, Gandhi, Einstein, Jesus.* Lanham, MD: Rowman & Littlefield, 2014.

———. "Imagining Hope: William F. Lynch's Psychology of Hope." *Pastoral Psychology* 65 (2015) 143–65. http://link.springer.com/article/10.1007%2Fs11089-015-0653-5. Published online May 8, 2015.

———. *Jesus: A Psychological Biography.* 2000. Reprinted, Eugene, OR: Wipf & Stock, 2010.

———. *Jesus the Village Psychiatrist.* Louisville: Westminster John Knox, 2008.

———. *Laughter Ever After: The Ministry of Good Humor.* 2008. Reprinted, Eugene, OR: Wipf & Stock, 2014.

———. *Living Stories: Pastoral Counseling in Congregational Contexts.* Minneapolis: Fortress, 1998.

———. *Men and Their Religion: Honor, Hope, and Humor.* Harrisburg, PA: Trinity, 2002.

———. "The Mortification of the Self: Erving Goffman's Analysis of the Mental Hospital." *Pastoral Psychology* 66 (2016) 103–26. http://link.springer.com/article/10.1007/s11089-015-0665-1. Published online June 20, 2015.

———. "Nervous Laughter: Lament, Death Anxiety, and Humor." In *Lament: Reclaiming Practices in Pulpit, Pew, and Public Square*, edited by Sally A. Brown and Patrick D. Miller, 70–79. Louisville: Westminster John Knox, 2005.

———. "Pastoral Images: The Good Samaritan and the Unjust Judge." *Journal of Pastoral Care & Counseling* 63 (2009) 1–11.

———. *The Resourceful Self: And a Little Child Shall Lead Them*. Eugene, OR: Cascade Books, 2014.

———. "Riddles and Jokes: Growing Children's Use of Humor in Response to Societal Demands for Rational Thinking." *Sacred Spaces* 6 (2014) 142–70. http://www.aapc.org/_templates/74/capps_sacredspaces_last.pdf/.

———. *Still Growing: The Creative Self in Older Adulthood*. Eugene, OR: Cascade Books, 2014.

———. *A Time to Laugh: The Religion of Humor*. New York: Continuum, 2005.

———. "Trees and Us: Poetic Metaphors and Pastoral Images." *Pastoral Psychology* 60 (2011) 437–49. http://link.springer.com/article/10.1007%2Fs11089-011-0338-7#/page-1/.

———. *Young Clergy: A Biographical-Developmental Study*. Haworth Series in Chaplaincy. New York: Routledge, 2009.

Capps, John, and Donald Capps. *You've Got to Be Kidding! How Jokes Can Help You Think*. Malden, MA: Wiley-Blackwell, 2009.

Carhart, George S., and Paul A. McGhee, eds. *Magic Casements*. New York: Macmillan, 1926.

Christie, George L. "Some Psychoanalytic Aspects of Humor." *International Journal of Psycho-Analysis* 75 (1994) 479–89.

Cohen, Patricia. "A Company Copes with Backlash against the Raise That Roared." Business Day. *New York Times*, July 31, 2015. http://www.nytimes.com/2015/08/02/business/a-company-copes-with-backlash-against-the-raise-that-roared.html?_r=0/.

———. "One Company's New Minimum Wage: $70,000 a Year." Business Day. *New York Times*, April 13, 2015. http://www.nytimes.com/2015/04/14/business/owner-of-gravity-payments-a-credit-card-processor-is-setting-a-new-minimum-wage-70000-a-year.html/.

Cohen, Ted. *Jokes: Philosophical Thoughts on Joking Matters*. Chicago: University of Chicago Press, 1999.

Collicutt, Joanna, and Amanda Gray. "'A Merry Heart Doeth Good Like a Medicine': Humor, Religion and Wellbeing." *Mental Health, Religion & Culture* 15 (2012) 759–78.

Cousins, Norman. *The Anatomy of an Illness as Perceived by the Patient*. New York: Norton, 1979.

Craffert, Pieter F. *The Life of a Galilean Shaman: Jesus of Nazareth in Anthropological-Historical Perspective*. Matrix 3. Eugene, OR: Cascade Books, 2008.

Crossan, John Dominic. *The Dark Interval: Towards a Theology of Story*. 1975. Reprinted, Sonoma, CA: Polebridge, 1988.

———. *The Historical Jesus: The Life of a Mediterranean Jewish Peasant*. San Francisco: HarperSanFrancisco, 1991.

Daniels, John W., Jr. "Gossip in John's Gospel and the Social Processing of Jesus' Identity." *Journal of Early Christian History* 1 (2011) 9–29.

———. "Gossip in the New Testament." *Biblical Theology Bulletin* 42 (2012) 204–13.

———. *Gossiping Jesus: The Oral Processing of Jesus in John's Gospel.* Eugene, OR: Pickwick Publications, 2013.

Davies, Christie. "The Protestant Ethic and the Comic Spirit of Capitalism." In *Jokes and Their Relation to Society*, edited by Christie Davies, 42–62. Humor Research. Berlin: Mouton de Gruyter, 1998.

Deckers, Lambert, and Willibald Ruch. "Sensation Seeking and the Situational Humor Response Questionnaire (SHRQ): Its Relationship in American and German Samples." *Personality and Individual Differences* 13 (1992) 1051–54.

Demos, John. *A Little Commonwealth: Family Life in Plymouth Colony.* New York: Oxford University Press, 1970.

Derville, André. "Humor." In *Dictionnaire de la Spiritualité: Ascétique et Mystique*, 7:1188–92. Paris: Beauchesne, 1969.

De Sousa, Ronald. "In Praise of Gossip: Indiscretion as a Saintly Virtue." In *Good Gossip*, edited by Robert F. Goodman and Aaron Ben-Ze'ev, 25–33. Lawrence: University Press of Kansas, 1994.

Diener, Ed, et al. "Subjective Well-Being: Three Decades of Progress." *Psychological Bulletin* 125 (1999) 276–302.

Donnelly, Doris. "Divine Folly: Being Religious and the Exercise of Humor." *Theology Today* 48 (1992) 385–98.

Doody, John A., and John Immerwahr. "The Persistence of the Four Temperaments." *Soundings* 66 (1983) 348–59.

Dufflo, Colas. *Jouer et Philosopher.* Pratiques théoriques. Paris: Presses Universitaires de France, 1997.

Dworkin, Earl S., and Jay S. Efran. "The Angered: Their Susceptibility to Varieties of Humor." *Journal of Personality and Social Psychology* 6 (1967) 233–36.

Dykstra, Robert C. et al. *Losers, Loners, and Rebels: The Spiritual Struggles of Boys.* Louisville: Westminster John Knox, 2007.

Eco, Umberto. *The Name of the Rose.* Translated by William Weaver. San Diego: Harcourt Brace Jovanovich, 1983.

Edmonds, Ed M., and Delwin D. Cahoon. "Effects of Religious Orientation and Clothing Revealingness on Women's Choice of Clothing." *Journal of Social Behavior and Personality* 8 (1993) 349–53.

Elkins, James. *On the Strange Place of Religion in Contemporary Art.* New York: Routledge, 2004.

Erikson, Erik H. "The Galilean Sayings and the Sense of 'I.'" *Yale Review* 70 (1981) 321–62.

———. *Toys and Reasons: Stages in the Ritualization of Experience.* New York: Norton, 1977.

———. *Young Man Luther: A Study in Psychoanalysis and History.* New York: Norton, 1958.

Ernest, P. Edward. *The Family Album of Favorite Poems.* New York: Putnam, 1959.

Eysenck, H. J. "The Appreciation of Humour: An Experimental and Theoretical Study." *British Journal of Psychology* 32 (1942) 295–309.

Felleman, Hazel, ed. *The Best Loved Poems of the American People.* Garden City, NY: Doubleday, 1936.

Foot, Hugh C., and Anthony J. Chapman. "The Social Responsiveness of Young Children in Humorous Situations." In *Humor and Laughter: Theory, Research and*

Applications, edited by Anthony J. Chapman and Hugh C. Foot, 141–75. London: Wiley, 1976.

Ford, Richard Q. *The Parables of Jesus: Recovering the Art of Listening*. Minneapolis: Fortress, 1997.

Franklin, Benjamin. *Poor Richard's Almanack*. Mount Vernon, NY: Pauper, 1988.

Freud, Sigmund. *The Ego and the Id*. Translated by Joan Riviere. Revised and newly edited by James Strachey. New York: Norton, 1962.

———. "Humor." In *Character and Culture*, edited by Philip Rieff, 263–69. Collected Papers of Sigmund Freud 9. New York: Collier, 1963.

———. *The Interpretation of Dreams*. Edited and translated by James Strachey. 1900. Reprinted, New York: Avon Books, 1965.

———. *Jokes and Their Relation to the Unconscious*. Edited and translated by James Strachey. New York: Norton, 1960.

———. "The Uncanny." In *On Creativity and the Unconscious: Papers on the Psychology of Art, Literature, Love, Religion*, edited by Benjamin Nelson, 122–61. Harper Torchbooks. New York: Harper & Row, 1958.

Gelkopf, Marc et al. "Laughter in a Psychiatric Ward: Somatic, Emotional, Social, and Clinical Influences on Schizophrenic Patients." *Journal of Nervous and Mental Disease* 181 (1993) 283–89.

Gilman, Sander L. *The Case of Sigmund Freud: Medicine and Identity at the Fin de Siècle*. Baltimore: Johns Hopkins University Press, 1993.

———. *Freud, Race, and Gender*. Princeton: Princeton University Press, 1993.

Gilmore, David D. "Anthropology of the Mediterranean Area." *Annual Review of Anthropology* 11 (1982) 175–205.

Gluckman, Max. "Gossip and Scandal." *Current Anthropology* 4 (1963) 307–16.

Goffman, Erving. *Asylums: Essays on the Social Situation of Mental Patients and Other Inmates*. Garden City, NY: Doubleday, 1961.

Goodman, Robert F., and Aaron Ben-Ze'ev. *Good Gossip*. Lawrence: University Press of Kansas, 1994.

Götz, Ignacio L. *Faith, Humor, and Paradox*. Westport, CT: Praeger, 2002.

Greene, Mel. *The Greatest Joke Book Ever*. New York: Avon Books, 1999.

Gritsch, Eric W. *The Wit of Martin Luther*. Facets. Minneapolis: Fortress, 2006.

Haerich, Paul. "Premarital Sexual Permissiveness and Religious Orientation: A Preliminary Investigation." *Journal for the Scientific Study of Religion* 31 (1992) 361–65.

Harris, Henry F. "The Absence of Humor in Jesus." *Methodist Quarterly Review* 57 (1908) 460–67.

Hausherr, Irénée. *Penthos: Le Doctrine de la Componction dans l'Orient Chrétien*. Orientalia Christiana Analecta 12. Rome: Institutum Orientalium Studiorum, 1944.

Heller, Ena Giurescu. *Reluctant Partners: Art and Religion in Dialogue*. New York: Gallery at the American Bible Society, 2004.

Herskovits, Melville J., and Frances S. Herskovits. *Trinidad Village*. New York: Octagon, 1976.

Herzog, William R., II. *Parables as Subversive Speech: Jesus as Pedagogue of the Oppressed*. Louisville: Westminster John Knox, 1994.

Holliday, Robert Cortes, ed. *Memoir and Poems*. Joyce Kilmer 1. New York: Doran, 1918.

Hyers, Conrad. *And God Created Laughter: The Bible as Divine Comedy.* Atlanta: John Knox, 1987.

———, ed. *Holy Laughter: Essays on Religion in the Comic Perspective.* New York: Seabury, 1969.

———. *The Spirituality of Comedy: Comic Heroism in a Tragic World.* New Brunswick, NJ: Transaction, 1996.

Jackson, Laurence E., and Robert D. Coursey. "The Relationship of God Control and Internal Locus of Control to Intrinsic Religious Motivation, Coping and Purpose in Life." *Journal for the Scientific Study of Religion* 27 (1988) 399–410.

James, William. "The Gospel of Relaxation." In *Talks to Teachers on Psychology and to Students on Some of Life's Ideals*, 99–112. Mineola, NY: Dover.

Kelly, William E. "An Investigation of Worry and Sense of Humor." *Journal of Psychology* 136 (2002) 657–66.

Kilmer, Aline. *Candles That Burn.* New York: Doran, 1919.

Kilmer, Annie Kilburn. *Memories of My Son Sergeant Joyce Kilmer.* New York: Brentano's, 1920.

Kilmer, Joyce. *Trees and Other Poems.* New York: Doubleday, 1914.

Kislev, Lior. Birding Tours and Bird-watching in Israel (website). 2015. http://www.tatzpit.com/site/en/pages/homePage.asp/.

Kuhlman, Thomas L. *Humor and Psychotherapy.* Homewood, IL: Dow Jones-Irwin, 1984.

Kuschel, Karl-Josef. *Laughter: A Theological Essay.* London: SCM, 1994.

Laird, Charlton Grant et al. *Webster's New World Roget's A–Z Thesaurus.* New York: Macmillan, 1999.

Lefcourt, Herbert M. and Rod A. Martin. *Humor and Life Stress: Antidote to Adversity.* New York: Springer, 1986.

LeGoff, Jacques. "Laughter in the Middle Ages." In *A Cultural History of Humour: From Antiquity to the Present Day*, edited by Jan N. Bremmer and R. Roodenburg, 40–53. Cambridge: Blackwell, 1997.

———. "Le Rire dans les Règles Monastiques du haut Moyen Age." In *Haut Moyen-Age Culture, Education et Sociéte*, edited by J. M. Sot, 93–103. La Garenne: Publi-dix, 1990.

Leventhal, Howard, and Martin A. Safer. "Individual Differences, Personality and Humor Appreciation: Introduction to Symposium." In *It's a Funny Thing, Humour*, edited by Anthony J. Chapman and Hugh C. Foot, 335–49. Elmsford, NY: Pergamon, 1977.

Levin, Jack, and Arnold Arluke. *Gossip: The Inside Scoop.* New York: Plenum, 1987.

Linss, Wilhelm C. "The Hidden Humor of St. Paul." *Currents in Theology and Mission* 25 (1998) 195–99.

Longfellow, Henry Wadsworth. *Favorite Poems of Henry Longfellow.* Garden City, NY: Doubleday, 1947.

Lupton, Martha, ed. *The Treasury of Modern Humor.* Indianapolis: Droke, 1938.

Lynch, William F., SJ. *Images of Hope: Imagination as Healer of the Hopeless.* A Mentor-Omega Book. New York: New American Library, 1965.

Marmysz, John. *Laughing at Nothing: Humor as a Response to Nihilism.* Albany: State University of New York Press, 2003.

Martin, James, SJ. *Between Heaven and Mirth: Why Joy, Humor, and Laughter Are at the Heart of the Spiritual Life.* New York: HarperOne, 2011.

McNeill, Don. *Breakfast Club Family Album.* Chicago: McNeill, 1942.
Ménager, Daniel. *La Renaissance et le Rire.* Perspectives littéraires. Paris: Presses Universitaires de France, 1995.
Miller, Alan S., and John P. Hoffmann. "Risk and Religion: An Explanation of Gender Differences in Religiosity." *Journal for the Scientific Study of Religion* 34 (1993) 63–75.
Morreall, John. "Comic and Tragic Religions." Paper presented at the Eighth International Society for Humor Studies Conference, Edmond, Oklahoma, July 8–13, 1997.
———. "Enjoying Incongruity." *Humor: International Journal of Humor Research* 2 (1989) 1–18.
———. "Gossip and Humor." In *Good Gossip,* edited by Robert F. Goodman and Aaron Ben-Ze'ev, 56–64. Lawrence: University Press of Kansas, 1994.
———. "Humor and Emotion." In *The Philosophy of Laughter and Humor,* edited by John Morreall, 212–24. Albany: State University of New York Press, 1987.
———. "A New Theory of Laughter." In *The Philosophy of Laughter and Humor,* edited by John Morreall, 128–38. Albany: State University of New York Press, 1987.
———, ed. *The Philosophy of Laughter and Humor.* SUNY Series in Philosophy. Albany: State University of New York Press, 1987.
Mullen, Wilbur H. "Toward a Theology of Humor." *Christian Scholar's Review* 3 (1973) 3–12.
Nevo, Ofra, and Baruch Nevo. "What Do You Do When You Are Asked to Answer Humorously?" *Journal of Personality and Social Psychology* 44 (1983) 188–94.
Niebuhr, Reinhold. *Discerning the Signs of the Times: Sermons for Today and Tomorrow.* New York: Scribner, 1949.
———. "Humor and Faith." In *Discerning the Signs of the Times: Sermons for Today and Tomorrow,* 111–31. New York: Scribner, 1949.
Nieting, Lorenz. "Humor in the New Testament." *Dialog* 22 (1983) 168–70.
Norem, Julie K. *The Positive Power of Negative Thinking: Using Defensive Pessimism to Manage Anxiety and Perform at Your Peak.* New York: Basic Books, 2001.
Olson, Richard P. *Laughter in a Time of Turmoil: Humor as a Spiritual Practice.* Eugene, OR: Wipf & Stock, 2012.
Oring, Elliott. *The Jokes of Sigmund Freud: A Study in Humor and Jewish Identity.* Philadelphia: University of Pennsylvania Press, 1984.
Palmer, Earl F. *The Humor of Jesus: Sources of Laughter in the Bible.* Vancouver, BC: Regent College Publishing, 2001.
Phipps, William E. *The Wisdom & Wit of Rabbi Jesus.* Louisville: Westminster John Knox, 1993.
Provine, Robert R. *Laughter: A Scientific Investigation.* New York: Penguin, 2000.
Pruyser, Paul W. *The Play of the Imagination: Toward a Psychoanalysis of Culture.* New York: International Universities Press, 1983.
Reader's Digest Association. *Laughter Really Is the Best Medicine: America's Funniest Jokes, Quotes, and Cartoons from Reader's Digest Magazine.* Pleasantville, NY: Reader's Digest Publishing, 2011.
———. *Laughter Still Is the Best Medicine.* New York: Reader's Digest Publishing, 2014.
———. *Laughter: The Best Medicine.* Pleasantville, NY: Reader's Digest Association, 1997.
Reik, Theodor. *Jewish Wit.* New York: Gamut, 1962.

Renan, Ernest. *The Life of Jesus*. 1935. Reprinted, Great Minds Series. Buffalo, NY: Prometheus, 1991.

Rennison, Nick. *Freud and Psychoanalysis*. Harpenden, UK: Pocket Essentials, 2001.

Rescher, Nicholas. *Luck: The Brilliant Randomness of Everyday Life*. New York: Farrar Straus and Giroux, 1995.

Roberts, Robert C. "Humor and the Virtues." *Inquiry* 31 (1988) 27–49.

———. "Sense of Humor as a Christian Virtue." *Faith and Philosophy* 7 (1990) 177–92.

Roof, Wade Clark. *Community & Commitment: Religious Plausibility in a Liberal Protestant Church*. New York: Elsevier, 1978.

Rosenzweig, S. "The Treatment of Humorous Responses in the Rosenzweig Picture-Frustration Study: A Note on the Revised (1950) Instruction." *Journal of Psychology* 30 (1950) 139–43.

Rosnow, Ralph L., and Gary Alan Fine. *Rumor and Gossip: The Social Psychology of Hearsay*. New York: Elsevier, 1976.

Rovin, Jeff. *1001 More Great Jokes*. New York: New American Library, 1989.

Rubin, Joan Shelley. *Songs of Ourselves: The Uses of Poetry in America*. Cambridge, MA: Harvard University Press, 2007.

Ruch, Willibald, ed. *The Sense of Humor: Explorations of a Personality Characteristic*. Berlin: Mouton de Gruyter, 1998.

Ruch, Willibald, and Franz-Josef Hehl. "Attitudes to Sex, Sexual Behavior and Enjoyment of Humor." *Personality and Individual Differences* 9 (1988) 983–94.

Rudnytsky, Peter L., ed. *Transitional Objects and Potential Spaces: Literary Uses of D. W. Winnicott*. Psychoanalysis and Culture. New York: Columbia University Press, 1993.

Salamon, Julie. *Rambam's Ladder: A Meditation on Generosity and Why It Is Necessary to Give*. New York: Workman, 2003.

Saroglou, Vasilis. "Being Religious Implies Being Different in Humor: Evidence from Self- and Peer-Ratings." *Mental Health, Religion, and Culture* 7 (2004) 255–67.

———. "Humor Appreciation as a Function of Religious Dimensions." In *Archiv für Religionpsychologie*, edited by Nils Holm, 144–53. Göttingen: Vandenhoeck & Ruprecht, 2003.

———. "Humor, Religion, and Personality." PhD diss., Catholic University of Louvain, 1999.

———. "Religion and Sense of Humor: An a Priori Incompatibility? Theoretical Considerations from a Psychological Perspective." *Humor* 15 (2002) 191–214.

———. "Religion and the Five Factors of Personality: A Meta-analytic Review." *Personality and Individual Differences* 32 (2002) 15–25.

———. "Religiousness, Religious Fundamentalism and Quest as Predictors of Humor Creation." *International Journal for the Psychology of Religion* 12 (2002) 177–88.

———. "Rêve et Spiritualité chez Jean Climaque." Master's thesis, Catholic University of Louvain, 1992.

Saroglou, Vassilis, and Lydwine Anciaux. "Liking Sick Humor: Coping Styles and Religion as Predictors." *Humor* 17 (2004) 257–77.

Saroglou, Vassilis, and Jean-Marie Jaspard. "Does Religion Affect Humor Creation? An Experimental Study." *Mental Health, Religion & Culture* 4 (2001) 33–46.

Scherer, Klaus R. "Les Émotions: Functions et Composantes." In *Les Émotions*, edited by Bernard Rimé and Klaus R. Scherer, 97–133. Textes de base en psychologie. Neuchâtel: Delachaux et Niestlé, 1989.

Schweitzer, Carol Schnabel L. "Gossip: The Grace Notes of Congregational Life." In *From Midterms to Ministry: Practical Theologians on Pastoral Beginnings*, edited by Allan Hugh Cole Jr., 191–203. Grand Rapids: Eerdmans.

Smaridge, Norah. *Pen and Bayonet: The Story of Joyce Kilmer*. New York: Hawthorne, 1962.

Snyder, C. R. *The Psychology of Hope: You Can Get There from Here*. New York: Free Press, 1994.

Snyder, C. R., et al. "Development and Validation of the State Hope Scale." *Journal of Personality and Social Psychology* 70 (1996) 321–35.

Spacks, Patricia Meyer. *Gossip*. New York: Knopf, 1985.

Stangland, E. C. *Red Stangland's Norwegian Home Companion*. New York: Barnes & Noble, 1987.

Stotland, Ezra. *The Psychology of Hope: An Integration of Experimental, Clinical, and Social Approaches*. San Francisco: Jossey-Bass, 1969.

Stroebe, M., and M. Hewstone, eds. "Social Sharing of Emotion: New Evidence and New Questions." Special issue, *European Review of Social Psychology* 9/1 (1998) 145–89.

Strong, George A. "The Modern Hiawatha." In *Martin Gardner's Favorite Poetic Parodies*, edited by Martin Gardner, 91–92. Amherst, NY: Prometheus, 2001.

Suls, Jerry M. "Cognitive Process in Humor Appreciation." In *Handbook of Humor Research*, edited by P. E. McGhee and J. H. Goldstein, 1:39–57. 2 vols. New York: Springer, 1983.

Tapper, Albert, and Peter Press. *A Guy Goes Into a Bar....* New York: MJF Books, 2000.

———. *A Minister, a Priest, and a Rabbi*. Kansas City, MO: McMeel, 2000.

Thorson, James A., and F. C. Powell. "Relationships of Death Anxiety and Sense of Humor." *Psychological Reports* 72 (1993) 1364–66.

———. "Sense of Humor and Dimensions of Personality." *Journal of Clinical Psychology* 49 (1993) 799–809.

Tibballs, Geoff, ed. *The Mammoth Book of Humor*. New York: Carroll & Graf, 2000.

Veatch, Thomas C. "A Theory of Humor." *Humor: International Journal of Humor Research* 11 (1998) 161–215.

Vilaythong, Alexander P. et al. "Humor and Hope: Can Humor Increase Hope?" *Humor: International Journal of Humor Research* 16 (2003) 79–89.

Webb, Lance. *Conquering the Seven Deadly Sins*. New York: Abingdon, 1955.

Wikipedia. "Don McNeill's Breakfast Club." http://en.wikipedia.org/wiki/Don_McNeill's_Breakfast_Club/, 2015.

Wikipedia. "Joyce Kilmer." http://en.wikipedia.org/wiki/JoyceKilmer/, 2015.

Winnicott, D. W. "The Location of Cultural Experience." In *Playing and Reality*, 95–103. New York: Routledge, 1982.

Wolfenstein, Martha. *Children's Humor: A Psychological Analysis*. Glencoe, IL: Free Press, 1954.

Ziv, Avner. "The Effect of Humor in Aggression Catharsis in the Classroom." *Journal of Psychology* 121 (1987) 359–64.

Zuckerman, Marvin. *Sensation Seeking: Beyond the Optimal Level of Arousal*. Hillsdale, NJ: Erlbaum, 1979.

Zuver, Dudley. *Salvation by Laughter: A Study of Religion and Sense of Humor*. New York: Harper, 1933.

Index of Names

Abel, Ernest L., 119–20, 167
Adams, Douglas, xii, 80–81, 85–90, 99, 114, 167
Agnes, Michael, ix, 2, 11, 14–15, 51, 121, 123, 135, 157, 167
Alexander, Jeff, vii, 149, 167
Allport, Gordon W., 119–21, 137, 167
Anciaux, Lydwine, 46, 77, 174
Anderson, Paul N., 167
Apte, Mahadev L., 50, 167
Argyle, Michael, 51, 167
Arluke, Arnold, 127–29, 172

Bakan, David, 79, 167
Baker, Russell, 145, 167
Barclay, William, 84, 167
Bartlett, I. J., xiii, 153, 167
Basil, Saint, 55, 167
Beck, Aaron T., 28, 167
Becker, Brian, 34, 112, 167
Beers, Mark H., 3, 15, 167
Beit-Hallahmi, Benjamin, 25, 51, 167
Ben Ze'ev, Aaron, 134, 167
Berger, Peter L., 38–40, 45, 50, 54, 167
Berlyne, D. E., 52, 168
Berman, William H., 168
Bizi, Smadar, 25–26, 168
Blatt, S. J., 99, 168
Bradley, Margaret M., 32, 168
Brooks, Cleanth, Jr., 150–52, 168
Brooks, Michael, 6, 168
Brooks, Phillips, 115, 158–62, 168

Cahoon, Delwin D., 58, 170
Calvin, John, 70, 79, 83–84, 168
Campiche, Roland J., 58, 168
Capps, Donald, xi, xiii, 2, 11, 16, 31, 34, 52, 65, 79–80, 89, 100–101, 104, 110, 119–20, 122, 126, 134–35, 142–44, 152–53, 157–58, 168–69
Capps, John, vii–viii, 157, 169
Carhart, George S., 150, 169
Chapman, Anthony J., 78, 170
Christie, George L., 56, 169
Clouston, Thomas Smith, ix
Cohen, Patricia, 115, 169
Cohen, Ted, 76, 117, 142–44, 169
Collicutt, Joanna, 2, 65, 169
Coursey, Robert D., 15, 172
Cousins, Norman, 1–2, 169
Craffert, Pieter F., 135, 169
Crossan, John Dominic, 101–2, 115, 169

Daniels, John W., Jr., 135, 169
Davies, Christie, 50, 170
Deckers, Lambert, 53, 170
Demos, John, 123, 170
Derville, André, 57, 170
De Sousa, Ronald, 134, 170
Diener, Ed, 58, 170
Donnelly, Doris, 37, 170
Doody, John A., 12, 170
Dufflo, Colas, 53, 170
Dworkin, Earl S., 55, 170
Dykstra, Robert C., 102, 170

Index of Names

Eco, Umberto, 51, 170
Eddy, Nelson, 150
Edmonds, Ed M., 58, 170
Efran, Jay S., 55, 170
Elkins, James, 35, 170
Emery, Gary, 28, 167
Erikson, Erik H., 52, 75, 80, 100, 132, 170
Ernest, P. Edward, 158, 170
Eysenck, H. J., 43, 170

Felleman, Hazel, , 170
Fine, Gary Alan, 126, 174
Foot, Hugh C., 78, 170
Ford, Richard Q., xii, 91–100, 102–4, 113–15, 168, 171
Franklin, Benjamin, 122, 171
Freud, Sigmund, viii, xii, 24–25, 54–56, 76, 99–115, 139, 163, 171

Gelkopf, Marc, 30–31, 171
Gilman, Sander L., 104, 171
Gilmore, David D., 101, 171
Glover, R. W., 153
Gluckman, Max, 126, 171
Goffman, Erving, 126, 171
Goldstein, J. H., 175
Goodman, Robert F., 134, 137, 170, 171, 173
Götz, Ignacio L., 36–37, 171
Gray, Amanda, 2, 65, 169
Greenberg, Ruth L., 167
Greene, Mel, 116, 155, 171
Gritsch, Eric W., 79, 171

Haerich, Paul, 58, 171
Harris, Henry F., xii, 68–77, 79–82, 84, 171
Hausherr, Irénée, 51, 171
Hehl, Franz-Josef, 56, 174
Heller, Ena Giurescu, 35, 171
Herskovits, Frances S., 133, 171
Herskovits, Melville J., 133, 171
Herzog, William R., II, 96, 171
Hewstone, M., 175
Hoffmann, John P., 53, 173
Holliday, Robert Cortes, 149, 171

Hyers, Conrad, 36, 50, 172

Immerwahr, John, 12, 170

Jackson, Laurence E., 15, 172
James, William, ix–x, 15, 33, 90, 147, 172
Jaspard, Jean-Marie, 40–41, 44, 77, 174
Joyce, Alfred, 149

Kelly, William E., 27–29, 172
Kilmer, Aline, 151, 172
Kilmer, Annie Kilburn, 149, 172
Kilmer, Frederick, 149
Kilmer, Joyce, viii, 148–52, 157–58, 172
Kislev, Lior, 157, 172
Knox, John, 70, 79
Kuhlman, Thomas L., 91, 172
Kuschel, Karl-Josef, 50, 172

Laird, Charlton Grant, x, 172
Lang, Peter J., 32, 168
Lefcourt, Herbert M., 14–19, 22, 24–25, 31, 60–61, 172
LeGoff, Jacques, 51, 172
Leventhal, Howard, 53, 172
Levin, Jack, 127–29, 172
Linss, Wilhelm C., 80, 172
Longfellow, Henry Wadsworth, 145, 172
Lupton, Martha, 34, 108, 116, 172
Lynch, William F., SJ, 11, 172

Marmysz, John, 14, 172
Martin, James, SJ, 79, 172
Martin, Rod A., 14–19, 22, 24–25, 31, 60–61, 172
McGhee, Paul A., 169
McGhee, Paul E., 150, 175
McNeill, Don, 124, 173
Ménager, Daniel, 51, 173
Miller, Alan S., 53
Miller, Patrick D., 169
Morreall, John, 13–14, 22, 50, 52–54, 72, 119, 134, 137–41, 144, 173

Index of Names 179

Morton, Julius Sterling, 148
Mullen, Wilbur H., 37, 173

Nevo, Baruch, 42, 55, 173
Nevo, Ofra, 42, 55, 173
Niebuhr, Reinhold, 37–40, 63–65, 131, 137
Nieting, Lorenz, 69, 173
Norem, Julie K., 28, 173

Olson, Richard P., 1–2, 79, 173
Oring, Elliott, 77, 173

Palmer, Earl F., xii, 81–84, 87–90, 99, 173
Penny, W. E., 153
Phipps, William E., 83–84, 173
Postman, Leo, 119–21, 137, 167
Powell, F. C., 2, 27, 56, 175
Press, Peter, 36, 66, 104, 110, 157, 175
Provine, Robert R., 77–78, 173
Pruyser, Paul W., 62, 173

Reik, Theodor, 77, 110, 113, 173
Renan, Ernest, 72–73, 174
Rennison, Nick, 163, 174
Rescher, Nicholas, 63, 174
Roberts, Robert C., 36–37, 174
Robeson, Paul, 150
Roof, Wade Clark, 122, 174
Rosenzweig, S., 42, 174
Rosnow, Ralph L., 125–26, 174
Rovin, Jeff, 113, 174
Rubin, Joan Shelley, 150–51, 174
Ruch, Willibald, 51, 53, 56, 174
Rudnytsky, Peter L., 133, 174

Safer, Martin A., 53, 172
Salamon, Julie, 108, 174
Saroglou, Vasilis, xi, 40–41, 43–44, 46, 49–63, 67, 77, 174
Scherer, Klaus R., 54, 174
Schumann–Heink, 150
Schweitzer, Carol Schnabel L., 134, 175
Smaridge, Norah, 149, 175
Snyder, C. R., 32, 175
Spacks, Patricia Meyer, 122–23, 129–34, 140–41, 175
Stangland, E. C., 30, 175
Stotland, Ezra, 11, 175
Stroebe, M., 175
Strong, George A., 145–46, 175
Suls, Jerry M., 52, 175

Tapper, Albert, 36, 66, 103, 110, 157, 175
Thomas, John Charles, 150
Thorson, James A., 2, 27, 56, 175
Tibballs, Geoff, 110, 166, 175

Veatch, Thomas C., 57, 175
Vilaythong, Alexander P., 31, 77, 85, 175

Warren, Robert Penn, 150–52, 168
Webb, Lance, 100, 175
Winnicott, D. W., 132, 175
Wolfenstein, Martha, 157, 175

Ziv, Avner, 55, 175
Zuckerman, Marvin, 53, 175
Zuver, Dudley, 37, 175

www.ingramcontent.com/pod-product-compliance
Lightning Source LLC
Chambersburg PA
CBHW031433150426
43191CB00006B/496